WORK AND INEQUALITY
IN URBAN CHINA

SUNY SERIES IN THE SOCIOLOGY OF WORK

RICHARD H. HALL, EDITOR

WORK AND INEQUALITY IN URBAN CHINA

YANJIE BIAN

STATE UNIVERSITY OF NEW YORK PRESS

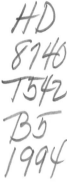

Published by
State University of New York Press, Albany

© 1994 State University of New York

For information, address State University of New York Press,
State University Plaza, Albany, N.Y. 12246

Production by M. R. Mulholland
Marketing by Fran Keneston

Library of Congress Cataloging-in-Publication Data

Bian, Yanjie, 1955—
    Work and inequality in urban China / Yanjie Bian.
        p.   cm. — (SUNY series in the sociology of work)
    Revision of thesis (doctoral).
    Includes bibliographical references (p.   ) and index.
    ISBN 0-7914-1801-4 (Ch : acid-free). — ISBN 0-7914-1802-2 (PB:
acid—free)
    1. Labor—China—Tientsin. 2. Social status—China—Tientsin.
3. Occupational prestige—China—Tientsin. 4. Social surveys—
—China—Tientsin. I. Title. II. Series.
    HD8740.T542B5 1994
    331'.0951'154—dc20   93—14708
                                                               CIP

10 9 8 7 6 5 4 3 2 1

CONTENTS

FIGURES AND TABLES

Figure

ACKNOWLEDGMENTS

I would like to thank Richard D. Alba, Christine E. Bose, Richard H. Hall, Nan Lin, and John R. Logan, who kindly served as members of my doctoral dissertation advisory committee. Although this book has an entirely different look and substance from the dissertation ("Work Units and Status Attainment: A Study of Work-Unit Status in Urban China"), it was this dissertation with which the study presented in the book started. I particularly feel indebted to Nan Lin, who served as chair of the advisory committee and with whom I worked closely as his teaching and research assistant during the years of my graduate program at the State University of New York at Albany and later as a postdoctoral research associate at Duke University. His continuing academic and financial support at both institutions was instrumental in allowing me to pursue the research project that led to my dissertation and the writing of this book. Without Nan the work would not have been completed, nor perhaps even begun.

I am grateful to Xinheng Yang and members of his research team at Nankai University, Tianjin, China, for their help in the 1988 Tianjin survey analyzed in this book; to my interviewees for their willingness to provide information about their personal experiences associated with their jobs and work units; and to Fuqin Bian, Jianhong Liu, and Xun Wang for their participation in coding the survey data into the computer. I owe particular thanks to Deborah Davis, Nan Lin (again), Maurice N. Richter, Jr., and Andrew G. Walder for their helpful comments on drafts of several chapters and for their sincere support and encouragement during the writing and revising of the manuscript. I am greatly indebted to Cynthia Cramsie and Rosalie M. Robertson for their editing assistance. I also wish to express my gratitude to Richard H. Hall and Rosalie M. Robertson for their efforts in making this publication possible. I feel extremely fortunate to have worked with these two individuals.

The 1988 Tianjin survey was supported in part by a grant from the State University of New York at Albany. A postdoctoral fellowship from Duke University made it financially possible for me to analyze the data and work on the manuscript. A summer faculty research grant from the University of Minnesota's College of liberal Arts enabled me to revise the manuscript for publication.

Finally, I wish to acknowledge four special individuals in my family for their love and support: my wife Qinghong, my son Feng, and my parents. My parents, both of whom worked in state factories in China before retirement and provided me with their vivid stories of working in socialist enterprises, have always encouraged me in developing this study. Not only their own lives were affected by their workplaces, but also their children's. As one of them, I lived in homes rented from my father's factory, grew up in neighborhoods where all the families worked in the same place, went to elementary and high schools with the children of my father's colleagues, read books that my father and mother borrowed from their work units' libraries, and used the workplace facilities such as medical centers, bath houses, meal halls, and gymnasiums. When I told my parents that I was writing this book, they encouraged me to concentrate on my work and not to "worry" about them. Through letters and telephone calls, my father always inquired how my project was progressing. While I worked on this book project, since early 1990, my wife Qinghong took all responsibilities at home, first in Durham, North Carolina and later in Minneapolis. Her firsthand knowledge about the implementation of Chinese labor and wage policies and their practices at the company and factory levels was also invaluable to me. My son Feng, who was between the ages of five and seven during this project, always wanted to play with me but understood that I needed time for my work. He sometimes complained to his mom about his daddy "always sitting in front of the computer working" (his words) with no time for him. I should have made myself available to him more than I did—something I am determined to do now, because pretty soon he won't be making himself available to me! I love you, Feng.

1

STRUCTURAL SEGMENTATION AND SOCIAL STRATIFICATION

The Communist revolution of 1949 marked the beginning of a new regime in China. By 1956, this regime completed its mission of transforming the country's profit-making and nonprofit organizations into publicly owned institutions. The result was a dominant state sector composed of vital industries and firms, and a dependent collective sector of small businesses. Organizations in both sectors were operated by central or local government agencies. Communist party cadres were sent to head these organizations, and party apparatuses were established in them. Not only were economic resources, properties, and products controlled by these work organizations, but they also distributed all incentives. Both state and collective sector workers, who made up 98 percent of the urban labor force for more than two decades, depended on their workplaces for continued employment, promotions, wages, welfare benefits, and housing. Their workplaces were also the source for party membership and political mobility. Individual laborers even depended on the government offices to issue their employment licenses and direct their work and nonwork activities.

This is a study of the impact of work organizations on the social stratification of urban workers in the People's Republic of China. In the modern era, work organizations play a crucial role in social stratification systems in all societies. As Stolzenberg (1978, p. 813) has pointed out, "the jobs they [employers] provide are the primary mechanism by which individuals are distributed among occupations and by which earnings are distributed among persons." In a planned economy such as China's, enterprises run the society (qiyie ban shehui). This popular Chinese expression refers to a unique phenomenon in urban China: work organizations provide not only jobs and earnings but also a wide array of goods and services for employees and their families, and these goods and services include not only material rewards but also ideological and organizational incentives. In the following pages, I reveal the extent to which socioeconomic and political inequalities among Chinese urban workers are generated by their workplaces. Why do work organizations have different abilities and potential for offering labor rewards? What factors determine who gains and who loses in the urban workplace?

Structural Segmentation as a Perspective of Stratification

A useful framework for this study is the segmentation perspective of social stratification. In contemporary sociology, *economic segmentation* is defined as the unequal distribution of resources and opportunities among industries or firms (Wallace and Kalleberg 1981). *Labor market segmentation*, which in part derives from economic segmentation, refers to distinct employment patterns, inequalities in earnings and benefits, and career ladders (Althauser and Kalleberg 1981). In order to theorize about segmentation structures in China, it is necessary to briefly review earlier analyses available on economic and labor market segmentation in market capitalism.

Economic Segmentation in Market Capitalism

Both Marxist and non-Marxist economists credit the profit-seeking behavior of the capitalist enterprise as the underlying force of economic segmentation. Chandler (1962, 1977) argued that the maximization of profits is the reason why small firms merged into giant corporations, and why bureaucratic mechanisms emerged to coordinate these giant corporations. "Multiunit business enterprise replaced small traditional enterprise when administrative coordination permitted greater productivity, lower costs, and higher profits than coordination by market mechanisms" (Chandler 1977, p. 6). Edwards (1979, viii), from a neo-Marxist point of view, argued that profitability is *the* reason behind the transformation from simple forms of control of workers to bureaucratic control: "Hierarchy at work exists and persists because it is *profitable*" (italics in original). According to Gordon, Edwards, and Reich (1982), segmentation analysis is concerned with the connections between capitalist development and working-class life and is generally intended to develop "a sufficient theory of capitalist development."

Institutional economists contend that the consequence of capitalist development is a dual economic structure. Researchers have used different terms to describe two distinct sectors: core and periphery (Averitt 1968), concentrated and unconcentrated (Bluestone 1970), planned and market (Galbraith 1973), and monopoly and competitive (O'Connor 1973). According to Hodson and Kaufman (1982), these various terms all apply to the same features of two basic sectors. The core sector (the most commonly used term) consists of firms and industries with a large number of employees, high capitalization, large profits and sales, monopolistic positions in product and labor markets, advanced technologies, high productivity, and high rates of unionization. The periphery sector, on the other hand, consists of firms and industries with a small number of employees, low capitalization, and low profitability and productivity. Although others (e.g., Edwards, Reich, and Gordon 1975; Gordon, Edwards, and Reich 1982) have suggested a "segmentation" model in which more than two sectors are possible, their theoretical interests in devising a model for capitalist development remain primary.

From a Marxist point of view, Gordon, Edwards, and Reich (1982, chap. 1) have argued that economic segmentation was the inevitable result of the historical development of capitalism. To these researchers, the American economy experienced a transition from entrepreneurial to corporative capitalism, or from a competitive to a monopoly economy, roughly between 1890 and 1920. Consequently, in their view, American workers were segmented between jobs in the primary (monopoly) and secondary (competitive) segments, and between independent and subordinate jobs within the primary segment.

Labor Market Segmentation in Market Capitalism

The important question regarding labor market segmentation is: Why do individuals who have the *same characteristics* but are positioned in different segments of the labor market structure enjoy *different sets of rewards*? Institutional economists have offered a "firm ability" theory. They contend that firms and industries with monopoly positions in commodity markets promote sales and profits, and therefore have a greater ability to offer earnings and benefits than do "peripheral" firms and industries. This ability to offer earnings and benefits to workers is affected by firm characteristics such as capital intensity, concentration, production duration, and size.[1] Earnings and benefits are viewed as a mechanism for controlling labor by the capitalist class (Edwards 1979; Gordon, Edwards, and Reich 1982), or as a means of maintaining labor stability, which is seen to be essential to a firm's productivity (Doeringer and Piore 1971) and long-term profitability (Chandler 1977).

New structural sociologists use a "worker power" theory to argue that selfish capitalists are not so much interested in as constrained to providing more rewards. As Bibb and Form (1977, p. 978) point out, "the economic stratification of enterprises is matched by the organizational power of occupational groups." Union membership, tenure with the firm, skills, occupational licensing, and managerial positions are all seen to contribute, both collectively and individually, to worker power, which in turn generates earnings (Kalleberg, Wallace, and Althauser 1981). Because these forms of worker power are more feasible and effective in monopoly or advantaged firms and industries, it has been argued that structural features of the workplace are "resources" not only for capitalists and management to manipulate workers, but also for workers to bargain with the capitalist and managerial classes for rewards (Hodson 1983, chap. 3).

Many have argued that labor market outcomes are more directly a result of internal organizational dynamics than of economic segmentation (Chandler 1977; Edwards 1979; Baron and Bielby 1980, 1984; Hodson 1983). In contrast to the economic dualists, who emphasize industrial segmentation as causes of labor market inequalities, new sociological structuralists examine internal labor markets along with organizations, classes, occupations, and industries (Althauser and Kalleberg 1981; Baron 1984). Researchers generally agree that there is a direct relationship between internal labor markets and workers' outcomes such as firm tenure, turnover, earnings, benefits, and promotion, but their interpretations about causes and consequences of that relationship differ. Internal labor markets are seen in various ways: as mechanisms to transfer work skills from senior to junior workers to maintain the firm's productivity (Doeringer and Piore 1971); as administrative coordination necessary to promote profits for giant firms (Chandler 1977); as a reflection of market imperfection that favors hierarchical promotions rather than perfectly competitive mechanisms (Williamson 1975); as an effort by the capitalist class to control workers (Edwards 1975, 1979); or as unions' efforts to protect job security, earnings, and benefits for workers (Hodson 1983).

Segmentation Research in Eastern Europe and China

Despite a neo-Marxist position that economic and labor market segmentation are derived from capitalist development, in state socialist societies where there is a lack of capitalist enterprises and a capitalist class, these types of segmentation may well exist. For example, Hungary's income distribution in the 1970s was a function of its political-economic organizations; it favored government bureaucrats and deprived the working classes in factories and villages (Szelenyi 1978; Jenkins 1987). In Poland, data collected in the 1980s show that the likelihood of workers receiving material incentives was contingent on workers' placement in certain industries and economic sectors (Domanski 1988, 1990). In China, differentials in wages and fringe benefits have existed for workers in the state and collective sectors (Whyte and Parish 1984, chap. 4; Davis-Friedmann 1985; Walder 1986, p. 41). The sectoral difference in income distribution continued to be significant in China through the 1980s (Hu, Li, and Shi 1988; Walder 1990), and workplace identification has become a more desirable way of achieving status than occupation per se for urban workers (Lin and Bian 1991). These various country data suggest that the absence of market capitalism does not rule out the segmentation phenomenon.

The existence of the segmentation phenomenon in Eastern Europe and China does not necessarily mean that economic and labor market segmentation in planned societies are implemented with the same processes and mechanisms as in market societies. These processes are, in fact, either nonexistent or greatly altered in planned economies. First, individual firms in planned economies are not oriented toward profits. Socialist firms operate under bureaucratic rather than market coordination. In a socialist state, the government controls and allocates resources needed for production, assigns projects and output quotas, sets prices of products to meet designated goals, collects all profits, and redistributes income to individuals. Government subsidies are guaranteed to maintain all enterprises.

Second, internal labor markets are largely nonexistent in the planned economies. For example, before 1978 in China, jobs were guaranteed through government assignments, and employers were not allowed to lay off workers. Wages and benefits were centrally regulated, salary increases were determined by state budgets, and career promotions followed ranking systems imposed by central planners. It was only during the economic reforms of the 1980s that internal labor markets were being used for the distribution of material incentives and promotions (see Stark 1986 for Hungarian practices; Walder 1989 and Davis 1993 for China).

Third, worker power in planned economies is limited. In pre-reform China, job turnover between workplaces was restricted through organizational procedures in order to protect labor stability, as required by central planning (Davis 1990). Also, worker unions were subject to the Communist party, and cooperated with the government and workplace management to control rather than serve workers[2] (Walder 1986, p. 96). Tenure in the workplace was unimportant, because of low job turnover (Davis 1990). Occupational licensing was nonexistent in the state and collective sectors, and rendered unnecessary because of the bureaucratic allocation of labor (Lin and Bian 1991).

Domanski (1988, 1990) has advanced an explanation of labor market segmentation in Poland. He observed that earnings were higher in the Polish state sector than in nonstate sectors, and higher in the mining sector than in any other manufacturing and non-manufacturing sectors. Domanski explained these wage differentials with a labor shortage argument: the Polish government, with the intent of protecting its state sector, consciously provided material incentives to stimulate the influx of workers into industries and firms "preferred" by the government. A similar argument was offered by Burawoy and Lukacs (1985) for Hungary, where worker benefits were used to discourage the outflow of labor from the Hungarian state sector.

This argument assumes that a neoclassical relation between labor supply and demand existed in Poland and Hungary, which in turn implies that the "worker power" explanation may be plausible for Eastern Europe. Such a relationship was greatly altered in pre-reform China, where oversupply of labor was sustained by the bureaucratic process (Walder 1986; Davis 1990; Lin and Bian 1991). Under these circumstances, interfirm job turnover, when it did occur, was more often the result of workers avoiding potentially negative effects on their careers than having adopted overt strategies for advancement (Davis 1990, 1993). In addition, there were no independent labor unions in China such as there were in Poland. What, then, are the dynamics of the labor process in China?

Workplace Segmentation in Pre-Reform China

Workplace segmentation here is understood as the unequal distribution of resources and opportunities among work organizations. This terminology is preferable to the widely used "economic segmentation" because segmentation processes within a state socialist framework in general, and in the Chinese context in particular, are indeed less economic than administrative in nature. In fact, I will show how workplace segmentation in pre-reform China stemmed from and was sustained by a bureaucratic process.

System-Oriented Goals and Strategies

A socialist state, unlike its market counterpart, bases its economy on a wide range of public ownership. Since the state has full control over resources, firms become subordinate "work units" of the centrally planned system. Within the Stalin model of high centralization, socialist firms had little motivation to pursue profits; instead, they operated under "soft budget constraints" that led to high production costs (Kornai 1986). Even during the economic reforms of the 1980s, enterprises in Hungary (Kornai 1989) and China (Lin 1989) were still strongly controlled by state bureaucratic processes of decision making. Firms in the United States may have state-sponsored projects and be subject to government pressures and influences, but these capitalist firms are doing business with the government, operating the state-sponsored projects as transactions in market terms. They can negotiate prices of the products to sell to the government in reference to market values, and their business relationships with the government are terminated after the completion of such projects. Enterprises under classical state socialism are in a very different situation. State and collective organizations are not viewed as independent firms, and they must take all direction from the state.

In such a command economy, developmental goals and strategies are system-oriented. In China, these goals and strategies were laid out in the documents of the Communist party or in the speeches of its leadership, even if sometimes in vague terms and reflecting unrealistic ambitions. In the early 1950s, China's goal was to restore the economy after the war years of 1937 to 1949. The basic strategy adopted was to develop various types of economic organizations, including private corporations. By the late 1950s, the national goal was "to catch up with the United States and surpass Britain" and, because China's industrial development was then and still is considerably lower than the United States' and Britain's, and because outside support of advanced technologies was not available, China's strategy was to mobilize a large-scale work force committed to labor-intensive mass production. Throughout the 1960s and 1970s, the "socialist construction of four modernizations"[3] was declared several times by the leadership as a statement of the national goal, and tighter state control of business enterprises and activities was the fundamental strategy adopted. The current regime under Deng Xiaoping's leadership is committed to a more measurable goal: to increase gross national output fourfold over the twenty years from 1980 to 2000, a growth rate that has been artificially and politically projected. The new leadership is committed to a strategy of developing a "planned commodity economy," in which state planning and governmental control are accompanied and supplemented by market coordination (Perkins 1986; Lin 1989).

The Allocation of National Resources and Incentives

These system-oriented goals and strategies require that economic resources and incentives be distributed according to government interests. Three government interests are critical: (1) ideological interests of the Communist party, (2) national interests of state planners, and (3) control interests of government administration.

Ideological Interests of the Communist Party. One feature that distinguishes state socialist economies from other nonmarket economies is that they are operated by Communist parties. The ideological interest of the Chinese Communist party in maintaining state ownership over the means of production has guided the restructuring of work organizations. After the Communist revolution in 1949, the state took over all industrial and financial firms that had been controlled by leading figures in the former Nationalist government or by foreign capitalists. At the same time, the nationalization of telecommunications, education, scientific research, entertainment, and sports took place to allow the party to control these "superstructures" of the state. During the socialist transformation in 1956, all vital firms in the private sector were turned over to the state. The rest of the economy was organized within a supplementary "collective" sector and a tiny private sector. For the last forty years, the state sector has been given priority over the collective sector in the supply of finance, material, and labor. Also, state sector workers have been provided with higher wages and benefits than collective sector workers. Individual laborers had been deprived of both resources and incentives for quite some time before the policy changes of the late 1970s.

National Interests of State Planners. Whereas the Communist party is ideology-driven, its state planners are oriented more toward a set of national interests, namely, the increase of state capital, economic growth, and industrialization. These national interests require that resources and incentives be allocated to certain industries whose products are essential to the country's overall economic plan. In China, state budgets favor heavy industries over light industries because their products, such as energy, steel and iron, and machinery, are the material basis for industrialization. Export industries have been favored over import industries because the foreign currency generated from international trade allows state planners to buy technologies from the West. In short, not only are sufficient budgets guaranteed for favored industries, but also prices of products, government subsidies, retention of profits, and wage standards are biased in their favor (Walder 1986, chap. 2; Li 1991, pp. 77–128).

Control Interests of Government Administration. All government bureaucracies have an interest in controlling the economic resources and incentives under their jurisdictions. In China, state and collective organizations are operated by each of the five levels of government administration. Central ministries operate large industrial complexes. At the next three levels are the governments of provinces (or municipalities or autonomous regions), cities or prefects, and urban districts or rural counties, all of which operate vital firms at each level. The lowest level is composed of small businesses operated by urban subdistricts or rural townships. This administrative structure forms the hierarchy in which national resources and incentives are allocated from the central command to the various levels of local governments, and favors accrue to the higher levels of government jurisdictions and their subordinate work organizations. In wage determination, for example, state-fixed wage standards have been set at the highest rate for workers in central ministry-run organizations and are lowest for those in the lowest levels of local-run enterprises (Li 1990, p. 85).

At all levels of the hierarchy, work organizations are assigned bureaucratic ranks similar to those used to rank military organizations. This ranking method defines the power and authority of work organizations within and across administrative boundaries, and consequently the power and authority of the individuals who head them. Ranking also facilitates another control interest: under the same government jurisdiction, organizations with a higher bureaucratic rank can obtain more resources and incentives than organizations with a lower bureaucratic rank. In addition, work organizations with a higher rank have greater ability to cross administrative boundaries to obtain resources and incentives from government agencies and other organizations.

Labor, Management, and Incentives in Pre-Reform China

Ideological interests of the Communist party, national interests of state planners, and control interests of government administration determine how resources and incentives tend to be distributed to work organizations in the state sector, in certain industries,
and at high levels of the government bureaucracy. Thus, organizations with these interests are often able to provide more incentives
to their managers and workers. But why do they *want* to do so?

Labor as a National Resource

The Chinese Communist regime recognizes a citizen's right to
work. But this regime also denies an individual's private labor rights.
In official economics textbooks, labor has been defined as a commonwealth of the state, not as a private right of the individual. In
practical terms, labor has been treated as a national resource, not as
a commodity. Like the allocation of financial and material resources, the allocation of labor reflects the ideological interests of
the party, the national interests of state planners, and the control
interests of government jurisdictions. Therefore, organizations in
favored sectors, industries, or bureaucratic levels obtain and hoard
more and better labor resources.

Obtaining Labor Resources Through Job Assignments. Government job assignments have been the primary mechanism for the
allocation of labor resources in China. Before economic reforms in
the 1980s, state labor agencies had the ultimate authority to control
labor supply and demand. On the supply side, students were required to enroll in government job assignment programs after graduation from high school or college. Individual job searches were prohibited in both state and collective sectors. Urban youths did not
look for jobs but waited for an assignment from their local state
labor agencies. On the demand side, state labor agencies controlled
and distributed labor quotas to work organizations. Administratively, it was illegal to hire workers outside of quotas. Food rationing was also an effective economic means to maintain administrative control. With these mechanisms, the government was able to
control and allocate labor resources according to its ideological, national, and control interests.

State labor agencies were not the only actors in the job assignment process. Work organizations also influenced government decisions on the allocation of new workers. Formally, work organizations were allowed to submit proposals to government labor

agencies for labor quotas, and request new workers with specific qualifications. Informally, managers of these organizations bargained with government officials for favorable assignments. Although the more formal type of influence favored organizations with government priorities, informal bargaining favored only those organizations with a higher bureaucratic rank: the managers of these organizations had the ability to contact and influence high-ranking officials.

Hoarding Labor Resources Through Organizational Control. As a national resource, Chinese labor was collectively "owned." The ownership of labor by the work unit (*danwei suoyouzhi*) was the basic form of this collective ownership of labor. These work units were given the ownership rights of the labor force they used in their production of goods and services. A staff member or worker could not leave for another job without the permission of his or her current employer. Another form was the ownership of labor by government jurisdictions (*bumen suoyouzhi*). At the local level, a municipal bureau or a company had the authority to permit job switching between work organizations, within the government jurisdiction or across it.

These organizational barriers to interfirm job turnover led to "hoarding" behavior: work organizations intentionally kept their experienced management staff, technicians, and skilled workers. Such hoarding behavior took away an individual's freedom to change jobs. But at the same time, it also limited the flexibility of work organizations to distribute human resources across organizations, simply because each and every work organization tended to hoard its personnel whether it used them effectively or not. Under these circumstances, work organizations have had to rely on job assignments for recruitment. In addition, new businesses relied on their government jurisdictions to "transfer" experienced technicians and skilled workers, or to exchange technicians and workers with other organizations for mutual benefit. In China, this practice was known as a "two-way transfer."

Incentives as a Strategy of Management

Administrative barriers to interfirm job switching were effective for hoarding labor resources. But this does not mean that workers being hoarded in their workplaces would definitely have positive work commitments. Incentives were needed both for preventing negative and promoting positive work behaviors. Negative behaviors included intentional slowdown of work schedules, the engagement of personal work during working hours, the hiding of scarce tools for exclusive personal use, the wasting of raw materials, inattention to output quality, and the damaging of machinery or other facilities. These were the ways workers used to express dissatisfaction with wages, benefits, working conditions, political atmosphere, and managerial inabilities to provide incentives (Haraszti 1979; Walder 1987). The extensive use of punishment to resolve worker problems broadened and worsened them in the long run. Instead, "state-of-the-art" leadership attempted to use incentives as the primary strategy to prevent these negative behaviors (Li 1990).

Incentives were largely provided to stimulate positive work behaviors that affected workplace performance, which in turn was used by government authorities to evaluate workplace party secretaries and managers. For promotion purposes, party secretaries and managers made strong efforts to stimulate employees with various sets of incentives, whether political, material, or organizational.

Political Incentives. Chinese work organizations also established a comprehensive "model worker" program. To be a model worker was a social and political honor. Each year, model workers were selected by mass elections, or by appointment of the party secretaries and managers, or both. These model workers could be all-around models as well as models for specific aspects of work life. The same kind of program was conducted to select model cadres, model women workers, model youth league members, model party members, model work teams, model work units, and model companies or bureaus.

Another political incentive was Communist party membership. Model workers and politically active workers were granted party memberships as a result of better performances or for their loyalty to party branch secretaries and management (Walder 1986). Both party members and activists were promised promotions for their efforts and their success in inspiring, correcting, and directing workers (including monitoring any negative behavior of other workers and reporting it to party and managerial authorities in the workplace).

Material Incentives. Political incentives were provided only to a minority of the work force. Management in China used material incentives to reinforce positive behaviors from the majority of the work force. Although cash-income incentives were largely controlled by central planners, workplace management had "strategies" to break free from this bureaucratic control. One strategy was to bargain for a lower output quota in order to produce a greater chance of retaining above-quota bonuses (Walder 1986, p. 111). Another strategy was to use piece rates rather than time rates, which allowed workers to earn extra wages after completion of assigned quotas (Li 1991, p. 231). Finally, workers were assigned extra hours of work at the end of each month, quarter, or year, which allowed them to receive more pay (Yuan 1990, p. 189).

Noncash incentives were largely available in the workplace. First, workers were rewarded with material prizes, which were less restricted than cash bonuses.[4] Second, work organizations, particularly large enterprises and high-ranking agencies, controlled housing units and used them as rewards to their managers and workers. Third, comprehensive welfare programs were developed in the workplace to satisfy the daily needs of workers. These welfare programs included meal halls, medical clinics, bathing facilities, retail services, infant day care and kindergartens, sports and entertainment activities, and libraries. Fourth, work organizations used production resources for the welfare of employees and their families. A few examples illustrate this point: railway companies offered free train tickets to employees and their dependents; universities opened subsidiary high schools and elementary schools for the children of their employees; appliance manufacturers sold their products (which were in short supply in the market) to their employees at discount prices. Finally, many work organizations opened supplementary units to hire their employees' spouses and children.

Organizational Incentives. This final set of incentives refers to measures of rewards associated with one's tenure. Tenure in a work unit may not be important for wages or fringe benefits, because the distribution of wages and benefits followed government regulation. Seniority, however, could be a significant determinant of wages and benefits (Hu, Li, and Shi 1988; Walder 1990). But tenure in a work unit is a critical criterion for any patron-client relationships between party secretaries and political activists, between workplace managers and their administrative and technical subordinates, and between shop-floor supervisors and their workers. The longer one stays in a work unit, the greater the chance of developing instrumental ties with one's leaders, and the higher the likelihood of gaining the trust of one's leaders. These patron-client relationships were important not only for one's career promotions but also for acquiring the political and material incentives already mentioned (see also Walder 1986).

Segmentation in a Planned Commodity Economy

China's market-oriented reforms since 1978 have affected both rural and urban economies. These reforms, like those in Hungary and Poland, were initiated to overcome the difficulties resulting from a highly centralized economy (Brus 1989; Kornai 1989). The current central reform directive has been to transform administrative control into market coordination. In China, such a process has taken place only partially, resulting in a "planned commodity economy" in which both administrative and market forces alter economic activities (Perkins 1986). Szelenyi (1989) argues that this mixed economy will characterize state socialist societies for rather a long time, because the transition to market coordination, in which private ownership is dominant, will not be easy and cannot be accomplished in a short period. This is particularly true for urban China. After a decade of market reform, private sector workers were, according to the official statistics, only about 4 percent of the urban labor force in 1987, the year that witnessed the peak of market reforms. Thus, in this research, I pay special attention to the state and collective sectors, which absorb more than 95 percent of the labor and produced the same percentage of the industrial output values (State Statistical Bureau of China 1989, p. 19).

Income-Oriented Incentives and Sustained Segmentation

Extensive measures have been introduced since 1979 to distribute incentives in state and collective workplaces. For profit-making enterprises, the old *profit-turnover system*, in which enterprises turned over all profits to their government jurisdictions, has been replaced by a tax system, in which profits are divided between the government and enterprises on agreed contracts. Profits retained by industrial enterprises on average increased from 1.7 percent in 1978 to 44.6 percent in 1987, and about one-third of this amount was used in the form of bonuses (Liu and Xu 1991, p. 358). The remaining two-thirds was invested in the production, housing, and welfare facilities and benefits. Nonprofit institutions, upon completion of contracted missions with the government, are allowed to engage in income-oriented activities, and earnings made through these activities are distributed in the form of bonuses (Han, Ren, and Tian 1990, p. 193). Government agencies, however, are not provided with these incentives.

Workplace directors and workers respond to these reform initiatives by becoming increasingly profit-seeking and income-oriented. According to a 1986 Tianjin survey, salaries accounted for 70 percent of total earnings (Walder 1990), and were distributed according to strict government regulations. But retained profits motivate workplace managers to reward workers with bonuses for two reasons. In social-political terms, there is a greater expectation by workers that a manager will be able to generate bonuses in the new economic environment (Walder 1989). Thus, rewards are intended to promote worker performance, which in turn can lead to increased profits. This has now become the primary criterion of career promotion for managers (Liu and Xu 1991, p. 374). In addition, managers benefit from raising bonus funds in economic terms because the more funds they raise, the more money will go into the managers' pockets (Liu and Xu 1991, p. 383). Enterprises, then, are able to generate bonuses as the direct result of retained profits.

But institutional economists' firm ability theory does not fully account for this relationship between firm profitability and bonuses in the current reform era in China. One reason is that profit retention at the firm level is still in part affected by vertical relations with the government bureaucracy. Retained profits result from a case-by-case bargaining process with the government (Walder 1989, pp. 253–59; Li 1990, pp. 176–83). The lower the profits contracted to turn over to the state, the higher the profits retained by enterprises. Moreover, enterprises capable of getting resources from the government at a low state-fixed price, and then selling their outputs in commodity markets at a higher state-guided price (or at an even higher, negotiated price), will enjoy increased profits and greater retention of those profits (Walder 1987). Finally, retained profits are usually associated with price subsidies, tax benefits, and special funding that enterprises may receive from the state (Li 1990, p. 253). Because a "father-son" relationship still characterizes the socialist state and its production units (Li 1990, p. 176), enterprises with government priorities in the past continue to be favored in these vertically structured relations that now affect profit determination.

New Patterns of Economic Inequalities in the Urban Workplace

Bureaucratic coordination is not as deterministic in China as it was before market reforms. These reforms have substantially altered the basis of workplace segmentation and social stratification. Nee (1989) argues that the market transition will shift power, incentives, and opportunities from the central redistributive structure into the marketplace. Equally important, Nee (1991) argues that "partial reforms" retain the effects of the redistributive forces, and consequently require the coordination of the bureaucracy and markets to determine the distribution of resources and rewards in this early stage of transition. For example, in a study of rural households in South China, Nee discovered that the richest were peasant entrepreneurs who at the same time held village administrative positions.

The market transition theory should be useful in explaining changes occurring in the urban sector because it defines general rules of social stratification in state socialism.[5] But urban reforms do differ from rural reforms: decision-making power is partially decentralized to urban work units, rather than individual households. Just as peasant households are actors in the rural marketplace, work units are the direct producers in the cities. Work units, rather than individual workers, contract with the government bureaucracy and participate in markets. Workers are organized within their workplaces to produce profits and bonus funds, and, in turn, they are rewarded with bonuses and other incentives through the workplace, rather than in the larger marketplace. These developments are producing a new pattern of labor-reward distributions in urban China: the workplace is a primary initiator of labor rewards as a result of the shift from central control of incentives to enterprise autonomy; workplace managers are the new redistributors, in response to the shift of decision-making power from government bureaucrats to workplace authority; and workers gain power to demand rewards if they have greater political and human resources. I elaborate on these points in the sections that follow.

Workplaces as the Primary Initiators of Labor Rewards. There has been a remarkable shift in the workplace from the central control of incentives to an enterprise autonomy. The production and distribution of bonuses is one of the most visible areas where individual workplaces have gained decision-making power. At one time, workplaces influenced government decisions on the distribution of wages and incentives in only limited ways. Now enterprises and institutions actively organize their workers to produce profits and above-contract earnings. These profits and earnings, as documented already, are largely translated into bonuses and distributed. Just as peasants increase their earnings by becoming increasingly active in the rural market (Nee 1989, 1991), urban workers rely on their work units for improving their income. Specifically, urban workers depend on both the government and work units to increase salaries, but they rely solely on their workplaces for bonuses. In the analysis of Tianjin workers, this suggests that one's work unit would be associated more strongly with one's bonuses than with one's salary. As described earlier, the ability of work units to generate bonus funds varies considerably from one unit to the next. Thus, I anticipate that workplace segmentation will have greater effect on the distribution of bonuses than on that of salaries.

Workplace Managers as New Redistributors. Since 1979, workplace managers have gradually acquired more decision-making powers from government bureaucrats. One of these is the distribution of bonuses. Despite government regulation on bonuses in the workplace, party cadres and managers, who are now in control of sizable bonus funds, have the power to distribute these funds according to their own interests. In such a case, workplace management tends to gain redistributive power as government bureaucrats lose it. A further implication is that although overall social and economic inequalities may be reduced because reform has benefitted peasants and workers by removing the privileges of government redistributors (Szelenyi 1978), there in fact may be new inequalities generated between newly established redistributors and workers in the urban workplace.

Worker Power in the New Environment. Workers have gained power to demand rewards in light of the new environment in the workplace. When incentives were previously controlled by government authority, workers lacked effective autonomous organizations, such as unions in the United States (a market society) or Poland (a formerly socialist society), and could do little but protest by means of negative or uncooperative work behavior.[6] Now they are interacting with new redistributors: workplace managers, who depend on workers to produce profits and bonuses. For workers, this interdependence is their source of power for demanding rewards.

In the pre-reform period, the most effective worker power relationship, if any, was with one's work-unit party leader. Walder's "party clientelism" (Walder 1986, p. 162–86) predicted a pattern in which rewards were provided to party members and activists. But now workplace managers are more interested in a worker's performance and how it affects profits and bonuses, than in a worker's relationship with party secretaries or with the managers themselves. It appears that the basis of worker power may have been altered: as labor rewards once favored party members and political activists in pre-reform periods, they now favor workers who have exceptional abilities.

Sources of Data and Related Issues

The focus of analysis in this study is on the effects of work-place segmentation on the stratification of urban workers in the 1980s. The key data analyzed in this study come from a 1988 representative sample of 1008 adult residents in Tianjin, China. A description of the sampling and data collection procedures, along with a copy of the questionnaire, appear in Appendix A. Supplementary data include official statistics and in-depth interviews, which I conducted in Tianjin between 1983 and 1985 and in the United States between 1988 and 1992. Information about the in-depth interviews can be found in Appendix B.

Changing Situations in China and the Timing of the Survey

China has been politically, economically, and socially dynamic since the founding of the People's Republic in 1949. The country has also been in constant party-led campaigns. These major campaigns included (1) the Suppress Counter-Revolutionaries Campaign in 1950; (2) the Elimination of Counter-Revolutionaries Campaign from 1950–52; (3) the Land Reform Campaign from 1950–52; (4) the Ideological Remolding of Intellectuals Campaign in 1951–52; (5) the Anti-"Three Evils" Campaign against corruption, waste, and bureaucracy within the Communist party, government, army, and mass organizations in 1951–52; (6) the Anti-"Five Evils" Campaign against bribery, tax evasion, theft of state property, cheating on government contracts, and stealing of economic information in 1952–53; (7) the Agricultural Communalization Campaign from 1955–58; (8) the Socialist Transformation of Capitalist Industrial and Commercial Enterprises from 1956–58; (9) the Anti-Rightists Campaign to purge open-minded intellectuals in 1957; (10) the Great Leap Forward for rapid industrialization in 1958–59; (11) the Anti-Rightists Campaign within the Communist party in 1959; (12) the Socialist Education Campaign in rural and urban organizations in 1964–65, otherwise known as the "Four Clean-Ups" Campaign; (13) the Great Proletarian Cultural Revolution between 1966 and 1976; (14) the campaign against Deng Xiaoping for his intention and actions taken to reverse the principles of the Cultural Revolution from 1975–77; (15) the nationwide discussions focusing on the principle that "practice is the only criterion for testing the truthfulness of knowledge" in 1978–79; (16) the Campaign of Anti-Spiritual Pollution by the Bourgeoisie in 1983; (17) the Rectification Campaign of the Chinese Communist Party from 1984–86; and (18) the Campaign for the Elimination of Bourgeois Liberalization in early 1987. After the prodemocracy movement of April–June 1989, there was a party-led campaign to ferret out activists.[7] These campaigns altered political atmospheres and affected people's work and nonwork activities. Because of these campaigns, it is difficult to draw conclusions from a cross-sectional social survey, such as the one presented in this book, about *general* patterns of Chinese workplaces and their effects on workers. Such conclusions may be limited to one period of time and are subject to further tests based on data collected at other times.

The year 1988 marked a decade of China's market-oriented reforms. This was also the year that witnessed the peak reforms. Over the ten years, "market economies" as related to individual laborers, family businesses, private companies or corporations, foreign investments, and international joint ventures grew drastically in both urban and rural areas. Industries in a "collective" economic sector also grew fast, while the state sector shrank. As a result, the state's control of industrial products was reduced from more than 80 percent to 60 percent for the entire nation. In southern provinces such as Guangdong and Fujian, this percentage was reduced to less than 50 percent (State Statistical Bureau of China 1989, p. 19). Politically, 1988 was also a significant time. Despite a left-wing campaign to eliminate "bourgeois liberalization" in the first half of 1987, the Thirteenth Congress of the Chinese Communist Party in the same year declared that the main line of work for the party in the next decade was to further the policies of economic reforms. *Gaige-Kaifang-Gaohuo* (Reform, Openness, and Unrestrainedness) were the approved party slogans. Although conservative leaders occupied some key positions in the party's Central Committee and its politburo, as well as in the central administration, the new party secretary general Zhao Ziyang, who was supported by the senior, paramount leader Deng Xiaoping, led the majority of reform-minded party cadres at both the central and local levels. Under these circumstances, the year 1988 reached the highest degree of political openness since 1949. This openness nourished the prodemocracy demonstrations of 1989.

These economic and political situations made 1988 a desirable time for conducting a study on Chinese workplaces and workers. Very often, responses to survey questions are affected in one way or another by the changing world around the respondents (Lin 1976; Bailey 1986). This is particularly true in China, where people are generally careful about what they say on nonprivate occasions in order to survive under authoritarianism. During the Cultural Revo-

lution between 1966 and 1976, for example, because of radical political agendas and political intensity throughout the country, it was
almost impossible to use survey techniques to collect valid and reliable data inside China about the Chinese people's life experiences,
characteristics, and attitude towards the Communist regime. In a
sense, the political and economic openness of the 1980s prior to
June 1989 provided a high degree of security for the Chinese people
to willingly give truthful information about their jobs, workplaces,
and political affiliations, as well as their *guanxi* (interpersonal connections) used in the process of status attainment, their perceptions
of occupational and family lives, and their evaluations of current
party policies. All of these topics were included in the 1988 Tianjin
survey. This high degree of security was one of the bases under
which survey techniques were successfully used in collecting valid
and reliable data.

Tianjin as the Research Site

Tianjin is China's third-largest city and is located on the east
coast of the country, approximately eighty miles southeast of Beijing. In 1988 Tianjin had about 8.5 million registered residents. The
city is known as the birthplace of modern manufacturing industries
in North China, and had been an industrial urban center long before
the Communist party came to power in 1949. Since then, Tianjin
has been a leader in the country's chemical, textile, manufacturing,
and consumer-goods industries, and its industrial output values
have been ranked second, next to Shanghai, among Chinese cities.
The 1982 Chinese Census showed that of the total civilian labor
force in the city, 60 percent were manufacturing and transportation
workers, 15 percent sales and service workers, 5 percent clerical
workers, and 19 percent professionals and administrators (Population Census Office of Tianjin 1984, p. 244). These percentages were
comparable to those of all Chinese cities for the same year: 60 percent, 14 percent, 5 percent, and 20 percent, respectively (State Statistical Bureau of China 1983, pp. 350–52).[8]

Tianjin is not representative of Chinese cities in many re-
spects. Because of its size, its leading role in industrial development
in the North, its strength in science, technology, and higher education, and its proximity to the national capital, Tianjin has been
designated as one of three municipalities (with Beijing and Shanghai) under the jurisdiction of the central government. Some 250
other cities fall under the jurisdiction of either a province, an autonomous district, or a prefecture. For many reasons, economic reforms

in Tianjin, like those in Beijing and Shanghai, have been rather moderate compared with cities in many southern provinces. In 1988, for example, 70 percent of Tianjin's industrial output values were produced by the state sector, compared with 60 percent for the nation and less than 50 percent for southern cities in Guangdong and Fujian provinces (State Statistical Bureau of China 1989, p. 19). Thus, Tianjin represents a core locality in a planned economy during the reform period.

Organization of the Book

This chapter includes theoretical hypotheses that will lead the analyses in subsequent chapters. In Chapter 2, I describe and analyze the structures and functions of Chinese workplaces. In Chapters 3, 4, and 5, I focus on employment and job-mobility processes in order to analyze exactly how individuals are channelled into favored organizations. I employ a status attainment model for analysis, but specify how the Chinese pattern of status attainment varies from others, such as the American one. In Chapter 6, I investigate the importance of the workplace to a person's political life, with particular attention paid to Communist party membership and cadre status. I next look at wages (Chapter 7) and collective consumption (Chapter 8) to analyze salaries, bonuses, labor insurance and benefits, collective welfare facilities, and housing as a function of workplace segmentation. In the final chapter, I draw conclusions and discuss research problems for further study.

2

STRUCTURES AND FUNCTIONS OF WORK ORGANIZATIONS

The workplace of an urban resident in China, whether a factory, store, school, or government office, is known as a "work unit" (*gongzuo danwei*, usually abbreviated as *danwei*). Its influence in Chinese life is pervasive, as I will demonstrate.[1]

In Chinese official statistics, the work unit is defined as an independent accounting unit with three characteristics: (1) administratively, it is an independent organization; (2) fiscally, it has an independent budget and produces its own accounting tables of earnings and deficits, and (3) financially, it has independent accounts in banks and has the legal right to sign contracts with the government or with business entities (Yuan 1989, p. 514). "Independence" is a misleading term to define work units. Although the intent is to distinguish work organizations from their related units, whose administrative, fiscal, and financial statuses are part of a single "host" organization, work units in China have never been independent of government control. On the contrary, one can only understand the nature of work organizations through their relations to the government bureaucracy.

Work organizations are officially classified into three broad categories in terms of strategic functions: (1) profit-making enterprises, which are businesses engaged in the production and distribution of material commodities; (2) nonprofit institutions, which offer nonmaterial services, namely, education, research, cultural and fine arts, health and medicine, sports, banking, mass media, and the like; and (3) party and government agencies, which include administration, legislatures, courts, prosecutorial and security organs, political parties (the Communist party and recognized democratic parties[2]), and mass organizations (workers' unions, women's federations, and youth leagues[3]). Government administration is the core of these agencies. Most relevant is the fact that enterprises and institutions

are "owned" in varying degrees by the state, and state-owned organizations are operated directly by the government's system of
administration.

In the remainder of this chapter, I examine two *formal* structures of work organizations. The first is *ownership structure*, and
concerns the degree to which the state claims its ownership rights
over the economic properties of work organizations. The second is
bureaucratic structure; this type concerns the ways in which enterprises and institutions are organized, both horizontally and hier-
archically, by the government administration. I then analyze aggregate and individual data to show how these formal structures affect
the allocation of economic resources and labor rewards. Finally, I
describe some non-economic functions of work organizations.

The Ownership Structure

The elimination of private ownership over the means of production is a goal proclaimed by all Communist regimes. China is no
exception. After the Chinese Communist revolution in 1949, the
state took over firms that were controlled by leading figures in the
former Nationalist government or by foreign investors. Private businesses were still allowed to exist, but their activities and developments were limited by the government. In 1955, collectively owned
People's Communes began to spread in rural areas, and they became
the dominant form of economic organizations in the countryside. In
the cities, a government campaign called the "Socialist Transformation of the Capitalist Industrial and Commercial Industries"[4] was
underway. The aim was to transform vital private enterprises and
institutions into state-owned ones. Other private and corporate
businesses formed a "collective" sector in which the properties of
enterprises were owned, as interpreted by the Chinese government,
by employees. By 1956, the primary course of the economic transformation was completed. Although several transitional forms of ownership were initiated during the reforms, the Chinese urban economy contained a predominant state sector, a dependent collective
sector, and a tiny private sector. Not until the late 1970s did private
businesses, foreign investment, and domestic and international
joint ventures reemerge. Table 2.1 shows this historical trend in the
distribution of China's urban labor force from 1949 to 1988.

Historians and economists have provided detailed accounts of
these transformation processes (Fairbank 1986, chap. 15; Chamberlain 1987; Lin 1989). My purpose here is different. Rather than dis-

TABLE 2.1

Distribution of the Urban Labor Force by Sector, China, 1949–1988

Year	Total (in ten thousands)	Percentage* of Urban Labor in:			
		State	Collective	Individual	Other
1949	1533	32.2	0.6	66.2	. . .
1952	2486	63.6	0.9	35.5	. . .
1953	2754	66.3	1.1	32.6	. . .
1954	2744	68.5	4.4	27.0	. . .
1955	2802	68.1	9.1	22.8	. . .
1956	2993	81.0	18.5	0.5	. . .
1957	3205	76.5	20.3	3.2	. . .
1958	5300	85.5	12.5	2.0	. . .
1959	5389	84.6	13.2	2.1	. . .
1960	6119	82.4	15.1	2.5	. . .
1961	5336	78.2	18.7	3.1	. . .
1962	4537	72.9	22.3	4.8	. . .
1963	4603	71.5	23.4	5.0	. . .
1964	4828	71.8	23.5	4.7	. . .
1965	5136	72.8	23.4	3.3	. . .
1966	5354	73.5	23.6	2.9	. . .
1967	5446	73.6	23.9	2.6	. . .
1968	5630	74.1	23.7	2.2	. . .
1969	5825	74.4	23.7	1.9	. . .
1970	6312	75.9	22.6	1.5	. . .
1971	6868	77.4	21.4	1.2	. . .
1972	7250	77.4	21.0	0.9	. . .
1973	7388	78.5	21.5	0.7	. . .
1974	7687	78.1	21.4	0.5	. . .
1975	8222	78.2	21.6	0.3	. . .
1976	8692	78.9	20.9	0.2	. . .
1977	9127	78.8	21.0	0.2	. . .
1978	9514	78.3	21.5	0.2	. . .
1979	9999	76.9	22.7	0.3	. . .
1980	10,525	76.2	23.0	0.8	. . .
1981	11,053	75.7	23.2	1.0	. . .
1982	11,428	75.5	23.2	1.3	. . .
1983	11,746	74.7	23.4	2.0	. . .
1984	12,229	70.6	26.3	2.8	0.3
1985	12,808	70.2	26.0	3.5	0.3

(continued)

TABLE 2.1   (Continued)

Year	Total (in ten thousands)	Percentage* of Urban Labor in:			
		State	Collective	Individual	Other
1986	13,292	70.2	25.7	3.6	0.4
1987	13,787	70.0	25.3	4.1	0.5
1988	14,267	70.0	24.7	4.6	0.7

*All percentages were calculated from tables.

Source:
(1) Data for 1952–1988: *Statistical Yearbook of China: 1989*, State Statistical Bureau (1989, p. 101).
(2) Data for 1949: State Statistical Bureau (1984, p. 107 and p. 111).

cuss how each sector came into being, or exactly how each sector has risen, declined, or reemerged, I focus on those general features of each sector that are important in the social stratification of urban workers.

Between State and Collective Sectors

State and collective organizations share two features in common. First, no individual can claim ownership rights over property in state or collective organizations. Second, organizations in both sectors are operated by government agencies. But these two sectors vary significantly in the degree to which they are subject to government control, both before and after the economic reforms of the 1980s. This degree can be measured by the following variables: ownership rights, profits and finance, labor and material resources, and wages and fringe benefits.

Ownership Rights. The properties of a state organization are owned by "all the people" of the country (*quanmin suoyou zhi*). The state claims to be the only representative of the people in the country, and therefore retains ownership rights over "all the people's" firms. Traditionally, a state firm was not allowed to sell, lease, or transfer its properties and products; only the government had the jurisdiction and the right to do so. In a modified *planned commodity economy* in China under current reforms, the state still claims ownership rights over the properties of state firms, but it allows them to operate by themselves on agreed contracts with the government. In contrast, a collective organization's economic assets, capital, and products are owned by its employees. The organization itself is allowed to make transactions with these economic resources, even though it is required to notify its government jurisdiction of any transactions made.

Profits and Finance. Traditionally state firms turned their profits over to the government, which in turn supplied them with finance, materials, and labor. Government subsidies were guaranteed. In the modified planned commodity economy, these state firms contract with the government for production projects and for the supply of bank loans, materials, and labor. They negotiate with the government for tax rates that are tailored to enterprises. They also are allowed to retain profits after the government contract has been fulfilled. If they encounter deficits that are "policy-permitted," they are entitled to government subsidies. In contrast, whether in traditional or modified planned economies, a collective firm is treated more as an independent business entity: it pays taxes to the state, remits a management fee to its government jurisdiction, resumes ownership rights over profits after taxes, and is solely responsible for any losses. Collective enterprises may apply for state loans for emergencies such as bankruptcy.

Labor and Material Resources. Through the recent periods of economic change in China, labor and materials needed for the production of goods and services have remained under the control of the government. By means of quotas and job assignments, labor resources are guaranteed to state organizations, and better-qualified workers are channeled into state firms rather than collective enterprises. On the other hand, available material resources are classified into four categories (described in the next section), and each of them is subject to government control, from central to local administration. Through a quota system, state firms are given the privilege of having better and more materials; collective firms do not necessarily participate in this allocation process and must rely more on the markets for the supply of materials.

Wages and Fringe Benefits. Wages for state workers have been regulated by the central government's labor department both before and after the 1985 wage reforms (discussed in Chapter 7 in detail). Wage increases before the reforms were determined by the state. After the reforms, and pending government approval, profit-making enterprises were allowed to raise wages, using money from their retained profits. For fringe benefits, state workers continue to be protected by a national labor insurance and welfare system of pensions, medical care, and various welfare benefits. A different wage and fringe benefit system has been used for collective sector workers, in which their wages are subject to local regulation. Basically, standard wages in the same occupation for the same industry are lower for collective workers than they are for state workers, and wage increases are dependent not only on government approval but also on their budgets. There is no government protection of insurance and fringe benefits for collective workers. Workers in large and high-ranking collectives have certain limited benefits, and those in small and lower-ranking collectives have virtually none.[5]

Summary. The disparities between organizations in the state and collective sectors are dictated by the ideological interests of the Communist party, whose purpose is to maintain state ownership over the means of production and consumption. Although both state and collective organizations are regarded by the party as publicly owned, to Chinese leadership the state sector is ideologically "more advanced" (Mao 1957; Chen 1956). In the traditionally planned economy, economic resources, business opportunities, and incentives were all subject to government allocation. Being controlled by the government meant that state organizations had the privilege of retaining these resources, opportunities, and incentives. As a result, collective enterprises, under less government control, received fewer resources, opportunities, and incentives. This pattern has continued in the new planned commodity economy, although collective enterprises do enjoy greater freedom in increasing wages. This only benefits workers in collective firms that have the ability to pay higher wages.

Businesses in the Private Sector

Domestic Private Businesses. The domestic private sector is composed of (1) individual laborers (self-employed), (2) family businesses (*getihu*), and (3) private companies (*siren gongsi*). Officially, this third type of business is one in which investment capital comes from individual investors and the company hires eight or more employees. It can be individually owned, co-owned and cooperative, or a limited corporation. In Tianjin as in other cities, these three types of domestic private businesses are licensed by the Bureau of Managing Industrialists and Merchants.

Workers in the domestic private sector come from several sources. There are those who have not found jobs in the state and collective organizations. Others are retired state and collective workers. A third source is people who have quit their jobs in state or collective work units. However, many of these people have kept their names on the employee list in their former work units. This arrangement, with the support of the government, allows these workers to come back when they decide to. The fourth source is people who acquire second jobs in the private sector. Government officials and employees are not permitted to engage in this type of arrangement. The fifth source is the massive number of peasant workers who come to work in small cities and towns. Because of population pressures, large cities have typically restricted the hiring of peasant workers.

Systematic data on the composition of these sources of private-sector workers are not available. However, observations by individual researchers (Gold 1990) have clearly shown that increasing personal income is the driving force behind domestic private businesses. These private businesses have been concentrated in the retail service sector, in which the shortage of various commodities and services has favored sellers rather than buyers. Furthermore, private businesses find ways to avoid being taxed. Consequently, private-sector workers have been able to raise their wages higher than those in the state and collective sectors.

Foreign Capital Investment. Businesses that receive foreign investments are known in China as "three capitalist enterprises" (TCE). "Three" here refers to the three ways in which foreign capital can be invested in a China-based firm: (1) Chinese-foreign jointly shared businesses, in which the stock of the business is shared by Chinese and foreign investors; (2) Chinese-foreign contract businesses, in which the distribution of profits foreign capital enterprises; and foreign businesses. Chinese partners in the first two types are limited to business enterprises and individual investors. Government agencies and nonprofit institutions are not permitted to develop joint ventures with foreign investors.

Three capitalist enterprises are the primary mechanisms used by the Chinese government to attract foreign capital investment. The government has provided tax exemptions for imported materials needed by TCEs and has also offered property and income tax deductions. For example, all China-based international joint ventures are offered income tax exemptions for the first two years in which these firms have profits. For the next three years, income taxes are cut in half. Only from the sixth year on are these firms required to pay full taxes. Independent foreign capitalist firms are offered similar tax benefits (Huai 1991, chaps. 14 and 15; Chen and Wei 1991, chap. 10). These benefits, among other factors such as advanced technology and more efficient management, reduce the production costs and increase earnings. As a result, TCEs have the ability to pay higher wages than domestic state and collective enterprises. Because of the higher wages offered, many state and collective workers quit their secured jobs in order to work in TCEs.

Summary. There has been a remarkable growth of workers in the domestic private sector and the three capitalist enterprises since market reforms began in 1978 (see Table 2.1). However, private-sector workers are still only a small portion of the urban labor force. In 1988, when the Tianjin survey was conducted, workers in Tianjin's private and "other" sectors comprised only 2.0 percent of the total labor force (State Statistical Bureau of China 1989, pp. 112–19), which was lower than the 5.3 percent of the country as a whole. These workers, however, are not central to the present study, which focuses on the impact of *socialist* workplaces on urban workers. For this reason, I examine in depth the state and collective sectors in my description and analysis of the bureaucratic structure.

The Bureaucratic Structure

In China, the government administration is composed of five bureaucratic levels: (1) central; (2) province, autonomous municipal city, or autonomous district; (3) city or prefect (nonexistent for autonomous municipal cities such as Beijing, Shanghai, and Tianjin); (4) urban district or rural county; and (5) urban subdistrict or rural township. Within each level, administrative branches (i.e., central ministries and local bureaus) are established to control work organizations and coordinate economic activities. Every enterprise or institution belongs to an administrative ministry or bureau at one of the given levels of administration. Figure 2.1 illustrates a simplified bureaucratic structure of work organizations in Tianjin.

An Illustration of the Bureaucracy: Tianjin

In the figure, terms boxed in rectangles symbolize government agencies, whereas those without rectangles refer to enterprises and institutions. An arrow with a solid line denotes direct command and fiscal relations: a lower-level unit receives commands and budgets from the next-higher level of the hierarchy. A diagonal arrow with a broken line denotes vertical coordinating relationships. In such relationships, a higher level in the hierarchy sends tasks, requests, or instructions to the next-lower level of the hierarchy to

FIGURE 2.1

Bureaucratic Structure of Work Organizations in Tianjin

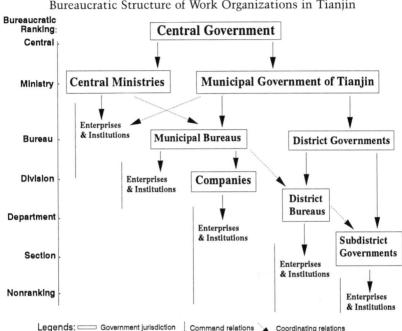

coordinate "business," but the higher level is not responsible for the budgets of the lower-level units it coordinates. For example, the municipal bureau of education in Tianjin receives orders and budgets from the municipal government. It also receives instructions, tasks, and technical support from the central government's ministry of education, and reports its work performance back to the ministry. The level of the hierarchy to which a government agency, enterprise, or institution belongs is indicated by its official bureaucratic ranking (the vertical scale on left side of figure).

Below the central government in the hierarchy are two systems: the central ministry system and the municipal system. The central ministry system has a simple structure; enterprises and institutions in this system are operated directly without intermediate management agencies. The central government has some fifty ministries, each being identified with a major industry or a major function of the government. Industrial ministries such as machinery, chemical, textile, petroleum, power and water, transportation, railroad, and light industries all have operations in Tianjin (as well as in other large urban centers in the country). Nonindustrial ministries such as education, health, finance, research academies, and the China News Agency have universities, research centers, or agencies operated in the city. These ministry-operated organizations have high bureaucratic ranks, ranging in positions close to the rank of ministry (for an industrial complex) down to the rank of division (for single-unit factory or branch office).

The municipal system is subdivided into three government levels: municipal, district, and subdistrict. The municipal level commands some sixty bureaus. Vital enterprises and institutions in Tianjin are operated directly by municipal bureaus. Any variation in bureaucratic ranking is slight, ranging in position close to half-bureau down to half-division. All other enterprises and institutions are operated by companies within each bureau. These companies on average have the same bureaucratic rank as those for firms operated by bureaus. Company-managed enterprises are mainly industrial enterprises. There is great variation in the bureaucratic ranking for these enterprises, which may vary by size, sector, industry, history, reputation of products, and/or the head of the organization, but usually falls between the lower ranks of department and "not ranked."[6]

There are nine urban districts in Tianjin. Each of these commands industrial and nonindustrial bureaus, which in turn operate enterprises and institutions. These enterprises and institutions are service-oriented operations, such as schools, retail services, medical centers and clinics, and small and middle-size factories. The bureaucratic ranking of these operations is relatively low, ranging from the rank of half-department to nonranked. Finally, at the lowest level of government administration are 124 subdistricts (as of 1992). These subdistrict governments operate small workshops producing goods such as garments and craft products, and service centers such as daycare facilities and kindergartens. There is a concentration of women workers (who were previously housewives) in these lowest-ranked workshops and service centers.

The Allocation of Economic Resources

The bureaucratic structure of work organizations operates like a command system. Commands are sent from the central government to enterprises and institutions through the ministry and municipal (provincial) systems. Similarly, commands from the municipal government are sent to locally based enterprises and institutions through the municipal bureau and district systems. These command flows are replicated at the lower district and subdistrict levels. The system consequently nurtures the process by which resources and incentives are allocated from a higher level of government to a lower level, and from government jurisdictions to their subordinate enterprises and institutions. Here I describe four of these administrative-economic processes: financial, material, labor, and wages.

The Financial Process. In the traditional planned economy before 1978, state enterprises turned profits over to government jurisdictions, who then turned them over to the next-higher level of government, and on until they reached the central government. Collective enterprises contributed to state revenues in the form of taxes and management fees, also paid to their government jurisdictions. These profits and taxes formed the revenue basis of the central government's budget.

The central government's budget supplied finances for central ministries and municipal (provincial) governments. Central ministries, in turn, supplied finances downward, for their subordinate enterprises and institutions. In the municipal system also, the municipal government supplied finances for municipal bureaus and district governments, which in turn supplied finances for the firms operated by them and the next-lower level of government. Such a financial process was replicated at the district and subdistrict levels. In this manner, the budget for the central government encompassed the whole country, the budget for a municipal government covered the city, and the budget for a district or subdistrict government covered the smallest locality. The financial well-being of any given enterprise or institution was determined by the financial capabilities of its government jurisdictions.

In the modified planned commodity economy after 1978, the financial process for government agencies and nonprofit institutions has remained relatively unchanged. New mechanisms have appeared to operate for state enterprises; starting in 1979, the profit turnover system was gradually replaced by a tax system, and retained profits are available for investment in plant development, welfare benefits and workplace subsidies, and bonuses. By 1986, reformed enterprises no longer needed to rely on their government jurisdictions for the supply of finances. But this does not mean that state enterprises are now truly independent businesses. Rather, their financial status is still affected by their government jurisdictions for three reasons. First, tax rates are justified on an individual basis, and government jurisdictions play an important role in determining these taxes. Second, enterprises need their government jurisdiction's permission for bank loans (which were previously allocated to them by quotas). Third, government jurisdictions can provide special funding to support enterprises. For these reasons, the financial well-being of an enterprise is still affected by its relationship with its government jurisdiction.[7]

The Allocation of Material Resources. Production materials in China have been classified into four categories, each under a different level of control. *First-category materials (yilei wuzi)*, which are also known as "centrally allocated materials" *(tongpei wuzi)*, are under the control of the State Council's Planning Commission. These include all metals, manufacturing machinery, and energy. *Second-category materials (erlei wuzi)* are ministry-managed materials *(buguan wuzi)*, under the control of the central ministries. On the average, some six hundred industrial products (e.g., steel and iron, coal, chemicals, etc.) belonged to these two categories before 1979. In 1985, this number was reduced to sixty first-category items and some 250 items in the second category (Perkins 1986; Yuan 1989, pp. 486–88). State-controlled industrial supplies then comprised about 70 percent in large cities, 50 percent in medium-size cities, and 40 percent in small cities (Yuan 1989, pp. 489–90).

The *third category materials (sanlei wuzi)* are controlled by local governments. In Tianjin, these locally controlled materials include fuel, metal supplies, chemical materials, light industrial products, woods, mechanic and electric equipment, construction materials, auto parts, and electronic supplies. Enterprises and institutions must apply to the municipal government's Planning Commission through their bureaus or companies for these locally controlled materials. The *fourth category materials (silei wuzi)*, which are assumed to be the least important for state planning, are available for purchase and sale in local markets. In Tianjin, these "marketed" materials include supplementary metal equipment, paint and dyestuff, telecommunication equipment, chemical fertilizer, agricultural chemicals, and used industrial equipment and spare parts. Since retail stores featuring these "unplanned" materials are operated by the municipal or district commercial bureaus, the product markets are in reality monitored by the local governments. A common practice is for an enterprise or private business to obtain coupons or permission from its municipal or district bureau in order to buy materials for which there is a shortage (Yuan 1989, pp. 232–35).

The Allocation of Labor. Labor planning is part of China's overall state plan. Enterprises and institutions at all levels must apply to their government jurisdictions for labor quotas, which are controlled by the central and local government labor offices. There are two processes for the allocation of labor, and both are affected by the bureaucratic structure of work organizations. The first is the job assignment process. In Tianjin, as in all cities, the municipal government's labor bureau assigns new workers to municipal government offices, ministry-run organizations, municipal bureaus, and district governments. These organizations retain a sufficient number of assignees for themselves and redistribute others to the work organizations under them. This process is replicated down to the level of subdistrict governments.

The second process is that of job turnover between work organizations. Each work organization has "ownership rights" over its workers for the production of goods or services. Thus, a person must obtain permission from his or her work-unit leaders in order to leave the unit. Moreover, government jurisdictions have ownership rights over the workers in their enterprises and institutions also. Hence, one must additionally acquire the government jurisdiction's permission to move to another work unit. To move into a work unit in a different government jurisdiction, an individual not only must obtain permission from the new work unit but also from the government that has jurisdiction over it. These bureaucratic processes also apply to government agencies.

The Distribution of Wages. Wages for state and collective employees are affected by the bureaucratic structure of work organizations through two processes. One process is that standard wages are set by the government administration. Standards for government officials, staff members in nonprofit institutions, and staff and workers in large and middle-size state enterprises are the responsibility of the central government. Standards for workers in small state enterprises and in all collective enterprises are set by local governments. Before 1985, standard wages for the same occupation in the same industry were set higher for workers in ministry-operated firms, lower for workers in provincial (municipal) bureau-operated enterprises, and even lower for workers in city (or city district) bureau-operated enterprises (Li 1990, p. 84). In addition, wage standards were set much lower overall for workers in collective enterprises. After 1985, the first two levels of standard wages were integrated, whereas the third level was reserved for local regulation.

The second process is salary raises. Before 1985, salary raises followed central plans on an irregular basis. Each time, quotas for salary raises were distributed from the central to local governments. Each level of government increased salaries for the workers in their subordinate enterprises and institutions according to the wage quotas they retained. After 1985, such processes remained relatively unchanged for government agencies and nonprofit institutions. Enterprises were allowed to increase wages with money from retained profits. However, such increases were dependent upon government approval, and were recognized only as "floating wages" and not part of standard wages determined by the government. (Chapter 7 provides detailed information about this practice.)

Formal and Informal Mechanisms in the Allocation of Resources

The allocation of resources and incentives favors organizations that are operated by a higher level of government and, within each level, by work organizations with a higher bureaucratic rank. There are formal and informal mechanisms that explain this pattern of differential distributions.

Formal Mechanisms. The first formal mechanism is multilevel state planning. Each level of government plans the financing, materials, labor, and wage bills for the organizations under its jurisdiction. The higher the level of government, the greater the authority, and the larger the budget. Therefore, a higher level of government has greater ability to acquire economic resources and incentives, and thus allocate them to the enterprises and institutions under its jurisdiction. A lower level of government and its subordinate enterprises and institutions retain fewer resources and incentives. This is the primary formal mechanism that explains the variation in resources and incentives among organizations that are operated by different levels of government.

The second formal mechanism is the degree to which each level of government depends on its subordinate enterprises and institutions for revenues, products, and noneconomic activities (which will be discussed in the last section of this chapter). During routine evaluations, government officials favor those firms that are "important" to the government jurisdiction. A common practice is for government officials to select such firms as research sites, where they visit frequently or stay for a period of time to gain firsthand experience in guiding overall work. These firms are treated as models and are favored in the allocation of resources and incentives. This is the mechanism that explains the variation of resources and incentives between organizations with different bureaucratic ranks.

Informal Mechanisms. The bureaucratic structure also facilitates an informal process of influence, which again favors high-ranking organizations. First, party secretaries or managers of high-ranking enterprises tend to be members of the government decision-making bodies (their party committee or administrative councils). These individuals can therefore directly influence government decisions.

Second, government agencies, which are on central restrictions to limit their permanent staff, frequently "borrow" office staff from their subordinate enterprises and institutions. High-ranking enterprises, which are usually large and have a rich pool of educated and experienced staff, tend to send their own staff to work in government offices. While on the government staff, these people still receive salaries, bonuses, allowances, and housing from their work units and therefore can function as "lobbyists" or "informants" for them.

The third mechanism is personal networks. The leadership of a workplace may influence government decisions when its managers have a higher civil service rank, placing them closer to government officials.

The Distribution of Resources and Incentives

In the section that follows I examine the bivariate relationships between the formal structures of work organizations, on the one hand, and the well-being of these organizations and the employees in them, on the other. These analyses are exploratory in nature. Later, in Chapters 4 to 8, I apply multivariate techniques, based on various status attainment models, to estimate the independent effects of work-unit variables on an individual's attained status, controlling for the individual's family and personal characteristics.

Resources and Incentives for the Workplace: Aggregate Data

Table 2.2 presents official statistics for nine indicators measuring enterprise well-being, by sector and by level of government jurisdiction. The data are from a 1985 national census of industrial enterprises (in the mining and manufacturing sectors). In 1985, China's industrial sector contained 45 percent of the total urban labor force, and was responsible for 70 percent of the nonagricultural national income (State Statistical Bureau of China 1989, p. 32). Although

TABLE 2.2

Enterprise Well-Being by Sector and Level of Government Jurisidiction in Chinese Industry, 1985

Sector and Level of Government Jurisdiction	Industrial Indicators				Wage and Labor		Collective Consumption		
	Gross Output (1)	Invested Capital (2)	Sales Earnings (3)	Sales Profits (4)	Total Wages (5)	College Degrees (6)	Welfare Funding (7)	Medical Expenses (8)	Collective Benefits (9)
State sector									
Centrally operated (3825)	19.0	25.8	17.8	8.8	13.3	62.8	382.9	78.2	64.3
Locally operated (66,517)	15.0	13.6	14.4	1.8	11.2	33.2	319.9	73.2	44.6
Urban district/rural county (35,263)	11.5	11.3	10.5	0.9	9.4	11.0	204.2	61.5	21.2
Collective sector									
Urban district/rural county (33,548)	10.0	7.7	8.7	0.6	8.2	3.8	—	—	—
Urban subdistrict (30,518)	5.2	5.2	7.2	0.8	8.9	4.0	—	—	—
Township (170,364)	6.1	5.0	5.4	0.6	7.8	0.8	—	—	—
"Three capitalist enterprises" (516)	46.9	37.0	46.7	3.4	21.4	27.6	—	—	—

Notes:
(a) Sources are from Yuan (1989): Table 2 (p. 528), Table 12 (p. 539), Table 34 (p. 561), Table 39 (p. 567), and Table 42 (p. 572).
(b) Units of measurement: (1) to (4) in thousand yuan; (5) in hundred yuan; (6) in thousand employees; (7) to (9) per capita.
(c) Collective benefits include subsidies for collective welfare programs and expenses for collective welfare facilities.
(d) Figures in parentheses next to row headings are number of enterprises.

nonindustrial enterprises might show a somewhat different pattern, official statistics for this broader coverage do not exist.

Industrial Indicators. State enterprises had higher values in gross output, investment capital, sales earnings, and sales profits than collective enterprises. Sector differences in these industrial indicators hold even for enterprises at the same level of government jurisdiction: at the urban district/rural county level, state-owned enterprises fare better than collective enterprises. Within each sector, enterprises that were operated by a higher level of government had higher industrial indicators. Finally, "three capitalist" enterprises had much higher industrial indicators than enterprises in the state and collective sectors.

Wages and Education. For state and collective sectors, the average wages and number of employees with college degrees was higher for enterprises in the state than in the collective sector, and for enterprises under higher levels of government jurisdiction. The effects of sector and of level of government jurisdiction are independent: wage or education differentials by sector existed for enterprises at the same level of government jurisdiction (urban districts/rural counties), and differentials by hierarchy existed for enterprises within each sector. Foreign capitalist firms had the highest average wage and employee educational level. An additional multivariate analysis of individual-level data is offered in Chapter 7 to show the independent effects of workplace variables on wages, controlling for education and other characteristics of the labor force.

Collective Consumption. Welfare funding, medical expenses, and collective benefits are labeled here as collective consumption. The funds for these expenses are supplied by enterprises. Data for collective enterprises and foreign capitalist firms were not available, but most of these businesses did not usually offer these types of collective consumption. Nonetheless, collective consumption in the state sector was positively associated with the level of government jurisdiction. Thus, the higher the level of government jurisdiction, the greater the ability of enterprises to provide funding for collective consumption.

Resources and Incentives in the Workplace: Individual Data

Table 2.3 presents data on the status characteristics of the respondents to the 1988 Tianjin survey, using four characteristics of their work units. The purpose here is to show the association between the status characteristics of the respondents and those of

TABLE 2.3

Labor Market Characteristics of the Respondents by Work-Unit Variables, Tianjin, 1988

Work-Unit Variables	Percent Males	Percent Party Members	Average Occupation Status	Average Level of Education	Average Monthly Salary	Average Monthly Bonuses
Total (950)	54.95	20.43	79.80	3.52	85.58	24.72
Ownership [N = 950]						
State (76.1%)	60.30	24.48	82.25	3.65	89.22	26.51
Collective (22.6%)	36.45	6.54	71.84	3.10	69.40	19.71
Private (1.4%)	61.54	23.08	76.94	3.08	146.77	6.53
R	.17	.16	.28	.15	.12	.13
Eta	.30	.29	.30	.25	.31	.23
Rank [N = 938]						
Higher than bureau (2.9%)	64.17	46.43	84.52	3.89	106.21	27.29
Bureau (25.8%)	60.82	27.76	83.12	3.73	90.63	25.71
Division (25.3%)	57.14	27.08	84.42	3.80	89.18	29.40
Department (26.0%)	49.80	11.74	75.81	3.36	79.20	23.54
Section (14.8%)	41.13	10.64	74.17	3.08	74.52	18.24
Not ranked (5.2%)	34.90	8.16	70.10	2.86	60.06	17.83

	C1	C2	C3	C4	C5	C6
R	.24	.31	.25	.27	.24	.10
Eta	.27	.33	.29	.29	.31	.14
Industry (N = 938)						
Government agency (2.8%)	80.77	80.77	93.02	3.92	119.50	14.74
Noneducational (14.9%)	56.83	38.13	87.85	4.01	95.99	26.17
Educational (9.2%)	46.51	26.74	102.98	4.56	97.33	20.65
Industrial (50.4%)	61.57	18.26	78.42	3.42	82.88	26.45
Commerce/service (22.8%)	38.97	3.76	66.79	2.96	72.17	24.00
R	.11	.35	.55	.36	.31	-.02
Eta	.21	.37	.69	.44	.33	.09
Size (N = 938)						
50 or fewer employees (8.1%)	42.11	17.11	78.23	3.29	85.36	22.51
51–100 (5.7%)	50.00	24.07	82.37	3.59	83.70	23.95
101–500 (28.7%)	52.03	22.51	83.51	3.68	89.44	21.39
501–1000 (20.8%)	58.67	21.94	79.18	3.47	84.01	23.79
1001–3000 (25.6%)	56.43	16.18	77.96	3.48	81.23	27.12
3001–5000 (4.9%)	63.04	18.70	72.24	3.28	85.93	34.64
5001 and more (6.3%)	62.71	32.20	78.12	3.56	92.59	31.66
R	.10	-.01	-.11	-.02	-.01	-.11
Eta	.11	.12	.12	.12	.10	.17

Note: Private-sector workers (12 cases) were excluded from the data on Rank, Industry, and Size.

their work units. I measure these associations with the Pearson coefficient (R) for linearity and the Eta coefficient for nonlinearity. Six variables were chosen to measure characteristics of the labor force: percentage of males, percentage of Chinese Communist Party members, average occupational status, average level of education, average monthly salary (in *yuan*), and average bonuses per month (in *yuan*). Measurements and descriptions of these variables can be found in Appendix C.

Sector. Only twelve respondents (eight males and four females) reported that they worked in private-sector jobs. Their average salary was double the figure for collective workers and 65 percent higher than that for state workers. These private-sector workers had less education, a lower occupational status, and fewer bonuses than state or collective workers. Similar to the state sector were the percentages of males and of party members. These descriptive data are merely informative at best, because the number of cases is so small that it is difficult to draw any definite conclusions from these data. These twelve cases of private-sector respondents are excluded from further consideration to eliminate errors. From this point on, I focus on the nonprivate sectors.

Seventy-six percent of the respondents worked in the state sector and 22.6 percent in the collective sector (Table 2.3). This skewed percentage is consistent with census data released by the municipal government of Tianjin (Duan et al. 1987, p. 666). State-sector employees had higher status in all six variables than did collective employees. There are three sharp contrasts between state and collective workers: male percentage (60.3 percent and 36.5 percent for state and collective workers, respectively), percentage of party members (24.5 percent and 6.5 percent), and monthly salaries (89 *yuan* and 69 *yuan*).

Bureaucratic Rank. Most respondents were located in middle-ranking work units, fewer at the top and bottom. The percentage of males increased with higher work-unit ranks. Similar associations occurred for the percentage of party members, occupational status, education, and monthly salaries. Figures for the linear measure of association (R) were close to those for the nonlinear measure of association (Eta), suggesting that work-unit rank is linearly associated with these labor market characteristics of the respondents. The association between work-unit rank and bonuses was considerably weaker. The average bonus increased up to the rank of division, and it decreased sharply at the bureau level before increasing at the highest level of the bureaucratic ranking. These results seem to suggest that the distribution of bonuses differs from that of salaries.

Industry. Respondents were classified into five broad categories. Half of them work in industrial enterprises (manufacturing, transportation, construction, and mining), and 22.8 percent in commercial and service sectors. The rest of the respondents work in government agencies (2.8 percent), noneducational nonprofit institutions (14.9 percent), or educational institutions (9.2 percent). This industry variable is a categorical variable; the rank-order was arbitrary.

Data showed that the five-category industry variable had fairly high linear correlations with four of the six variables of labor market characteristics: percentage of party members (R = .35), occupational status (.55), education (.36), and monthly salary (.31). The nonlinear measures (Eta), however, showed higher associations for occupation and education. These were tied to the significantly higher education (and thus occupational status) for employees in educational institutions than in other industries. The percentage of males was higher in government agencies and industrial enterprises than in educational institutions and in the commercial/service sector, because males are clearly more likely than females to be promoted into official positions in the government or in industrial jobs. Bonuses, however, did not correlate with the industry variable either linearly or nonlinearly.

Size. Although I do not consider the size of a workplace as a dimension of the *formal* structure of work organizations, it would be interesting to test whether workplace size is associated with the labor market characteristics of the respondents, because size has been considered one of the predictors of labor market segmentation in the United States. The Tianjin data showed that labor market characteristics of the respondents were not associated with workplace size. Except for the percentage of males and amount of bonuses, which had weak positive correlations with workplace size, none of the other characteristics was associated with size. The Eta coefficients for these four variables were also weak, although higher in absolute values than the Pearson coefficients; together these coefficients suggest that workplace size might have somewhat nonlinear associations with these labor market characteristics of the respondents. Similar patterns regarding the relationships between workplace size and labor market characteristics of the respondents were revealed when industrial sectors were controlled for.[8]

Social-Political Functions of the Workplace

Thus far, I have treated work organizations as economic organizations and have described and analyzed their structures. Work organizations in China are far more than that, of course. Here, I describe three noneconomic functions of the workplace: as an administrative unit, a political vehicle, and a social welfare organization.

The Workplace as an Administrative Unit

Every work organization falls under a particular level of government administration. Self-employed and family businesses are managed by a municipal or district bureau of industrialists and commercialists. Even foreign capital-invested firms are affiliated with a state ministry, bureau, or company. Work organizations have become administrative units precisely because the government takes advantage of the system of work organizations to carry out its initiatives and programs.

Carrying out Administrative Initiatives. Administrative orders, regulations, and policies of the central and local governments are sent to work organizations. Although mass media are used to publicize government documents, people are organized in their work units to study government documents. Importantly, rewards and punishments are available in work organizations to "encourage" compliance from citizens. The following examples will make this clear.

Family planning: The conduct of family-planning programs is to a large degree dependent on the involvement of work units. Although birth quotas are distributed to households through neighborhood organizations, rewards are given out by work units to those who comply, and penalties are assessed against violators of government birth-control policies. Under the policy of one child for one couple, every couple who has only one child receives a one-child bonus (about five percent of the average basic salary) from the husband's and the wife's work units (half and half) until the child is fourteen years of age. Those who do not comply face a number of penalties: participation in a special study session in the workplace, causing the participant to lose face; costs in career and political promotions; loss of one or more turns at salary raises; deduction of a certain percentage of one's regular salary (in some cases, no salary is paid to the violator); withholding of all bonuses; and withholding of some fringe benefits, such as the termination of one's housing lease by the work unit.

Government bonds: Quotas of government bonds, which are a method used continuously to help the state with financial deficits, are distributed to work units. Each work unit receives quotas of government bonds proportional to its annual wage bills. Work units then "inspire" their employees to buy government bonds proportional to their basic salaries. Those workers who are willing to buy more and actually do so are given priority in career and political promotions, salary and bonus raises, and other work-related considerations for their loyalty to the work unit, as well as to the nation.

Organized voluntary activities: Such activities include removing snow from city streets, planting trees in neighborhoods and along streets, combating floods, collecting donations to help areas suffering from natural disasters, and the like. Although the nature of these activities is voluntary, individuals are organized by their work units to participate. Leaders of work units can, once again, apply political, economic, and social pressures to encourage their employees to participate in these organized voluntary activities.

Representing Individuals. The direct consequence of work units as administrative organizations is that they serve as mediators between the state and the individual. In a civil society, citizens communicate directly with the state (e.g., a U.S. resident sends income tax forms to tax offices in the federal and local governments, and applies for a passport to travel abroad to a designated government office); but in the Chinese party-state, individuals are connected to the state and society through their work units.

Presenting individuals to the state: Citizenship identification cards are distributed to citizens through their work units and with their confirmation. When criminals are discharged from prison, they are received by the personnel from their workplaces, rather than by their families. Persons who need their birth certificates notarized by public notary agencies must first get approval from their workplaces. Students or scholars studying abroad and wishing their spouses, children, or parents to visit them are required to get approval letters from their formerly affiliated Chinese work units; without such letters the government will not grant passports to the applicants.

Presenting individuals in society: A letter of introduction from one's work unit, identifying one's work-unit affiliation and specifying one's objectives, is necessary in order to visit any other organizations. One cannot pass by security guards of organizations without showing an appropriate letter of introduction. Such a letter is also needed for individuals' access to many social services—for example, hotel reservations, the purchase of airline tickets, and the purchase of tickets for trains or passenger boats. A pregnant woman wanting an abortion is also asked to show such a letter in order for her to qualify for the operation.

The Workplace as a Political Vehicle

Unlike the United States, where political organizations are associated most closely with one's place of residence, in China one's political life is bound to the workplace. Several aspects of this political life are discussed in the following paragraphs.

Elections of People's Representatives. According to China's election law, government leaders are elected by people's representatives, who are themselves chosen by primary elections in urban districts and rural counties. In the cities, the basic electoral functions are handled by the administrative units of urban districts. In Tianjin, there are nine urban districts, in which people's representatives are elected through work organizations primarily and residential organizations secondarily. In other wards, working people of voting age (eighteen years and older) register and vote in their work units, rather than their residential blocks. Students eligible to vote participate in the elections in their schools. Only retirees, housewives, and adults who have no jobs go to the voting stations of their neighborhoods.

Furthermore, although people's representatives are elected to represent residents currently living or working in a city district, candidates for people's representatives are distributed to workplaces and not to residential organizations. Therefore, elected representatives actually represent their work colleagues. Because these representatives express opinions more in line with management, they are simply considered the *danwei* (work unit) representatives. In meetings of the People's Congress, these representatives tend to speak in the interests of their work organizations.

Political Parties and Memberships. The leading Chinese Communist Party (CCP) and its supplementary organization, the Chinese Communist Youth League (CCYL), and other democratic parties all have their organizations based on the workplace structure. The CCP and CCYL place their representative bodies, whether called committees (in large establishments) or branches (in small ones), in every work organization. CCP cadres comprise the core of workplace management at all levels, and CCP secretaries resume political leadership in the workplace. People apply to the party branches in their work units for CCP membership. Because the party only recruits a few loyalists, membership in the party has been a valuable political resource. One's chance of entering the party is affected primarily by two factors: the party secretary's ability to get quotas from the higher level of party authority and one's relationship with the party secretary. Chapter 6 will examine these interorganizational and intraorganizational factors in the process of party membership attainment.

Political Studies. The pursuit of the political control of management and workers is a major reason why the CCP maintains its organization in the workplace. Political study meetings and political campaigns are two basic means to pursue such control. When party documents, national leaders' speeches, administrative orders, regulations, and policies are sent to the workplace, employees are organized to study these materials in on- or off-work meetings. Such meetings are also held to study the constitution, amendments to the constitution, and laws that have been passed by the People's Congress.

In these meetings, participants are expected to express their attitudes toward the party's new guidelines or requirements. In addition, they are often asked to examine the deviations of their ideologies and behaviors from the party guidelines and to make confessions and self-criticisms. Attendance at the political study meetings and the performance of each employee in these meetings is considered in evaluations for job promotion, salary and bonus raises, application for party membership, and other work related statuses and resources. Passive attitudes and "wrong" opinions of the current party guidelines are recorded promptly and "corrected" in one way or another, sooner or later, in the work unit.

Political Campaigns. Political campaigns, a method frequently adopted to "correct" wrongs, are initiated by the CCP in central and, perhaps, local governments. Since 1949, nearly twenty large-scale national campaigns have been initiated (see Chapter 1), averaging one campaign every other year. Most have lasted several months to one year, the Cultural Revolution being the longest (ten years). These political campaigns are conducted in the workplace. In fact, factories, schools, stores, hospitals, and government offices become battlefields for political campaigns and struggles (Whyte and Parish 1984; Fairbank 1986, chap. 17). More political study meetings are also held during work and off-work hours during the campaigns.

Between 1967 and 1969, in the peaks of the Cultural Revolution, few workers worked in their jobs; the majority were instead totally involved in the political campaigns.

The Workplace as a Welfare Organization

The popular Chinese expression that "enterprises run the society" (qiyie ban shehui) refers to a unique phenomenon in urban China: workplaces offer a wide array of commodities and services. These include employee insurance and benefits, residential housing, and collective welfare programs and facilities. The result is a pattern in which urban workers must depend on their work units for collective consumption. This pattern is analyzed further in Chapter 8. Here I describe three major aspects of this form of collective consumption.

Labor Insurance and Welfare Benefits. Families that live in poverty apply to the father's or mother's workplace for financial aid. The welfare office at the work unit then examines the economic situation of everyone in an applicant's family and makes decisions about the kind of help to provide. These families may receive money on a regular or irregular basis, and the amount may vary from time to time, depending on the financial situation of the workplace. Housewives and children from these families may be recruited by the workplace as temporary or contract workers. Such financial aid and employment may also be available to families in special emergencies.

Besides pensions and various allowances, workplace-based benefits include medical facilities, dining halls, bath halls, entertainment centers, cultural clubs, and sports facilities that are available to employees and their families. Unlike U.S. companies that sponsor games and entertainment for commercial purposes, Chinese industrial companies, administrative bureaus, and enterprises support ball clubs, musical groups, and singing-dancing teams for their employees and their families.

When commodity markets face a crisis, the workplace intervenes to help its employees. Using its business networks, the workplace buys scarce goods wholesale and sells them to its employees at a price lower than market value. From seasonal vegetables and fruits to rice, lean meat, and high-priced liquor, these items are numerous and vary from one city to another. In addition, government-certified coupons for rationed and imported goods are distributed to various organizations, which can then redistribute them to potential customers. The workplace also often helps its employees to get tickets for entertainment shows, sports events, and even movies (particularly foreign-made ones), all of which are difficult to obtain.

Housing. Public housing is dominant in China's urban housing market. In the early 1980s, 84 percent of Tianjin's housing (in area) consisted of public estates (Gu et al. 1984, p. 374). Public housing can be either *work unit housing* (estates owned and managed by workplaces), or *city public housing* (apartments built and owned by the city government). The former is rented to employees, and the latter distributed to workplaces that pay the cost of housing construction and then redistribute apartments to their employees. Functioning as a residential developer and a real-estate agent, each workplace has a housing office that deals with affairs of public housing for the employees. Married couples apply to their workplaces for an apartment in work-unit housing or city public housing. Because of housing shortages, long waiting lists can be found in every workplace, and unmarried employees are excluded from applying. But housing is used as a reward to employees, and internal criteria can be applied to distribute public apartments in this fashion.

Collective Welfare Programs. Collective welfare programs that are offered in urban workplaces include medical facilities (hospitals, clinics, and health-care centers), meal halls, bathing facilities (because few homes have showers, and public bath houses are few in number), barber shops, nurseries, day-care centers, recreational activities (sports, movies, music, and performing arts), and libraries. There are also industry-sponsored schools (elementary, high, and technical schools and even colleges, which are for employees' children), nursing homes, and sanitariums. These are all subsidized commodities and services (see Chapter 8).

Summary

Workplaces in urban China constitute a complex organizational structure. I have examined the formality of the structure, and identify three dimensions of it. The ownership dimension is derived from the Communist party's ideological interests in maintaining state ownership over the means of production. The administrative-industrial dimension and the hierarchical dimension are institutional expressions of the national interests of state planners and the control interests of government jurisdictions, respectively. These three dimensions provide an institutional basis for the party-state to realize its goals through the workplace organizations.

What has been left unexamined is the structure of work organizations on a social-dynamic dimension: an examination of the connections among people who are active in the formal structure. For example, the social network or *guanxi* among people with the same or different positions in this formal structure is an important aspect of the social dynamics of the workplace. In Chapter 5, I examine *guanxi* and its impact on job placement and job mobility.

A work organization in urban China is a multifunctional institution. For the party-state, it serves as an economic enterprise to carry out national plans for economic development, as an organizational means to administer the country, as a political vehicle to control workers, and as a welfare organization to distribute goods and services. To be sure, the Communist party-state could not function without these multifunctional work organizations.

For individuals, their place of employment is a means to satisfy their material needs, a path to party membership, and a means to accumulate human and political resources for upward mobility and for the welfare of their families. Because workplaces are segmented and have different abilities to provide whatever individuals expect to attain from them, they are a type of social status. This raises the question of who gets where in this segmented workplace structure and why. I seek answers to this question in the next three chapters.

3

URBAN EMPLOYMENT: POLICIES AND PRACTICES

In Maoist ideology, labor is not a commodity but a *national resource*. This ideology has virtually eliminated private labor rights. Bureaucratic allocation of labor in China is based on this ideology. As a national resource, labor is matched to financial and material resources that are also allocated bureaucratically. The matching process is facilitated through job assignment programs, in which young people must await for government assignments rather than search for jobs on their own. This job placement process differs entirely from that in market societies.

In this chapter, after reviewing Chinese manpower policies in Mao's and Deng's eras, I describe job placement practices during the market reforms of the 1980s, focusing on three specific employment processes: (1) direct state assignments, (2) indirect state assignments, and (3) direct individual application. Personal interview data give depth to the description of each of the three practices.

Manpower Policies in Mao's Era: 1949–1976

The Communist government's manpower policies in the early 1950s were established with the intention of restoring economic order. In 1949, following the overthrow of the Nationalist government, there were 4.7 million people left unemployed. At this time, the unemployment rate reached 23.6 percent, excluding women homemakers (He 1990, p. 34; Tang 1990, p. 25). Businesses in all sectors were asked by the new government to create jobs, and unemployed staff and workers were encouraged to return to their previous places of employment. Through a government job-introduction program, people were given jobs in the newly established state sector, which absorbed about half the urban labor force in 1952. From 1949 to 1957, 16.7 million jobs were created, of which nearly one-third were government-introduced. The unemployment rate was reduced to 5.9 percent.

In order to prepare for a forthcoming government campaign to nationalize the economy in 1955, job-introduction programs were replaced by a more rigid policy of direct state assignments. The Communist party made the following remarks in a 1955 central government document:

> The deployment of manpower in every sector and every work-place must be planned. Recruitment of new workers must be approved by state labor agencies[1] according to a unified plan. No workplaces should recruit workers without approval. (He 1990, p. 7)

Thus, a centrally imposed labor quota system was implemented. Direct state assignments became the predominant method of job placement. Respondents from Tianjin in 1988 reveal that, during the 1949–52 period, 64.5 percent had found their first urban jobs through direct state assignment. This percentage increased to 76.1 percent in the 1953–57 period (see Table 3.1).

An important urban employment policy since the implementation of labor quotas in 1955 was the distinction between permanent and temporary workers. Permanent jobs were full-time, tenured jobs, and were offered exclusively to urban residents through state assignments. Quotas for permanent jobs were controlled by the central government. Temporary workers, on the other hand, were largely recruited from rural areas, and their employment contracts were on a quarterly, semiannual, or yearly basis. Workers who received contracts for longer terms were known as "contract workers." Labor quotas for temporary jobs were controlled by local governments. When their labor contracts expired or were discontinued, temporary and contract workers were sent back to their home villages.

A less rigid manpower policy was implemented during the Great Leap Forward in 1958 and 1959. Labor quotas were decentralized first to the provincial level, and then even further to local government agencies and workplaces. Direct state assignments were reduced by 5 percent. One result was a rapid growth of the urban population. From 1957 to 1960, China's city workers almost doubled, whereas the urban population increased by 30 percent. Serious food shortages developed in the cities. This prompted the central

TABLE 3.1

Respondents' Birthplaces and Employment Placement Methods by Years
of First Urban Jobs, Tianjin, 1988 (by percentages)

Year of First Urban Job	Total Cases	Place of Birth						Methods of Employment		
		I	II	III	IV	V	VI	VII	VIII	IX
Total	912	67.9	2.4	4.2	7.1	2.6	15.8	70.7	11.5	17.7
<1949	61	27.9	—	9.8	9.8	8.2	44.3	31.1	4.9	63.9
1949–52	64	31.3	4.7	9.4	10.9	4.7	39.1	64.5	4.8	30.6
1953–57	68	51.5	1.5	4.4	10.3	5.9	26.5	76.1	4.5	19.4
1958–60	70	54.3	4.3	8.6	7.1	4.3	21.4	71.4	7.1	21.4
1961–65	108	64.8	1.9	4.6	13.0	4.6	11.1	86.9	7.5	5.6
1966–76	266	75.9	1.9	3.0	6.0	1.1	12.0	88.5	6.5	5.0
1977–88	275	86.2	2.9	1.5	3.6	0.4	5.5	56.0	23.8	20.1

Keys to symbols:
I   = Tianjin's urban districts
II   = Tianjin's towns
III   = Tianjin's rural villages
IV   = Non-Tianjin cities
V   = Non-Tianjin towns
VI   = Non-Tianjin rural villages
VII   = Direct state assignments
VIII = Indirect state assignments
IX   = Direct individual application

government to regain direct control of labor quotas and job
assignments.

The period of economic adjustment between 1961 and 1963
saw a restoration of the centralized labor policy. Thirty-one percent
of the urban jobs were eliminated during the period, causing 18.3
million workers who had been recruited from rural areas to lose
their jobs and their residencies in the cities (He 1990, p. 12).[2] To
avoid unemployment problems, urban youth were encouraged to
take agricultural jobs in farms and rural communes. As a result, 1.3
million urban youth were sent to the countryside between 1960 and
1966 (He 1990, p. 14).

During the Cultural Revolution, between 1966 and 1976, the
policy of offering temporary and contact positions to urban workers
was criticized by a radical group of party leaders as a form of class

exploitation. As a result, millions of temporary and contract workers were granted permanent jobs (He 1990, p. 16). The dramatic
increase of permanent workers in the cities was one factor that gave
rise to the transferring of urban youths to rural areas. At the same
time, self-employment was reduced by 88 percent. Workers in the
collective sector decreased from 24 percent to 20 percent. Consequently, state workers comprised nearly 80 percent of the work force
in 1976. During this period, 88.5 percent of the respondents to the
1988 Tianjin survey had received jobs through direct state assignments, and only 5 percent found employment through individual
application. In addition, because of the economic crisis in the cities,
even greater numbers of urban, educated youth than in the 1960s
program were transferred to rural areas through a new government
program known as a movement "up to the mountains and down to
the villages" (Bernstein 1977). By 1976, twelve million urban young
people had been sent to the countryside.

Household Registration and Food Rationing

The implementation of urban manpower policies was largely
dependent on the household registration system. Beginning in 1950,
people were required to register at police stations in their place of
birth. This was considered a person's permanent residence, and was
used as a basis for hiring; permanent jobs were assigned only to local
residents. In order to move within a city, town, or village, one simply had to transfer his or her registration card, which listed vital,
household, and residential information for the police station in the
new district. Along with transfer of the registration card, routine
procedures included transferring all official booklets for rationed
grain, oil, meat, eggs, sugar, salt, bean products, and other primary
groceries.

Because of the permanent shortage of food supplies, moves to
urban places, particularly to large cities, were restricted. Relocating
to one of the largest cities was almost impossible. Limited immigrant quotas were controlled by municipal governments, and were
distributed to work units only upon request and subsequent government approval. When a person wanted to work in a city in which he
or she was not resident, it was necessary to find a powerful work
unit that had the potential to request an immigrant quota from the
government. Legal immigrants were guaranteed food rations. Illegal
immigrants who did not have residential registration cards granted
by the local police had no access to rationed foods.

The abolition of food rations in the 1980s weakened the household registration system as a controlling mechanism. Although there are still grain rations, a variety of grains can be bought in free farmers' markets. Restaurants no longer require government grain coupons. Primary foods such as oil, meat, eggs, sugar, and salt are no longer rationed because there have been sufficient supplies since 1983. By 1985, nonpermanent residents could live in cities with little trouble in getting food. A growing number of rural residents were motivated to seek jobs in towns and in economic developmental zones associated with large cities, and they did so without transferring their residential cards. Because of population pressures, however, large cities still use immigrant quotas to restrict the hiring of outside labor.

Data from the 1988 Tianjin survey provide evidence of the persistence of urban employment being related to one's place of birth. As shown in Table 3.1, 67.9 percent of the 912 respondents who had jobs in the city of Tianjin at the time of the survey were born in urban districts of Tianjin. Another 6.6 percent were born in towns or rural villages (including suburban towns and villages) in the Tianjin municipal area. Only 25.5 percent were born in places other than Tianjin. Historically, the majority of workers who entered the labor force before 1949 came from non-Tianjin areas. This was changed during the first Five-Year Plan period (1953–57), when Tianjin-born employees exceeded 50 percent. The percentage increased as time went on, and it reached a peak of 86.2 percent in the 1977–88 period.

Labor Policies in the Era of Market Reform: After 1976

Labor policies that prevailed during the Cultural Revolution were critically evaluated by new leadership in the post-Mao era. The policy of transferring urban youths to the countryside was abolished. School graduates were promised jobs in their cities of residence. Those who had been sent to the countryside were allowed to move back home. Unemployment became a serious problem in the cities. Although some 14.5 million new jobs were created in 1978 and 1979, by the end of 1979, 5.4 percent of the young population were still classified as "waiting for jobs" (He 1990, p. 21). Because of unemployment pressures, a *dingti* (which literally means "replacement and substitution") system was heavily used, in which parents retired early to allow their unemployed children to take over their jobs. The increasing use of indirect state assignments (23.8 percent) of Tianjin workers largely reflects the *dingti* practice.

Several party and government documents have been issued since 1979 to reform labor policies.[3] These documents focus on employment policy, recruitment criteria and methods, and a labor contract system.

Employment Policies

The previous system that aimed to limit collective businesses and eliminate the private sector was considered by the late 1970s to be incorrect policy. The government now supported a mixed economy, in which state, collective, private, and joint businesses coexisted. As a result, self-employment was encouraged and grew rapidly in the 1980s, particularly in the sales and service sectors. Self-employment increased from 150,000 in 1978 to 5.7 million in 1987, multiplying by thirty-eight. The overall increase of the urban labor force for the ten-year period was 83 percent. Workers in the collective sector increased from 21.6 percent to 25.3 percent, and state employees decreased from 78 percent to 70 percent (State Statistical Bureau of China 1988, p. 123).

A related policy enabled individuals to search for jobs in the state and collective sectors. In the 1988 Tianjin sample, 20.1 percent of the respondents who began their careers after 1977 got jobs through direct individual application, up from 5.0 percent during the Cultural Revolution period. Newly created employment service centers played a significant role in helping individuals to search for jobs. These centers were sponsored by various government agencies, institutions, and enterprises, and totaled 56,060 in 1987. Urban youths on job-waiting lists registered at these centers and received employment information as well as preoccupational training. By 1987, the centers sponsored 232,900 new businesses, absorbing 7.3 million workers and producing 55.2 billion *yuan* (or $10 billion) output values and 2.6 billion *yuan* (or $472 million) in revenues. From 1979 to 1987, newly employed workers in urban China totaled more than seventy million, and urban youths on job-waiting lists decreased from 5.4 percent to 2.0 percent (He 1990, pp. 21–23).

Recruitment Policies

In the reforming period, state labor quotas still provide the basis for state and collective workplaces to recruit workers. Under a new policy implemented in 1986, however, work units sign labor and wage contracts with the state. They may apply for labor quotas to hire workers, but their contracted total wages are fixed. Work units now are allowed to recruit new workers themselves from designated schools and residential areas. The *dingti* and *neizhao* (internal recruitment) practices, which will be discussed in detail later, were generally not allowed after 1986. The central government now demands that recruiting organizations hire the best-qualified new workers by conducting merit examinations. The examinations covered *de* (political thought and virtue), *zhi* (academic abilities), and *ti* (physical condition and health). Which of the three criteria is emphasized in hiring is determined largely by the recruiting organizations.

Despite these government-imposed criteria, the recruitment process has been affected increasingly by social factors. *Guanxi*, a term referring to a person's social connections, has played a significant role in the recruitment process. Ms. Fang (personal review 2), who was a factory labor and wage office staff member, said that

> In the past, our factory accepted new workers assigned to us. Now we are allowed to recruit workers by ourselves. We announce our preferences, conduct merit examinations, and select the best-qualified persons. This is good, but not completely. In the screening process, we have to pay special attention to those applicants who were endorsed by our factory party secretary, managers, engineers, team leaders, senior staff and workers, and even ordinary staff. There is no problem with hiring those who qualify. For the few unqualified, we must treat them as special cases. You really cannot say "no" to these people, because their endorsers are your supervisors, colleagues, and sometimes friends. In addition, we always receive *tiaozi* (a message) from "above" asking to accept someone. You'd better do whatever they ask, because our factory party secretary and managers would be mad if you don't; they are under a lot of pressure from "above" for hiring and such. Overall, we usually reserve 20 percent of our quotas to deal with these special cases.

Labor Contract System

A long-term problem that has existed in the urban economy is the Maoist "iron rice bowl" (*tie fan wan*)—bureaucratically protected job security that led to a passive work attitude and low productivity. A related problem was the "ownership of labor by the work unit" (*danwei suoyouzhi*), which refers to the monopolylike control over labor by work organizations. Reformers under the leadership of Deng Xiaoping initiated a labor contract system to overcome these problems. Since 1986, newly hired staff and workers are required to sign three- to five-year contracts with work units, and upon completion of the contract either side can terminate the agreement. Long-term contracts of more than five years are permissible, but more restricted. A probationary period of three to six months also applies to contracted staff and workers. Some workplaces require all current employees to sign labor contracts. By 1989, 11.6 percent of the state workers signed labor contracts with their work units (Tang 1990, p. 71).

Despite these policy changes, the labor structure has not been altered radically. By 1989 more than 95 percent of the urban workers remained employed in state and collective sectors, and nearly 90 percent of the state employees still had no labor contracts.

Methods of Job Placement

Government labor agencies, the recruiting work units, and people who want work are the three principal actors in the process of urban employment. The method of job placement explains *how* each of the three actors is involved in the process. *Direct state assignment (guojia fenpei)* is a method of job placement in which government labor agencies take control. Recruiting work units coordinate passively with government labor agencies, and people in need of work wait and accept assignments. *Indirect state assignment (jianjie guojia fenpei)* is a method in which recruiting work units take charge of targeting and screening candidates. Its basic forms include children being recruited by the work-unit system in which their parents are currently employed, which is known as *neizhao*, and children taking over their parents' jobs upon retirement, which is known as *dingti*. Finally, the third method of job placement is *direct individual application (zimou zhiyie)*.

In the 1988 Tianjin survey, the respondents were asked which method of job placement was utilized to find their first urban jobs.[4] As can be seen in Table 3.1, 70.7 percent of the respondents got their first urban jobs through direct state assignments. Between 1949 and 1976, the use of direct state assignments was on the rise, individual applications were declining, and the number of indirect state assignments stayed relatively stable. The 1977–88 period showed a clear departure from this long-term trend. During this period, direct state assignments declined to 56 percent, and there was an increased use of direct individual application (20.1 percent) as well as indirect state assignments (23.8 percent).

Direct State Assignments

Before 1979, students who did not go to college received job assignments right after graduation from high school. In the 1980s, especially after 1983, only college graduates and vocational-school students were guaranteed jobs after graduation. High-school graduates registered in government labor offices in their neighborhoods to wait for job assignments (*daiyie*). The waiting period, according to recent data from Wuhan and Shanghai (Davis 1990), ranged from three months to two years. Other people entitled to job assignments included demobilized soldiers, retired military officers, prisoners who have completed sentences, and handicapped people.

Stages of Job Assignments

Direct state assignment is a multistep process. It begins with the municipal labor bureau's investigation of supply and demand for labor. On the demand side, the labor bureau collects hiring requests from workplaces. On the supply side, school authorities and residential organizations report to the municipal labor bureau the numbers of people waiting for job assignments. Current government policies determine the matching of supply and demand. Artificial manipulations occur when supply and demand are not balanced. Thus, when supply exceeds demand, workplaces are required to inflate their labor demands in order to absorb more workers. An alternative policy has been to send educated urban youth to the countryside for rural work (largely used from 1968 to 1977). Still another alternative has been to maintain educated urban youths in urban areas and put them on job-waiting lists, a method that has been used since 1977. If demand exceeds supply, which was the case in 1958 and 1959 because of the Great Leap Forward campaign, homemakers in the cities were encouraged to participate in paid work, and peasants were mobilized to work in urban factories.

The second step of the job-assignment process is to distribute labor quotas to recruiting organizations. Four types of organizations receive labor quotas directly from the municipal labor bureau: (1) central and municipal government agencies; (2) ministry-run institutions and enterprises located in the city; (3) municipal bureaus that manage bureau-run companies, enterprises, and institutions; and (4) district governments' labor agencies, which will redistribute labor quotas to district-level enterprises and street workshops. This order of distinction represents priorities granted for job assignment.

Heads of these organizations are invited to meetings held jointly by the municipal planning commission and the local labor bureau for planning and assigning labor quotas. In these meetings, decisions are made about how many quotas each recruiting organization should receive, and which schools and residential areas each organization should go to in order to fill these quotas.

Similar planning and assignment meetings are held within bureaus and companies to distribute labor quotas to work units they manage. At this level, state-owned work units and organizations with higher bureaucratic ranks, which are favored in the allocation of financial and material resources, are also favored in the distribution of labor quotas.

The next stage of the job-assignment process is for recruiting organizations to send their hiring requests to designated schools or residential districts. Desired numbers and qualifications of new workers are specified in these requests. Usually, qualifications include sex, age, education, political background, and academic performance of candidates. Professional training or vocational skills are considered for college and vocational-school students.

Assignments in Colleges and Vocational Schools

Job assignments in colleges and vocational schools are conducted once a year at the end of the academic year. A week-long graduation session is held to educate students to cooperate with state assignments. During the session, students are allowed to express their preferences for working in certain geographical areas, types of workplaces, and occupations. Although in principle these preferences are considered in making assignments, students are still required to consent to final job assignments. Those who do not accept an assignment face the possibility of unemployment. Greater flexibility has existed since 1986, when college and vocational-school students were allowed to search for jobs by themselves.

Hiring information is announced by schools at different times. The overall process of assignment in a school may take one to three weeks, including the week of the graduation session. Students often use a number of strategies to get better assignments. The best strategy is to acquire hiring information in advance and contact authorities to send a *tiaozi* (a message) to one's school to "initiate" a specific assignment. These authorities usually are party cadres in government agencies and hiring organizations. The school is likely to accept such an initiative because it is "from above" (higher authorities).

The next best strategy is to use one's network in school. The homeroom political adviser, the department party secretary or chair, or a school authority are very useful resources because these individuals are key decision makers for job assignments at schools.

When students are unable to use these strategies, they often use their school performance, both academic and political, as bargaining chips for a desirable assignment. They carefully study government regulations regarding job assignments and particular hiring practices, and promote themselves as the most qualified candidates for a specific workplace and/or job. They may fail in the first try, but their aggressiveness may draw the attention of the school authorities, and therefore can improve their position in the next round of assignments.

There are many students who have neither social networks nor the credentials to take advantage of hiring practices. Instead, they must accept whatever jobs they are assigned.

Assignments in Residential Areas

Similar procedures to those for assignments in college and vocational school had been used in high schools before 1979. Since then, and in some cities after 1983, high-school graduates who fail to move on to higher education are sent back home to wait for later assignments. These educated youths must transfer their personnel dossiers, which state their political and academic performances in school, to the offices of the residential district in which they live, and must file as "youth waiting for an assignment" (daiyie qingnian) or job waiting.

Unlike the school procedures, job assignments in residential areas are conducted several times a year. When hiring information is circulated, youths who await jobs apply to enter the screening process. They are required to take merit and physical examinations, and the results are used as criteria in hiring decisions. Government officials in residential districts have little influence in these decisions, because the hiring organizations, which control the screening and decision-making process, exclude them.

Like college and vocational-school students, youths waiting for jobs use certain strategies to seek better assignments. The rules of the game are a little different from those in school, however. In school a student must act as quickly as possible during the job-assignment process, because it occurs only once a year and lasts for only one to three weeks each time. In residential areas, job openings at different workplaces are announced as they are available, and the job-assignment process is conducted several times a year. Because one cannot withdraw his or her candidacy from consideration, and because it is very difficult to change work units once assigned a job, gauging *when* to enter the job-assignment process is of critical importance. Social networks are used extensively to gain information on employment opportunities, as well as to influence hiring decisions. If applicants cannot obtain this information or influence, they must either adopt a wait-and-see attitude or enter the screening process at a time when the merit examinations might be easier to pass.[5]

Employment Notices and Occupational Assignment

Newly hired persons are notified of their place of employment by the municipal or subdistrict labor bureau on behalf of the hiring organization. They are also informed when first to report to the workplace, but not what their particular occupation will be. It is only after checking in at the assigned work unit that they are given a specific job.

Occupational assignment is affected by several factors, including education. A college graduate is likely to be assigned a job consistent with his or her educational background. Often, this is arbitrarily defined, because college education is perceived by practically-minded managers in broad categories, such as natural sciences and social sciences. A vocational-school graduate is likely to be assigned work based on training received. High-school graduates would be assigned any type of manual or nonmanual work, whatever is available in the work unit. Another factor is a new worker's performance in school, which is recorded in his or her personnel dossiers. As in the process of work-unit assignments, new workers may also use their networks during the occupational assignment process to attain a desired job.

Personal Experiences with Direct State Assignments

1. Mr. Wang (personal interview 33). Mr. Wang was a university lecturer in economics in China before coming to the United States for doctoral training in 1986. While in China, he had the experience of receiving job assignment four times.

I graduated from a junior-high school [in Tianjin] in 1973 and was sent to the countryside. I should have moved on to senior-high school, if academic qualifications alone were the criterion of selection. My elder sister was assigned a job in the city, and according to the policy it was my turn to work in the village. I was assigned to a rural county of Tianjin. My classmates and I were bused to the assigned commune's headquarters, and stayed there for two hours waiting for village assignments. I was told a year later by the commune's youth league secretary, who became a friend of mine, that I was assigned to the poorest village in the commune because my personnel dossier showed that I was an "outstanding student both academically and politically." The commune authority wanted to add me as "new blood" to the weak party leadership of the village. I was not a party member, but a youth league leader in school. At that time, party authorities took it for granted that youth league leaders were new blood for the party. This was the first job assignment I received.

The second assignment came four years later when I was recruited by the grain bureau of the county where my village was located. This time I had a purpose: I tried to get a job in a state-owned grain depot that was managed jointly by the county grain bureau and the municipal grain bureau of Tianjin, because rumors said that the depot would eventually be the property of the city and, in that case, I would have a better chance of coming back home to work. I did not care what job would be assigned to me; I just wanted to work in that depot. I had an uncle working in the municipal labor bureau and his office had direct authority over the labor office of the county. So, when I was assigned to a collective-owned factory that was managed by the county's industrial bureau, I asked my father to talk to my uncle about the "wrong" assignment. It took only two days to change it. In the end I became an office worker in the grain depot I wanted to be assigned to. Actually, all one hundred people who were assigned to the depot used their *guanxi* to get to the depot.

The third time I received a job assignment was when I graduated from college. It was in 1981. I wanted to be assigned to the economic planning commission of the municipal government of Tianjin. I told my homeroom political adviser about my desire. I was a party member then, had received an award from the university for a junior project, got two research articles published, and had never done anything wrong politically. I convinced the political adviser that I deserved the job.

The last assignment was simple. It was when I graduated from an economics institute after completion of a master's program. My institute hired me, although I did not want to work in the institute. But the institute leaders imposed their decision on me, and had no intention of releasing my dossier to any other place. So, I had to stay.

2. Ms. Fei (personal interview 5). Ms. Fei was a typist working in the general office of a factory for six years before being promoted to be a technician in the same workplace.

I was assigned to this factory right after I graduated from junior-high school during the Cultural Revolution. I was an outstanding student, but not so by political standards at that time. My homeroom teacher urged me to take this assignment because, she said, if I did not I would be assigned to a collective factory. No one wanted to be in a collective firm. I accepted the assignment and checked in at that factory on time. Its manager liked my school record and assigned me work as a typist. My colleagues thought I had a lot of *guanxi* from above.

3. Ms. Zhang (personal interview 21). Ms. Zhang was sent to the countryside after graduation from a senior-high school. She was rated "an outstanding student" by her school and evaluated as "excellent educated urban youth" by her village authority. She was recruited by a textile company in Tianjin and hired as a manual worker on a production assembly line in a state-owned factory within the company.

I worked in a village in one of the rural counties of Tianjin for two years. Then, labor quotas were sent to my village to recruit from "educated youth from Tianjin," of which I was a member. Thirty-seven of us competed for two quotas. We all applied to the village's party branch. The party branch published its records about each of us. These records contained information about each person's demographic data, the number of years of residence in the village, work attendance, and total work credits earned. These records were studied carefully by the authorities of the production team in which each of us worked. Both work and political performances by each of us were also evaluated by the team authorities. My team leaders even collected opinions from villagers to help them evaluate eight of us in the team. Then, the team leaders sent their recommendation to the village. The village's party branch made the final recommendation and announced it to the public. A male colleague and I won the recommendation. He was hired as a road construction worker, and I was assigned to the textile factory. None of us knew where we would be assigned beforehand. We cared less about where we would go than the fact that we were finally able to come back to our home city. I was lucky, though, not to be assigned to a collective textile factory in the same company.

4. *Ms. Li (personal interview 6).* Ms. Li graduated from a two-year technical school managed by the Second Manufacturing Industry Bureau of Tianjin. She was assigned to be a skilled worker in a factory of the bureau.

It was not a big deal to get a job right away after graduation from a technical school. Everybody got one. And everybody got a job within the Second Manufacturing Industry Bureau that managed our school. All that mattered was where we would be assigned. The best assignment was to go to the bureau headquarters. The next best one was to work in an office at the company level. But you must *you ren* (have some connections) to help you out in order to work at these two levels. Of course, most of us were assigned factory jobs, and in these cases it was a matter of which one we would go to.

I was trained as a machinist, and could be assigned to any factory. I ended up going to one of three bicycle factories in the bureau. I was happy about the assignment, because that meant I would have the privilege of receiving bicycle coupons from the factory. I really did. You know how difficult it was to buy a Tianjin-made bicycle at that time. There was a shortage, because Tianjin-made bicycles were exported abroad for foreign currency. A lot of products also had to be sold in other Chinese cities as planned. It would be better, however, if I was assigned to a television assembly plant; it was much harder to buy a color TV set in the store.

Indirect State Assignments

In both direct and indirect state assignments, recruiting organizations are granted labor quotas through an integrated government employment plan. During indirect assignments, however, government labor agencies oversee but do not get involved in the screening process.

One original form of indirect state assignments was *dingti*, in which children take over a parent's job when the parent retires. *Dingti* was created as a means of protecting the living standards of retirees' families. Recruited children worked in the same workplaces as their parents had, but did not necessarily perform the same duties. Instead, they could be assigned any job according to the need of the workplace.

The *dingti* practice was used heavily at the end of the 1970s and the beginning of the 1980s, during the periods when urban-born youth flooded back to their home cities from long-term stays in the countryside during the Cultural Revolution. Many parents were willing to retire earlier than they had intended (sixty years of age for men and fifty years of age for women) in order for their children to be hired. From 1978 to 1983, twelve million state and collective workers retired, and 80 percent of the vacant positions were filled by the children of retirees through the *dingti* practice (He 1990, p. 152).

A related form of indirect state assignments is *neizhao* (internal recruitment), in which children of employees are targets for recruitment, but the employees' jobs are not affected. Usually an employee can submit only one child's name for *neizhao* during his or her entire lifetime. Depending on the recruiting organizations, children may be recruited by their parents' work units, or by the bureau or company to which their parents' work units belong. Not every type of work unit is authorized to use *neizhao* to recruit new workers. The method is largely used to recruit unskilled workers, and then only when there are large numbers of employees' children waiting for jobs. National statistics show that from 1978 to 1987, nearly 50 percent of new workers were recruited through the *dingti* and *neizhao* practices (He 1990, p. 156).

Both *dingti* and *neizhao* have had serious side-effects for lowering the quality of the work force. Experienced and skilled staff and workers were retiring earlier, and the new workers lacked training. Among families, *dingti* and *neizhao* were regarded as a "salvation" to secure positions for the least capable children. Other children capable of getting jobs through state assignment programs or individual applications did not have to rely on their parents for jobs. School students who wished to take over their parents' jobs appeared to be those who were poorly motivated to strive for high educational achievement. For these reasons, the policy of *dingti* was officially terminated in 1986, and that of *neizhao* has since then generally not been allowed.

Personal Experiences with *Dingti* and *Neizhao*

To convey to the reader different situations in which youths found their employment through *dingti* or *neizhao*, I describe several cases I interviewed.

1. Mr. Guo (personal interview 3). Mr. Guo was sent to the countryside to take a rural job after graduation from a senior-high school. He came back to his home city of Tianjin in 1979, after his petition was approved by the government. He stayed jobless with his parents for three months before taking over his father's job in a soy sauce plant.

I could have waited for a government assignment if I had any idea how long the wait would be. I was twenty-three years old, had no job, no apartment to live in, and no girlfriend. But my older brother got everything that a man of his age would need: a job, a public apartment, and a fiancée. My mom (a housewife) was worried about me. She wanted my father to retire earlier so that I could take his job. That was how I got a job in my father's former work unit, a soy sauce plant. I was hired as a *cai gou yuan* (purchasing agent), because the plant's manager thought of me as being honest and hardworking.

2. Mr. Han (personal interview 4). Mr. Han is the second child of a family of four children and a mother. His father had died ten years previously, and his mother worked in a collective textile plant before he took her job through *dingti*.

I waited for jobs for nearly a year and still had no luck. I could not pass exams to take a state job. Nor could my school records help; I had a lot of *cha* grades (equivalent to *D*) in school. Finally, my mother wanted me to take her job, and I did. My brothers and sister did not need my mom's job. One brother graduated from a vocational school and got a job right away. Another brother got a state assignment after he was on the job waiting list for three months. And my sister was an outstanding student; she went to college. I was the only one my mom had to take care of.

3. Mr. Zha (personal interview 19). Mr. Zha failed the general entrance examination the year he graduated from a senior-high school. His parents did not want their first son to wait for an assignment but instead get a job right away. They would feel humiliated if their first son stayed home doing nothing. So, he was urged by his parents to take over his father's job in a railroad station in the city.

My parents just did not want me to stay home to "humiliate" them. So, my father decided to retire even though he was only fifty-four years old. His manager did not want him to go, because his skills were important to the railroad station in which he worked. But the manager had to give in because he understood how important my substitution for my father was to our family.

4. *Ms. Zhou (personal interview 25).* Ms. Zhou was a train conductor recruited through *neizhao.* Her experience with *neizhao* was a typical case.

I graduated from a senior-high school that was managed by the railroad bureau of Tianjin. The majority of students in that school were from families whose members worked in the railroad system; so was I. My father was a senior worker in a railroad factory. Everybody knew railroad jobs were better—a lot of prestige, higher salaries, and many benefits. It was easier to get an apartment in the railroad industry, too. I easily got assigned to the railroad bureau because I was from a "railroad family." It was considered a kind of *neizhao,* a tradition in the railroad industry. But it was harder to get a good assignment within the bureau. I got help from the chief of the bureau's labor office, who was a good friend of one of my mother's brothers. I was extremely happy to be assigned as a conductor in the Tianjin-Shanghai charter; that was the best line managed by the bureau.

5. *Mr. Zhao (personal interview 23).* Mr. Zhao quit his state farm job and was hired as a cargo van loader through *neizhao* in a transportation company where his father formerly worked. Although his father died of an illness five years before the company began using *neizhao* to recruit its employees' children, Mr. Zhao claimed his eligibility as an applicant. He got help from one of his father's former colleagues who was then on the office staff of the company.

I wanted to be recruited by that company because it was the only chance that I could come back to the city. I worked in a state farm. Although it was only eight miles from the city, residents there were considered "rural population" and outside of the residential system of the city. I could not just quit the state farm job, because if I did I would be unemployed and I had no father to support me. My mother then was a homemaker, dependent on a small amount of "hardship compensation" provided month by month from my father's former work unit. My older brother and I had to send money to support her.

My father's former company did not think I was eligible as an applicant for *neizhao* because my father was no longer an employee of the company. But I got help from one of my father's former colleagues, who was on the office staff of the company. He talked to the company authority and argued that I was not ineligible because the company still supported my mother. Besides, he said, I would be the only one in my father's family who would "bother" the company. It worked for me. I was hired as a cargo van loader, not a very good job. But it was okay for me, because it was much better than my farm job. Besides, I came back to live in the city.

Direct Individual Application

Direct individual application became a popular method of job placement in China in the 1950s. During that decade, workplaces posted employment advertisements on walls along major streets in the cities. Qualifications usually focused on age, sex, education, and state of health. Individuals applied directly to the adverting workplaces. If they had previously filled out general application forms in government labor agencies, the latter would forward these forms to the recruiting organizations upon request of the applicants. Usually, physical and educational examinations would be conducted to sort and select applicants. The results also would be used for assignments of occupations.

Direct individual application was all but eliminated for two decades before it reemerged in the 1980s. There are now several forms. The predominant form has been through personal contact or *guanxi*. Parents' networks, kin ties, friends, and acquaintances have been extensively used to locate a work unit and a job. Another form of individual application is through employment services centers, which help place urban youths on job-waiting lists. Special employment services also exist to recruit college graduates. A third form of individual application is formal application: individuals apply directly to desired work units, even if they are not aware of any specific openings. This form of individual job search is used primarily by college graduates.

Personal Experiences with Direct Individual Application

1. Mr. Liu (personal interview 8).

I wanted to be a lawyer. There was no law school in Tianjin at that time. So, my philosophy major was not a negative factor. In college, I read a lot of translated books on law. I took notes while reading. I showed these notes to the head of a newly established law center, whom I knew through a friend. This law center head graduated from Harvard Law School before 1949 and was an expert in business law. He liked my notes. But he told me he liked better the fact that I had motivation to study law by myself. He also admired my philosophy background. So, I was hired by his law center. It would be very difficult to get a job in our center now; too many people want a job here.

2. Mr. Qi (personal interview 10). Mr. Qi was a middle-school graduate. He failed to move on to senior-high school because his academic abilities were poor. With help from an employment service center, he became a construction worker.

I did very bad in almost every course I took. I was bored in school. I wanted to work, to make some money that I could spend. But I could not find a job with my school records. I went to an employment service center in the district in which I lived. I was told by a staff member that I could join others like me to organize a team to employ ourselves. I asked how. I learned that the center subcontracted with a powerful company that had a lot of contracts with the municipal government for building construction. As a team, we could sign a subcontract with the center to do the work for the company. All seasonal or even monthly contracts. But something is better than nothing. So, I found several people to form a team and got the first contract for three months.

We did a lot of work: loading and unloading, moving bricks, moving water hoses, cleaning buildings, and so on. Outdoor work, of course. But the company paid by piece rates. So, when we wanted more, we did more work. Also, once we gained experience, we bargained with the company for more. That's what other workers told us to do. We did it collectively. Permanent workers wanted us to cooperate with them. They liked experienced temporary workers, not only because of skills but because experienced workers knew how to cooperate with them to bargain for money. The employment center that we subcontracted with got a percentage of our pay. But it was not shown on our pay slips; it went directly from the company to the center. We did not care. I made several times more than my former classmates who got jobs in state factories. They were better students, but I worked on a better contract, I suppose.

Summary

Bureaucratic allocation of labor in China is based on the Maoist ideology that labor is not a commodity but a national resource. This ideology denies private labor rights. The resulting employment policies have centered around a rigid government job-assignment program in which labor is allocated to work organizations by state planners. It is only until the 1980s that individual application was accepted as a legal method of job placement. Even so, private labor rights are still not completely recognized. In fact, direct and indirect state assignments have remained the predominant methods of job placement in the 1980s, even though individual applications considerably increased.

A unique feature of the Chinese employment process is that labor is allocated to work organizations rather than types of occupations. Occupational attainment is pursued only after a person enters a work unit (e.g., Ms. Lei, Ms. Zhang, Mr. Guo, Mr. Han, Ms. Zhou, and Mr. Zhao). This is a very different process from the one found in market economies. In market economies, employment is occupation-directed, and social-class mobility is primarily a process of occupational attainment. Thus, the process of status attainment in China requires an examination of both work-unit and occupational attainments. This I investigate in the next chapter.

4

THE CHINESE VERSION OF STATUS ATTAINMENT

Locating a workplace and finding a job are two distinct aspects of employment in China. For a prospective Chinese worker, it is more important *where* you are than *what* you are. Different processes occur when the individual gives priority to one aspect over another. Employment tends to be occupation-directed in Western industrial countries, as a result of specialized training and job-related income distribution. "A man qualifies himself for occupational life by obtaining an education; as a consequence of pursuing his occupation, he obtains income" (Duncan 1961, p. 116). In the United States, although the literature on economic segmentation reveals the importance of workplaces for wage attainment, place of employment is considered a factor only *after* occupation is taken into account. In short, status attainment or social-class positioning in Western societies is primarily achieved through occupational choice.

A different process applies to China. As described in the previous chapter, the allocation of labor in the Chinese planned system is workplace-oriented. Although individuals pursue training for certain occupations, only a few college students and vocational-school students receive this type of training before entering the work force. For the large majority of urban youths, who do not receive this type of pre-occupational training, *occupational attainment occurs only after one enters a work unit.* For all urban youths, job hunting is directed toward finding a work unit, because working conditions, wage standards, fringe benefits, and access to housing and community resources are related more to workplace characteristics than to occupation. Also, entering the "right" work unit is a factor in eventually getting a more desirable job. Finally, a consistent bureaucratic bias in favor of the ownership of labor by the work unit has magnified the importance of the place of employment. Clearly, status attainment in urban China is not merely a question of occupational choice, but of who gets placed where in the work-unit structure.

In the previous chapter, I described Chinese employment policies and practices from an historical perspective. The effects of these
policies and practices for the employment process were examined
for the general population and in individual cases. In this chapter, I
provide a theoretical and statistical analysis of factors in the employment process using the 1988 Tianjin survey. Three factors in
particular are the focus: intergenerational influence, educational
achievement, and political criteria. Later, in the next chapter, I will
analyze the Chinese employment process further, with special attention to *guanxi* and social resources as predictors.

Status Inheritance and the Father's Work Unit

Debates and Evidence

Status-attainment scholars (Blau and Duncan 1967; Sewell and
Hauser 1975; Featherman and Hauser 1978) have argued that the
transmission of status from one generation to the next decreases as a
society becomes more industrialized. This is because, as Treiman
(1970, p. 218) put it, the complex labor-force structure in more industrialized countries "makes it more difficult for fathers to pass
their own positions directly on to their sons or even to arrange for
their sons to work at the same jobs they do." Data from market
societies lent support to this argument (Treiman and Yip 1989).

The industrialization argument predicts a stronger preference
for status inheritance in less industrialized *socialist* countries than
in the more industrialized *capitalist* countries. But studies of Eastern Europe and China provide contrary findings. Data from Hungary
and Poland show little direct effect of parental status on an individual's occupational attainment (Meyer, Tuma, and Zagorski 1979;
Zagorski 1984; Treiman and Yip 1989), and such a direct effect does
not exist at all in urban China (Xie and Lin 1986; Blau and Ruan
1990; Lin and Bian 1991). Earlier Chinese studies (Parish 1984;
Whyte and Parish 1984) show that the decreasing trend of parental
influence on occupational achievement was influenced by government policy changes rather than the industrialization process itself.

Lin and Bian (1991) argue that the controversy should be solved
by identification of status criteria meaningful to each society. With
a 1985 sample of Chinese urban workers in Tianjin, the researchers
show that although there was virtually no occupational inheritance,
there was a significant direct effect of the father's work-unit sector
on the son's work-unit sector. Also, the father's work-unit sector has
some indirect effect on the son's occupational status (via the son's

work-unit sector), but no direct effect.[1] Lin and Bian suggest that the *work unit* rather than occupation per se is a meaningful status criterion for the study of status inheritance in China.

Recruiting the Worker: Causal Mechanisms

In Chapter 3, I described mechanisms that explain why the parent's work unit has a direct effect on the child's work unit, but not on occupation. One mechanism is the practice of *dingti* and *neizhao*, by which urban youth are recruited into their parents' workplaces.[2] Until 1986, there had been an increasing use of these practices. Children recruited in this fashion, however, are not necessarily assigned the same type of work as their parents. Rather, occupational assignments are largely affected by the education and political background of the new workers.

The parent's work unit also determines place of residence. Public urban housing, which is predominant in Chinese cities, is distributed through work units. Family households whose members are employed in the same work unit are likely to live in the same neighborhood. Their children also go to the same school where, if they do not move on to vocational school or college, they receive job assignments after graduation. If these children do not receive assignments at school, they will return to the neighborhood to wait for later assignments. In both cases, through home and school locations, parents' work units affect children's job assignments, and serve as a mechanism to allocate the next generation's labor. This pattern of allocating labor to work units became more significant through time, along with a corresponding government monopoly of public-housing construction over the last forty years.

Still another mechanism is the path between parents' work units to parents' social networks and to children's employment. Work colleagues—those who work in the same work unit, company, or bureau—are used extensively as social ties in China (Blau, Ruan, and Ardelt 1991). Parents use work-colleague ties to help their children enter desirable work units, whether through state assignment programs or individual job searches (Lin and Bian 1989). The influence of these ties is particularly effective. Through this path, children are channelled into the sector and/or bureaucratic rank of work units of their parents. Since the opening of labor markets in the mid-1980s, there has been an increasing use of social networks in individual job searches. This implies that a stronger association exists between the parent's and the child's work-unit status, and can be attributed to the social networks of parents. Occupational assignments within work units also may well be affected by the social networks of parents.

Transmitting Status in the Workplace: Hypotheses

The mechanisms mentioned determine the transmission of status from one generation to the next in the Chinese urban labor force, and it is primarily achieved through one's work-unit status. Specifically, *the higher the parent's work-unit status, the greater chance the child has to enter a high-status work unit.* Furthermore, the child's work-unit attainment is not related to the industrialization process. Rather, it is associated with employment policies and practices implemented by the Chinese government. Specifically, because these mechanisms became more effective through the mid- or late 1980s, *intergenerational influence in status attainment is expected to be stronger for younger than for older cohorts of Chinese workers.*

Educational Achievement Versus Political Virtue

Debates and Evidence

Contemporary sociologists have debated at length the causes and effects of social stratification systems. Whereas functionalist scholars contend that status and privilege are awarded to individuals who have the potential to contribute to the society (Davis and Moore 1945; Blau and Duncan 1967; Treiman 1970), Marxist-conflict theorists argue that socioeconomic inequalities reflect class struggles over power and resources (Marx 1978 [1859]; Dahrendorf 1959; Wright 1978). To functionalist scholars, educational achievement contributes to upward mobility; but to Marxists, membership within or outside the dominant social class determines one's life chances.

The debate is represented in studies of social stratification and social mobility in postrevolution China by Shirk's (1982, 1984) conceptualizations of virtuocracy and meritocracy. Virtuocracy, she contends, is a reward system that favors those committed to the political ideology of the dominant bureaucratic class.[3] Meritocracy, on the other hand, is the system by which one's ability and credentials are rewarded. There is considerable documentation concerning which of the two is predominant in China, contrasting Chinese ideologies about "redness" (*hong*) against expertise (*zhuan*); class labels of the family (*jiating chushen*) against performance of the individual (*geren biaoxian*); or political background (*zhengzhi mian-*

mu) against educational achievement (Whyte 1975; Kraus 1981; Parish 1981, 1984; Shirk 1982, 1984; Unger 1982; Whyte and Parish 1984; Walder 1986).

This issue has been examined in different institutional settings and in different periods of time. In Chinese educational institutions in the 1960s, Shirk (1982, 1984) found that the virtuocratic principle of political morality and activism was mixed with academic achievements, and it soon became the primary criterion of student selections for higher education during the Cultural Revolution. Such a trend was reversed in favor of meritocracy during the market reforms of the 1980s, when academic merit examinations were restored in order to screen students for college admissions. In the current workplace, party membership, as an indicator of political virtue, and educational credentials are considered separate paths for upward mobility in terms of occupation (Blau and Ruan 1990; Lin and Bian 1991) and wages (Walder 1990).

Political Background, Education, and Job Assignments:
Causal Mechanisms

Of special interest here is the effect of an individual's political background and educational achievement on a first job assignment. There are basically three groups of youths. One group consists of youths with high profiles in both political background and education. These youths have received college or vocational education and are members in the Chinese Communist Youth League and, in particular, the Chinese Communist Party. They become available for recruitment by top agencies of the government hierarchy and institutions with strategic importance to the party-state, as well as for advancement into administrative and managerial positions.

Another small group of youths is those who perform poorly academically and are considered politically backward. My interviews with school officials and teachers in Tianjin (personal interviews 1, 9, 12, 16, 30, 31) show that students who are labeled "politically backward" are juvenile delinquents, those involved with street gangs, those who misbehave in school, and those who are passive in political studies and extracurricular activities. Students in this category are likely to receive undesirable job assignments, in terms of both work units and occupations.

A different situation applies to the greater majority of urban youths. These are graduates from middle, high, and vocational schools. They are neither party nor Youth League members, but they are also not labeled as politically backward. Thus, the issue of political virtue is not as relevant for the majority of urban youths as for the two smaller groups of high and low profile. As a practical matter, the majority of urban youths are recruited for manual work that is concentrated in numerous manufacturing and commercial units, and where political virtue is not really an issue for entry-level jobs. This means that educational credentials are the primary criterion for screening the majority of urban youths in their work-unit and occupational assignments.

Job Placement for Youths: Hypotheses

Because political virtue is irrelevant to the majority of urban youths in the process of job placement and education is an important screening criterion for workers, *the overall outcome of job assignments is expected to be associated more strongly with education than with political memberships.* The relative causal importance of the two factors in the job-placement process would vary from one labor cohort to another, as a consequence of employment policies during different time periods. Specifically, *the cohort who entered the labor force during the Cultural Revolution would experience a greater impact of political criteria on their job assignments than other cohorts, because of radical policies implemented during this decade of political hysteria.*

Modeling Status Attainment in the Chinese Context

The statistical analyses that follow are based on the 1988 Tianjin survey data. Descriptive data for variables used in the analysis are presented in Table 4.1. Multiple-regression models are employed. These models are appropriate to estimate independent effects of predictors and control variables on respondents' first work units and first occupations. Because one enters a work unit before one acquires an occupation, work-unit attainment is estimated before occupational attainment. Also, with a path analysis, the status of first work unit is used as a predictor of first occupation. In both work-unit and occupation estimations, the major independent variables are measuring inheritance, achievement, and political virtue. Variables of sex, year to enter the labor force, place of birth, and method of job placement are used as control variables.

These models are estimated for the total study group as well as for three labor cohorts separately. Labor cohorts are defined here as those who entered the labor force at a particular time. The three

TABLE 4.1

First Jobs for Entry-Level Workers in Tianjin, 1988:
Descriptive Data (N = 938)

Variables	Mean (Standard Deviation)	
Dependent Variables		
Fist work-unit sector (state = 1)	.72	(.45)
First work-unit rank	2.71	(1.15)
First occupational status	76.00	(12.90)
Variables for the Father's Status		
Father's work-unit sector (state = 1)	.57	(.49)
Father's work-unit sector (nonreporting = 1)	.28	(.45)
Father's work-unit rank (division or higher = 1)	.36	(.48)
Father's work-unit rank (nonreporting = 1)	.31	(.46)
Father's occupational status	58.96	(34.73)
Father's occupational status (nonreporting = 1)	.24	(.42)
Individual Characteristics		
Education by first job	3.29	(1.01)
CCYL membership before a first job	.15	(.36)
CCP membership before a first job	.05	(.22)
Direct state assignments	.71	(.45)
Indirect state assignments	.11	(.32)
Tianjin city-born	.67	(.47)
Sex (male = 1)	.54	(.50)
Year to have the first job	67.86	(12.20)

Note: CCP = Chinese Communist Party; CCYL = Chinese Communist Youth League.

cohorts are: (1) 1949–65, the first seventeen years of the People's Republic, during which political and economic reforms laid the groundwork for a new order of stratification; (2) 1966–76, the Cultural Revolution decade that precipitated political, economic, and social crises; and (3) 1977–88, the market reform era during which China struggled to reestablished itself.[4]

Measuring Work-Unit and Occupational Statuses

Ownership sector and bureaucratic rank of the work unit are used as indicators of work-unit status. These two indicators are available for both respondents and their fathers, which enables us to test hypotheses about the transmission of work-unit status from the older generation to the younger. Work establishment size is not considered, because the analysis from Chapter 2 demonstrated that the number of employees, represented in the 1988 Tianjin survey, was not a significant factor in workplace segmentation.

Ownership sector is a dichotomous variable, with 72.4 percent entering urban employment in the state sector (the omitted variable is nonstate sector; see Table 4.1). An alternative approach could have been to identify five ownership types: state, collective, private, foreign, and mixed; this would have required a log-linear analysis. Because there were too few cases in the last three categories (18 out of 919 cases), this strategy was not considered appropriate for the current study.[5] The bureaucratic rank of the first work unit is a five-level ordinal scale (excluding "nonranking") as shown in Appendix C.

Occupational status for the first job is on a nineteen-category scale (see Appendix C). The ranking of these occupations was obtained by using the Lin-Xie index (Lin and Xie 1988), which is a Chinese version of the Duncan Socioeconomic Index (Duncan 1961).[6] The average occupational status score for the respondent's first job is 76.0, with a standard deviation of 12.9. This is lower than the 79.2 score for the current job. The differential indicates a slight upward occupational mobility from the first to current job.

Measuring the Father's Status, Education, and Political Status

The father's work-unit sector, work-unit rank, and occupation by the time of the respondent's first job are used as indicators of parental status. Although these variables are also available for mothers, the variables for fathers are more strongly correlated with both sons' and daughters' status variables. Previous studies in both the United States (Blau and Duncan 1967; Duncan, Featherman, and Duncan 1972) and China (Blau and Ruan 1990; Lin and Bian 1991) show that the father's education does not have a direct effect on the child's first occupation, nor does it have an effect on the child's work-unit status (in Lin and Bian's study only). Thus, the father's education is not considered in the present analysis.[7] The serious technical problem in the analysis has been how properly to deal with "missing" cases for fathers' variables. Twenty-eight percent of the respondents did not report their fathers' work-unit sector, 31 percent did not report their fathers' work-unit rank, and 24 percent did not report their fathers' occupation. (The unreporting percentages are even greater for mothers because more than 50 percent of the mothers are homemakers). A dummy variable of "nonreport-ing" was created in order to include these missing cases in the analysis.[8]

Education at the time of the respondent's first job is defined here as a five-category rank. In Tianjin, the level of education rather than years of schooling has been the criterion for job assignments. This is related to the nearly perfect attendance and graduation rates at all levels of schools (Editors of Yearbook of China's Education 1989, p. 665 and p. 669). The sample shows 10.8 percent of the respondents indicating college or higher education, 32.4 percent high school/vocational education, 35.9 percent middle-school edu-cation, and 20.9 percent having had less than a middle-school education.

Commitment to party ideologies is the primary criterion for membership in the Chinese Communist Youth League (CCYL, for ages fifteen to twenty-five) and in the Chinese Communist Party (CCP, for age eighteen and older). These memberships are used as indicators of one's political status. The 1988 Tianjin sample showed 5.3 percent CCP membership and 15.5 percent CCYL membership by the time of a person's first job.

Measuring Demographic and Other Variables

As described in Chapter 3, people born in Tianjin had been given greater job security within the city of Tianjin, as a result of the household registration system. A dummy variable of place of birth is therefore created to test whether Tianjin city-born respondents would also have the privilege of entering high-status work units and high-status jobs. Respondents who were born in the city of Tianjin (67.4 percent) were coded "1," and the omitted category includes those born in Tianjin's suburbs and rural counties and other provinces.

Two dummy variables are used for method of job placement: direct state assignment (70.9 percent) and indirect state assignment (11.4 percent). The omitted category is direct individual application (7.7 percent). Jobs assigned through state programs are predomi-nantly state-sector jobs, and for this reason I expect that respondents who got jobs through direct state assignments had a greater chance of entering state work units than those who found jobs through independent application. There is no obvious effect of direct state assignments on work-unit rank and occupation, nor of indirect state assignments on sector, rank, and occupational attainments.

A great deal of the research literature demonstrate that sexual inequalities have been persistent in China's labor markets (Johnson 1976; Stacy 1983; Wolf 1985; Whyte 1984; Honig and Hershatter 1988; Lin and Bian 1991). For this reason, sex is used as a control variable in regression models. It is a dummy variable, consisting of 53.5 percent males (coded "1").

Finally, the last control variable is a continuous variable indicating the year one enters the labor force. Davis-Friedmann (1985) and Davis (1988, 1990, 1993) argue that the Communist system and the state bureaucracy have produced a reward system that favors the cohorts already in the labor structure and reduces competition between members of different generations. The implication of this "first comer hypothesis" for the present study is that older labor cohorts tend to enter work units in the state sector as opposed to the nonstate sector, and with higher bureaucratic ranks; they also have higher-status occupations than younger labor cohorts.

Entering the State Sector

Table 4.2 presents logistic coefficients estimating the likelihood that one enters work units in the state sector. I will discuss the effects of each of the predictors and control variables.

The Effects of Father's Work-Unit Sector on Sector Placement

The father's work-unit sector has a direct effect on the odds of one's entering a state work unit. The logit difference of .54 reveals that a person whose father worked in the state sector at the time when he or she was entering the labor force would increase his or her chance of getting a job in a state work unit by 71.6 percent (antilog of .716), compared to another person who had the same qualifications except that his or her father did not work in the state sector.[9]

The direct influence of the father's state sector on the child's first sector was on the rise from the 1949–65 period to the 1977–88 period. The logit coefficient of the father's sector increases from .44 (p < .05, one tailed) for the 1949–65 cohort and .52 for the 1966–76 cohort to .79 for the 1977–88 cohort. Interestingly, this trend corresponds to China's industrialization. From 1949 to 1985, China's industrial investment grew by forty-five times, the industrial output values grew by thirty times, and the industrial labor force increased by nine times (Yuan 1989, p. 2). Industries earned 25.2 percent of the country's gross national product and 12.6 percent of the national income in 1949, and these figures grew to 61.1 percent and 46.2

TABLE 4.2

Logistic Coefficients of Entrance into Work Units
in the State Sector, Tianjin, 1988

Predictors (N)	Total (919)	1949–65 (324)	1966–76 (262)	1977–88 (276)
Father's work-unit sector (state-owned = 1)	.537*** (.114)	.438 (.260)	.525* (.204)	.791*** (.202)
Father's work-unit sector (unreported = 1)	.484*** (.133)	.506* (.256)	.397 (.270)	.488 (.269)
Education	.370*** (.052)	.493*** (.089)	.535*** (.127)	.240* (.112)
CCYL	.279* (.131)	.142 (.236)	.300* (.141)	.267 (.179)
CCP	.163 (.219)	.599 (.543)	−.084 (.401)	.197 (.486)
Control Variables				
Direct state assignment	.433*** (.103)	.315 (.201)	−.149 (.381)	.529 (.178)
Indirect state assignment	.038 (.142)	−.123 (.303)	−.388 (.456)	.141 (.198)
Born in Tianjin	.006 (.099)	.017 (.179)	.190 (.187)	−.265 (.215)
Sex (male = 1)	.239** (.083)	.238 (.167)	.379* (.157)	.175 (.146)
Year to enter the labor force	−.019*** (.004)	−.052* (.021)	−.098** (.028)	.025 (.029)
Intercept	4.759*** (.301)	6.594 (1.180)	10.277*** (1.968)	1.605 (2.347)
Goodness-of-fit chi square	890.134	299.046	238.509	266.835
Degree of freedom	908	313	251	265

*p < .05, **p < .01, ***p < .001. Standard errors are in parentheses.
Note: Respondents who entered the labor force before 1949 are included in the "total" equation.

percent, respectively, in 1988. Correspondingly, agricultural output values decreased from 58.5 percent to 19.6 percent, and agricultural revenue contributions decreased from 68.4 percent to 32.4 percent for the 1949 to 1988 period (Yuan 1989, p. X-14 and X-21).[10] These

Chinese data fail to lend support to the industrialization-attainment argument (Treiman 1970), which predicts that status inheritance would be reduced with industrialization.

The strong effect of a father's work-unit sector on the child's work-unit sector for the Cultural Revolution decade contradicts an earlier study that focused on occupational inheritance (Parish 1984). In this earlier study, Parish found that the father's occupation had less effect on the child's for the post-1967 cohort than for the pre-1966 cohort. He explained this as the result of egalitarianism during the Cultural Revolution. I will demonstrate that such reduced intergenerational influence on a child's occupational attainment is not replicated in our 1988 Tianjin survey. Rather, the data show little evidence of transmission of occupational status from the father to the child through time.

The Effects of Education on Sector Placement

In Tianjin, education increases the likelihood of one's entering the state sector. Referring again to Table 4.2, the logit coefficient of .37 indicates that the higher the educational level one has, the greater the chances of entering a work unit in the state sector. Respondents with no schooling have a 59.1 percent chance of entering a state work unit; it increases to 67.7 percent for those with elementary school, 75.2 percent for those with middle-school education, 81.5 percent for those with high-school or vocational education, and 86.4 percent for college graduates.[11] Clearly, these are substantial differences in job opportunities.

The effect of educational achievement on sector attainment was about the same in magnitude for the 1949–65 and 1966–76 periods (logit coefficients of .49 and .53), but considerably reduced for the 1977–88 period (logit coefficient of .24). This reduced effect of education reflects changes in the education and labor market structures in the late 1970s and early 1980s. Academically oriented "general entrance examinations" were resumed in 1977 to select students for vocational schools and colleges. Students who were recruited according to political criteria in the mid-1970s were largely sent back to their previous work units after graduation in the post-1977 period. There was little positive effect of higher learning on sector attainment until 1981–82, when the first post-Cultural Revolution cohort of vocational school and college students had graduated. In the labor market structure, from 1977 to 1982 *dingti* and *neizhao* were the predominant methods of job placement, by which one's parent's work unit was the key criterion of recruitment, and the job applicant's education was rarely considered. The 1988 Tianjin data show logit coefficients for education of .31 for 1977–79 and .37 for 1980–82, which are considerably lower in magnitude than the .53 for the Cultural Revolution period.

From 1979 on, enrollments in various levels of vocational and college education were booming. When students graduated after 1982, they were exclusively assigned state jobs through state assignment programs. Between 1983 and 1985, *dingti* and *neizhao* were discouraged, and merit examinations were more widely used to recruit workers in the state sector. Urban youth who failed these examinations largely found jobs in the new "small collectives" and in the expanding private sector. In response to these changes, education became a significant predictor of sector attainment in the 1983–85 period, with a logit coefficient of .88.

In Chapter 3, I described the implementation of a labor contract system in 1986. This system challenged the long-term job security in the state sector. At the same time, more attractive foreign-capital enterprises and various forms of self-employment and corporate businesses were growing rapidly. Because college graduates were being given greater freedom to seek employment by themselves, they were encouraged to look for jobs in businesses other than those in the state sector. These changes in the labor market structure are responsible for the negative effect of education (logit coefficient of −.26) on sector attainment in 1986–88.

Similar findings have been reported by Lin and Bian (1990) in a 1983 study of urban residents in Beijing, Tianjin (in 1985), and Shanghai (in 1986). The 1977–83 cohort in Beijing showed a reduced effect of education on sector attainment.[12] The 1977–85 cohort in the 1985 Tianjin sample showed a much stronger effect (.351) than was found in Beijing, and the 1977–86 cohort in the Shanghai sample showed a weaker but statistically significant effect of education (.176). These findings once again demonstrate that, as far as post-revolutionary China is concerned, the effect of education on status attainment is associated with government policy changes rather than with the industrialization process.

The Effects of CCP and CCYL Memberships on Sector Placement

Youth League membership (CCYL) has a positive effect on the attainment of an individual's first work-unit sector. The logit coefficient of .279 in Table 4.2 indicates that CCYL members would have a 32-percent (antilog of 1.32) greater chance of entering work units in the state sector than non-CCYL members. The coefficient of par-

ty membership (CCP) is positive, although statistically insignificant. This means that although CCP members are more likely to get
jobs in the state sector than non-CCP members, a *significant* number of CCP members start their careers in nonstate sectors. This is
understandable, since CCP members are likely to be assigned administrative and managerial positions in state as well as nonstate
workplaces (as shown by the strong effect of CCP membership on
occupational status in Table 4.5, which will be discussed later).

As expected, the effect of CCYL membership on sector attainment varies across labor cohorts. It is weaker for the 1949–65 cohort
(.14), and stronger for the Cultural Revolution (.30) and post-1977
cohorts (.27). CCYL members had a 15-percent greater chance of
entering work units in the state sector than nonmembers during the
1949–65 period, a 35-percent greater chance during the Cultural
Revolution period in which virtuocracy was strengthened, and a 31-
percent greater chance during the post-1977 period in which market
reforms were launched. The persistence of this effect of CCYL membership for the youngest cohort indicates that political orientation
in job placement has not been greatly weakened during the 1980s
market reforms.

The Effects of Control Variables on Sector Placement

Direct state assignment increases one's chance of entering a
work unit in the state sector, but indirect state assignment does not.
This suggests that the *dingti* and *neizhao* practices, which have
been the basic forms for indirect state assignment programs, are
used in both state and nonstate sectors for recruitment of new workers. The effect of direct state assignments was moderate in the
1949–65 period, when direct state assignments were experiencing
ups and downs. The lack of effect of direct state assignments for the
subsequent 1966–76 period reflects the fact that jobs in the collective sector were also being controlled and assigned by the government. And the effect of direct state assignments was stronger in the
1977–88 period, when it became the policy that jobs in the collective sector and other nonstate businesses were to be excluded from
state assignment programs.

Consistent across labor cohorts, place of birth has no effect on
one's assignment to a work-unit sector. Thus, even though people
born in the city of Tianjin may find greater job security for urban
employment than people who were born in the suburbs, rural counties, and other provinces, their place of birth is not a significant
factor in the process of sector placement.

As expected, males were more likely to enter work units in the state sector than females. The finding is consistent with earlier observations (Whyte 1984; Lin and Bian 1991). A logit coefficient of .24 reveals that with other qualifications being equal, men would have a 27 percent greater chance of entering state work units than women. This gender effect is considerably higher for the Cultural Revolution cohort (.38), and is similar to the findings reported by Lin and Bian (1990) for Beijing and Shanghai. These findings fail to support the destratification hypothesis that predicts a reduced social inequality for the Cultural Revolution period (Parish 1984). Moreover, the gender effect on sector attainment was the lowest for the recent reform period (.18), as found by Lin and Bian for Beijing and Shanghai, suggesting that discrimination against females in the job-placement processes has been declining. The findings here contradict observations of individual cases from Beijing and Shanghai (Honig and Hershatter 1988).

Finally, the year of one's entrance into the labor force has a negative effect on sector attainment for the first two time periods, but it has no effect in the 1977–88 period. The results indicate that through time more and more people were assigned jobs in the state sector before market reforms. Such a trend was interrupted by the latest period of market reforms in which collectives and private businesses have grown more rapidly than state-owned businesses.

Entering a Higher-Ranked Work Unit

The process of work-unit rank attainment shows a similar pattern to that of work-unit sector attainment. Table 4.3 presents regression estimates for the respondent's first work-unit rank. The father's work-unit rank (a dummy variable) significantly promotes one's attainment of work-unit rank (a merit coefficient of .88).[13] The "unreported" father's work-unit rank also shows a positive coefficient of .20, suggesting that the category includes respondents whose fathers worked in high- and low-ranking work units, even through not identified as such. The effect of the father's work-unit rank on first work-unit rank increases in magnitude from the 1949–65 to 1977–88 period, which, once again, disproves the argument for the influence of industrialization (Treiman 1970).

Overall, education has a positive effect on work-unit rank attainment, but the effects of CCP and CCYL memberships on first work-unit rank are statistically insignificant. Interestingly, for the Cultural Revolution cohort, the effect of education disappears, and

TABLE 4.3

Regression Coefficients of First Work-Unit Rank, Tianjin, 1988

Predictors	(N)	Total (874)	1949–65 (311)	1966–76 (253)	1977–88 (264)
Father's work-unit rank		.889***	.726***	.868***	1.021***
(high ranking = 1)		(.082)	(.163)	(.128)	(.134)
Father's work-unit rank		.201*	.278	.025	.147
(unreported = 1)		(.095)	(.147)	(.181)	(.199)
CCYL		.084	.128	.437*	−.165
		(.098)	(.208)	(.200)	(.143)
CCP		.208	.208	.463*	−.023
		(.153)	(.230)	(.231)	(.347)
Education		.120**	.221***	.004	.143
		(.038)	(.057)	(.080)	(.093)
First state sector		.689***	.462**	.733***	.629***
		(.081)	(.164)	(.139)	(.137)
Control Variables					
Sex (male = 1)		.163**	.289*	.253*	−.032
		(.069)	(.120)	(.122)	(.120)
Born in Tianjin		.004	−.043	.159	−.049
		(.079)	(.124)	(.142)	(.171)
Direct state assignment		.071	.044	.230	.205
		(.094)	(.162)	(.303)	(.157)
Indirect state assignment		.009	−.169	.877*	−.028
		(.131)	(.268)	(.372)	(.180)
Year to enter the labor		−.012***	−.021	−.011	−.004
force		(.004)	(.014)	(.020)	(.023)
Constant		2.127***	2.422**	2.00	1.53
R squared		.273	.196	.372	.337

$*p < .05$, $**p < .01$, $***p < .001$. Standard errors are in parentheses.
Note: Respondents who entered the labor force before 1949 are included in the "total" equation.

it is the CCP and CCYL memberships that show strong direct effects. This suggests that ability had given way to political virtue as the criterion for entering high-ranking work organizations during the Cultural Revolution. These effects are obtained after the first work-unit sector is controlled for.

Neither direct nor indirect state assignment have an effect on work-unit rank attainment; all three methods of job placement (with individual application) are equally helpful in entering high-ranking organizations. This is despite the fact that direct state assignments are more helpful in entering the state sector. As before, place of birth has no effect on work-unit rank attainment.

As expected, males are more likely to enter work units with higher ranks than females. The gender differences in first work-unit ranks were comparable for the first two cohorts, but nonexistent for the post-1977 cohort. This is similar in form and trend to the gender effect of a particular job sector attainment. Finally, the earlier one entered the labor force, the higher the rank of the work unit in which one works. This effect, however, is significantly reduced within each cohort.

Getting an Occupation

Two equations provided information on occupational attainment in Tianjin. The first equation was based on a modified Blau-Duncan model (Blau and Duncan 1967), in which occupational status for the first job is regressed on the father's occupation and the individual's own education, controlling for sex. The second equation incorporated the father's and the individual's own work-unit sector and rank as additional predictors and other control variables. Cohort analyses are based on this last model, and the results are presented in Table 4.4.

As shown by the first column in Table 4.4, the effect of education on first-job occupation is evident. The father's occupation and gender, however, are not significant. The beta coefficient for education is .52, which is greater than the .44 reported by Blau and Duncan (1967, p. 170) for American males. However, the father's occupational status does not have the direct effect on the child's for the Chinese as it did for the Americans. The results from the Tianjin sample are consistent with recently published Chinese data (Blau and Ruan 1990; Lin and Bian 1991).

The second column of Table 4.4 presents results of a model that incorporates additional predictors and control variables. Several points deserve attention. First, none of the three types of status for the father (sector, rank, and occupation) has a direct effect on the child's first occupational status. This is a consistent finding across all three cohorts. The intergenerational influence on occupational attainment is only indirect: father's sector affects the child's job sector, which affects the child's occupational status. We can conclude that in terms of status transmission from one generation to the next, work-unit sector is the most important criterion.

TABLE 4.4

Metric Regression Coefficients of First Occupational Status, Tianjin, 1988

Predictors	[N]	Total (929)	Total (874)	1949–65 (311)	1966–76 (253)	1977–88 (276)
Father's state sector			.607 (1.150)	.155 (2.255)	3.780 (2.113)	−.004 (1.778)
Father's work-unit rank			−.104 (.004)	.328 (1.937)	.370 (1.757)	−1.750 (1.459)
Father's occupation		−.003 (.032)	.031 (.033)	.070 (.067)	−.024 (.065)	.058 (.048)
Education		6.610*** (.387)	6.904*** (.413)	7.811*** (.639)	5.410*** (.968)	6.234*** (.904)
CCP			5.223*** (1.630)	.588 (2.433)	11.489*** (3.405)	7.224* (3.266)
CCYL			−.014 (1.045)	.618 (2.222)	−2.351 (2.443)	1.187 (1.349)
First work-unit rank			.505 (.362)	−.353 (.615)	.522 (.780)	.857 (.594)
First state sector			2.401* (.907)	1.670 (1.764)	2.729* (1.304)	2.687* (1.379)

Control Variables

Sex	-.777	-.790	-1.153	-1.431	-1.555
	(.738)	(.758)	(1.300)	(1.490)	(1.139)
Born in Tianjin		-.782	-3.077	-.855	2.092
		(.853)	(1.357)	(1.719)	(1.628)
Direct state assignment		1.501	-.415	-4.371	3.376*
		(1.003)	(1.739)	(3.680)	(1.484)
Indirect state assignment		-.334	-2.971	1.058	-.951
		(1.397)	(2.863)	(4.564)	(1.699)
Year to enter the workforce		-.280***	-.281	-.289	.626**
		(.039)	(.147)	(.240)	(.219)
Constant	53.734	66.460	67.172	77.709	-11.462
R squared	.250	.354	.451	.277	.375

$*p < .05$, $**p < .01$, $***p < .001$. Standard errors are in parentheses.

Note: Respondents who entered the labor force before 1949 are included in the "total" equation.

Second, the effect of education remains significant after the other variables are controlled for. So does CCP membership. These effects do vary across the three cohorts. An interesting finding here is that education takes a U-shape effect through time and CCP membership has an upside-down U-shape effect for the three cohorts. These results testify to the historical trend that the principle of meritocracy was giving way to that of virtuocracy during the Cultural Revolution period, and that a reversed process was true during the market reforms of the 1980s. I prefer to be cautious in interpreting these results, and especially do not wish to overstate the effect of virtuocracy for the Cultural Revolution period. Even though the effect of CCP membership on job attainment increased and that of education decreased during the period, beta coefficients of the two variables indicate that education was a better predictor of occupational attainment than was CCP membership (.36 versus .20, as shown in Table 4.5). In fact, throughout postrevolutionary Chinese history the effect of education on occupational attainment has been greater than that of CCP membership. But it is not useful to underestimate the significance of virtuocracy either. During the current period of market reforms particularly, the effect of CCP membership has been considerably reduced and that of education has increased, but both variables remain significant predictors of occupational attainment.

Finally, direct state assignment, indirect state assignment, place of birth, and sex do not have effects on occupational attainment. This is not surprising, even for sex. Although men dominate the high-status jobs, such as professional, administrative, and managerial positions, they are also likely to be assigned low-status manufacturing jobs. Women's concentration in low-status service sector jobs is balanced by their predominance in technical fields such as nursing, teaching, and in low-ranking professional positions. The only control variable that has a significant effect on occupational attainment is the year one enters the labor force. Its negative effects for the 1949–65 and 1966–76 cohorts testify to the "first-comer hypothesis" (Davis-Friedmann 1985) that those entering the labor force earlier acquired better positions. Its positive effect for the 1977–88 cohort suggests a reversal of this historical trend. "First comers" in this more recent period have been predominantly urban youths who have come back to the cities from a long-term stay in the countryside. Together with high- and middle-school graduates, they were largely recruited for manual jobs. A significant number of urban youth took unskilled jobs in small collectives and family

TABLE 4.5

Beta Coefficients and Coefficients of Determination
for Regression Models in Table 4.2, 4.3, and 4.4

	Total	1949–65	1966–76	1977–88
Work-Unit Sector Model				
Father's sector	.22***	.10*	.15**	.31***
Education	.25***	.35***	.27***	.14**
CYCL membership	.08*	.05	.07*	.08*
CCP membership	.05	.02	.03	.03
R squared	.17	.18	.21	.18
Work-Unit Rank Model				
Father's rank	.37***	.27***	.38***	.44***
Education	.11*	.23***	.00	.09*
CCYL	.03	.03	.11*	.07*
CCP	.04	.05	.09*	.00
First sector	.27***	.16**	.30***	.26***
R squared	.27	.22	.37	.34
Occupation Model				
Father's sector	.02	.01	.14	−.01
Father's rank	.00	.01	.01	−.08
Father's occupation	.08	.19	−.06	.15
Education	.54***	.66***	.36***	.40***
CCP membership	.09***	.01	.20***	.11*
CCYL membership	.00	.01	−.06	.05
First work-unit sector	.10*	.05	.15*	.17*
R squared	.35	.45	.28	.37

Notes:
(1) Ordinary-least-square regression models are run to obtain beta coefficients in the work-unit sector model even though the dependent variable
is a dichotomous measure.
(2) *p < .05, **p < .01, ***p < .001.

businesses. Many "late comers" in the period who had higher education than those who entered the labor force earlier, on the other
hand, have taken positions in an expanding white-collar work force.

Summary

The urban employment process in China has a distinctive pattern compared to that in Western countries. Unlike the West, where
status attainment is oriented toward *what you are* (occupation), in

China the focus is on *where you are* (work-unit sector and work-unit rank). Thus, status inheritance is associated with work-unit attainment, rather than occupation per se. As summarized in Table 4.5, the father's work-unit sector and work-unit rank have significant effects on the child's sector and rank, respectively. Neither the father's work-unit sector, work-unit rank, nor occupation have any direct effect on the child's occupation. Another finding shown in this table is that intergenerational influence has become more significant through time, and the impact of education on attainment of work-unit statuses has been decreasing.

Because China has been making significant progress toward industrialization since 1949, these findings demonstrate that the industrialization-attainment argument is invalid in generalizing the historical trends (at least in a short run) in labor processes in socialist China. Government policies have been designed to stimulate the process of industrialization. Evidence here suggests that both the industrialization process and the process of status attainment can have different patterns and trajectories in the capitalist and socialist systems.

The Tianjin 1988 data disprove a long-held belief that political virtue is the primary criterion of social mobility in China. Party and Youth League memberships have not had consistent effects on status attainment through time (both in terms of work-unit measures and occupation). These memberships had *some* effects on work-unit sector, work-unit rank, and especially occupation during the Cultural Revolution decade. However, even during the Cultural Revolution period, the effect of education on these attained statuses was much stronger than the influence of party and Youth League memberships. Consistently, ability is a more important criterion of work-status attainment in China than is political virtue.

5

GUANXI AND SOCIAL RESOURCES IN JOB SEARCHES AND JOB MOBILITY

In the previous chapter, I examined intergenerational influence, educational achievement, and political membership as predictors of status attainment associated with one's first job. In this chapter I introduce a new factor into the process: *guanxi* (interpersonal connections). I first discuss the nature of *guanxi* through a theoretical framework of social networks and social resources, and then analyze how it is related to job searches and job mobility.

Guanxi as Social Networks and Social Resources

There has been considerable documentation concerning the use of *guanxi* to acquire power, status, and resources in China (Whyte and Parish 1984; Gold 1985; Yang 1986). *Guanxi* is a key variable in Walder's (1986) "party clientelism" model of authority structure in the Chinese workplace. Lin and Bian (1989) also analyze *guanxi* as a mechanism to explain status transmission from the older to younger generation. I have already described, in Chapter 3, the use of *guanxi* in the employment process. In our 1988 Tianjin study, 42.3 percent of the respondents reported that "someone" helped them to get their first jobs. When they were asked whether "someone" provided help when they changed jobs recently, 52.1 percent of the respondents said that this was the case. Clearly, *guanxi* is extensively used in job placement and job mobility processes.

Three Meanings of *Guanxi*

Guanxi is not a theoretical construct. In Chinese society, *guanxi* is a term used in everyday communication. It can basically be defined as "relation" or "relationship." In a social context, however, its meaning and significance go beyond any dictionary definition. In China, the term *guanxi* has three different, though related, meanings.

First, *guanxi* indicates the *existence of a relationship* between people who share a status group or are related to a common person. People in this type of *guanxi* may never come in contact with one another, but when they do, they start with a conversation that recognizes the preexisting relationship. "Did you graduate from Tianjin Nurses School? I did, too. We have a *guanxi*." "Mr. Zhang was my math teacher in middle school. You are his cousin? What a close *guanxi* we have!" This last expression is characteristic of indirect social ties.

A second usage of *guanxi* refers to *actual connections or contact* between people. How often they are in contact, how well they know each other, or how much they like each other reflects their degree of *guanxi*. "I know him well. Our *guanxi* is good." "She is my aunt. Although we rarely see each other, our *guanxi* is close." "He and I are working in the same store, but we don't get along with each other. Our *guanxi* is very bad." These expressions refer to *guanxi* as direct social ties, with an emphasis on their strength and intimacy.

The third usage of *guanxi* refers to *people with whom one has a strong connection.* "There is no problem in asking him for help. He is an old *guanxi* of mine." "Do you have any *guanxi* in that factory? I want my son to work there. Can you help?" "She is not my *guanxi*. It's no use mentioning my name to her. Forget it!" These expressions suggest that *guanxi* is a contact person.

As attached to these three meanings, *guanxi* represents what has been referred to as social networks in Western sociology. The use of social networks for expressive and instrumental purposes is common in human societies (Laumann 1966). China is no exception. But the process by which social networks are mobilized can differ from one sphere of social life to another, and between one society and another. In terms of the Chinese occupational structure, my interest is in how social networks serve as predictors of employment and job-mobility outcomes. But how is it possible in the first place to use social networks in a bureaucratically controlled labor market?

Guanxi in a Bureaucratically Controlled Labor Market

A Communist regime recognizes a citizen's right to work. But it does not recognize an individual's private labor rights. In Chinese economics textbooks, labor is defined as a commonwealth of the state, not as a private property of the individual; it is treated as a national resource, not as a commodity (Tang 1990; Han, Ren, and Tian 1991). Although a regulated labor market was initiated during the demographic and economic pressures in the early 1950s, the government produced strict administrative control of job assignments in the state sector by the mid-1950s. Since then, collective ownership of labor has been institutionalized in China.

Forms of Collective Ownership of Labor. Ownership of labor at the local level has three basic forms. First is ownership by the municipal government, whose labor agency has the ultimate authority to control labor supply and demand. Labor quotas, job assignments, and food rationing are mechanisms used to implement this control. Second is ownership of labor by various government jurisdictions. Municipal and district commissions, bureaus, and companies retain ownership rights of the labor force in the enterprises and institutions that they manage. Labor quotas and job assignments for these enterprises and institutions must be included in the employment plans of these government jurisdictions, which also grant permission for employees to switch jobs within the jurisdiction or across it. Finally, the third form of collective ownership of labor at the local level is by the work unit. Enterprises and institutions have ownership rights of their labor force for the production of goods and services. A staff member or worker cannot leave for another job without his or her current employer's permission, and it is illegal to hire anyone unless the new worker's personnel dossier is transferred from the previous employer. This system creates a web of government interests and bureaucratic barriers, in which individuals have very little power to control their own labor.

Guanxi as Access to the Cadre Class. Collective ownership of labor is, in fact, in the hands of the party cadres—government bureaucrats and workplace party secretaries and managers. It is these cadres who assign jobs and permits for job switching. Ideally, the cadres should work in the interest of the state: by assigning jobs according to party principles and ideals; by permitting job switching when, in their judgment, it results in the best use of labor; and by carrying out these tasks impartially. This ideal is not the reality, however. Personal interests permeate the system, and power is used in favor of the cadre's self-interests.

One set of self-interests served is a cadre's spouse, children, and relatives. The impetus comes not only from traditional Chinese family values, but from obligations to a broader web of kin relations (N. Lin 1989). Second, a cadre is interested in maintaining friendships for mutual benefits, for both short-term and especially long-term rewards. Third, cadres provide help for people in exchange for money, goods, or services.

These self-interests make it possible for *guanxi* to intervene in the bureaucratically controlled labor market. Unlike the Western labor market, labor value is not measured by economic variables such as skill, experience, or education, but by the ability of individuals to access power or influence, which in turn affect one's status-attainment outcomes. In urban China in the 1980s, when one waited for an assignment or wished to change jobs, one expected to use personal networks effectively to achieve the best outcome. *Guanxi* accessed could include direct social ties such as relatives, coworkers, neighbors, classmates, teachers and students, masters and apprentices, and people from one's hometown. Indirect ties are also sought after through relatives, friends, and acquaintances. There is one purpose for using these direct and indirect ties: to find someone who has the power or influence to break through the bureaucratic control of opportunities. But which individuals are likely to do so? It is useful first to review how social resources are accessed.

A Theory of Social Resources

Social resource theory (Lin 1982) provides a useful framework for the analysis of *guanxi* in the study of Chinese employment and job-mobility processes. My aim here is to specify exactly how to measure social resources relevant to the Chinese case, and how each of the following three hypotheses contained in the theory of social resources is usefully applied.

The theory of social resources offers an explanation of status attainment on two related questions: (1) why social resources, that is, power, status, or class characteristic of social ties, affect one's status attainment, and (2) why there is differential access to these resources.

For the first question, Lin (1982) perceives that there is a social structure, such as the labor market structure, that is a hierarchy of interrelated positions defined in relation to resources they command and access. This hierarchical structure tends to be pyramidal. In positions closer to the top, individuals have greater command of and access to resources, and there are also fewer of these positions. In actions taken for instrumental purposes, such as seeking a job, one can mobilize a social tie as a contact. The location of that contact in the hierarchical structure indicates the degree of assistance available (in terms of information and influence) to the job seeker. Therefore, a hypothesis concerning social resources states that the position or influence of one's social ties will have a direct impact on the outcome of a job search. This is the so-called *social resource hypothesis.* This hypothesis has largely been confirmed in studies from North America, Western Europe, and Taiwan (Lin, Ensel, and Vaughn 1981; Lin, Vaughn, and Ensel 1981; Xiong, Sun, and Xu 1986; DeGraaf and Flap 1988; Prengers, Tazelaar, and Flap 1988; Marsden and Hurlbert 1988; Wegener 1991).

For the second question, two factors were specified to explain differential access to social resources: strength of position and strength of ties. The *strength of position hypothesis* is straightforward: those from influential families or who have higher social positions will be able to contact people with better resources. The *strength of tie hypothesis* is more complex. Strength of tie is represented by either role relationships (i.e., relatives, friends, and acquaintances) or specified dimensions of strength (i.e., intimacy, frequency, intensity, and reciprocity of services; see Granovetter 1973; Marsden and Campbell 1984). Granovetter (1973, 1982) has argued that weak ties, rather than strong ties, positively affect status attainment because they afford an individual the opportunity to reach beyond the close social circle and gain the advantage of accessing greater information and influence. Lin (1982) argues that weaker ties are not directly related to status attainment, but rather they may facilitate access to better social resources, which in turn affect attained job status. The effect of strength of tie on social resources, however, does not hold for those whose original position is extremely high (Lin, Ensel, and Vaughn 1981) or low (Marsden and Hurlbert 1988).

A general implication of this theory of social resources for an analysis of *guanxi* in the Chinese employment process is that using *guanxi* or social ties does not necessarily lead to a better outcome of status attainment. For a *guanxi* user, an important question is what kind of *guanxi* he or she uses. Does one's *guanxi* have *influence* on job assignments and reassignments? Who is likely to have that influence? Where can they be found? How can they be found? In the following section, I offer a refinement of the social resource hypothesis, strength of position hypothesis, and strength of tie hypothesis by paying attention to these questions.

Guanxi and the Structure of Influence

Cadres as Social Resources. The primary measure of social resources for this study is the cadre status of the personal contacts. Job assignments and job mobility are controlled by a class of cadres, and access to this class is essential if individuals are to obtain any opportunities. In general, the higher the cadre's civil-service rank, the greater the power or influence, and the better the outcome one has for job assignment or job mobility. Specifically, when one contacts a cadre who is in charge of job assignments or job transfers, or who has authority over the cadres in charge of job assignment or job transfers, one will benefit directly from one's contact. When one's contact is a cadre in a different administrative branch from the one responsible for job assignments and job transfers, or in a different organization or bureau, this particular cadre can directly or indirectly, or both, influence decision makers through his or her ties. If one's contact is not a cadre, this influence will be reduced (with other factors being held constant). A general assessment is that individuals whose *guanxi* are cadres will have a greater chance of getting a desirable assignment or job transfer than those whose *guanxi* are not cadres.

Work-Unit Status of the Contact as a Social Resource. Power and influence of particular cadres are not limitless. A cadre's power or authority is associated with the office he or she holds, and his or her influence is most effective within the organizational system with which he or she is affiliated. This structure of influence would also be true for noncadres; ordinary staff and workers would have more influence, if any, within their work units than outside them. This leads to two processes. First, one locates those with whom one has social ties and who are in the workplace or system in which one seeks a job. Second, one's social connections will be helpful in getting a job in the workplace or system in which they themselves work. Both processes result in the same outcome: a contact's work-unit status (e.g., sector and rank) will strongly affect one's own work-unit status. This relationship between the contact's and one's own work-unit statuses should hold after the cadre status and other characteristics of the contact are taken into account.

Parental Status and One's Own Status as Predictors of Social Resources. For the strength of position hypothesis, my interest here is to test whether the father's status or one's own status is more important in accessing social resources for the first job. In the previous chapter I showed that one's father's work-unit status is a more important predictor of a person's first work-unit status than education and party membership. Is that because fathers working in the state sector or in organizations with higher ranks have access to more powerful *guanxi*? Or is it because the fathers themselves bring their children to the work units or the systems (sector or rank) in which they work? The specification of *guanxi* in the employment process will clarify that social networks are one mechanism for status transmission from one generation to the next in China.

Kin and Nonkin Ties as Predictors of Social Resources. For the strength of tie hypothesis, my interest is to test whether social resources are accessed more through acquaintances and friends than through relatives. Since these three types of social tie represent the strength of tie, the measure allows us to test whether weaker ties (acquaintances and friends) increase one's ability to access social resources (the contact's cadre status and work-unit status).

With these three types of social tie, I also look for substantive interpretations of the use of *guanxi*. I described previously that a cadre (as a contact) has different self-interests in these three types of social ties. Kin ties indicate a contact's interest in maintaining his or her family relations, and in many cases, helping relatives will not be based on rational calculation of costs and benefits. Friend ties represent a contact's interest in seeking a long-term investment in friendship, rather than short-term benefits. And acquaintance ties represent short-term benefits to the contact; such a contact exchanges power or influence for immediate rewards such as money, goods, or services. If kin ties are the most effective in accessing social resources, and given that Chinese society is known for its family-oriented tradition (Wong 1988), then *guanxi* could be viewed basically as an extension of family relations. On the other hand, China has also been known for its focus on comradeship and friendship during the postrevolutionary era (Vogel 1965; Gold 1985), suggesting that in our Tianjin survey we might also find that *guanxi* is primarily a long-term investment in friendship. Finally, acquaintances have also been considered a most effective tie in accessing social resources, because of the Chinese orientation toward instrumental uses of interpersonal connections since the Cultural Revolution (Gold 1985; Yang 1986; Walder 1986). In the analysis that follows, I seek to determine the relative importance of kin, friendship, or acquaintance ties that would help explain *guanxi*'s role in status attainment and job mobility in China.

Guanxi and First Job

As shown in Table 5.1, 42.3 percent of the respondents reported that "someone" helped them get their first urban jobs.[1] The percentage increased to 52.1 percent for job change. These percentages are similar to those obtained in studies in the United States,[2] but con-

TABLE 5.1

Characteristics of Personal Contacts
in the Employment Process, Tianjin, 1988

		First Job			Recent Job Change		
Variables	(N)	Total (938)	Male (502)	Female (436)	Total (451)	Male (240)	Female (211)
N using contacts		397	215	182	235	125	110
% use of contacts		42.3	42.8	41.7	52.1	52.2	52.0
Sex of contacts (%)							
Male		67.2	76.0	56.6	79.8	89.0	67.8
Female		25.4	16.1	36.5	16.8	8.5	27.8
Don't know		7.4	7.8	6.9	3.4	2.5	4.4
Respondents' relations with their contacts (%)							
Strong tie: relatives		43.3	40.9	46.2	21.4	19.3	23.6
Parents		25.3	25.1	25.6	5.8	7.6	3.3
Other relatives		18.0	15.8	20.6	16.3	11.9	22.2
Medium tie: friends		17.6	19.5	15.4	31.2	35.8	25.0
Weak tie: acquaintances		36.8	37.2	36.3	47.0	44.6	50.9
No answer		3.3	3.4	3.1	0.4	0.3	0.5
Status characteristics of contacts*							
% state sector		83.2	83.2	83.2	83.4	82.3	85.5
Work-unit rank		3.0	3.0	2.9	3.1	3.1	3.2
Occupational status		84.9	85.8	84.0	91.9	92.4	89.3
% cadres		36.8	39.7	33.3	60.5	67.6	51.1
% party members		30.8	30.7	30.8	53.8	64.4	40.0
Education		3.3	3.4	3.2	3.6	3.6	3.7

*Measurements for these variables are the same as those for the respondents. See Table 2.1.

siderably higher than the 20.3 percent (first job) and 23.0 percent (current job) found in a 1985 Tianjin sample (Lin and Bian 1989). There are reasons for the differential between the two Tianjin samples. First, a 1986 policy that recognized individual applications as a legal method of job search spurred the use of personal contacts for getting a job. When respondents began to get jobs through individual applications, 76.2 percent used personal contacts, compared with 26.9 percent by direct state assignment. Second, a less open political situation in 1985 might have caused underreporting of the use of personal contacts in the earlier study. In the 1988 Tianjin survey, 38.1 percent of the respondents who entered the work force before 1985 reported the use of personal contacts, nearly double the figure in the 1985 study.

Characteristics of the Contact

Of the personal contacts used in the first-job process, 67.2 percent were males and 25.4 percent females (Table 5.1). Some 7 percent of the respondents did not know the sex of their contacts. This suggests that the respondents themselves had no direct connection with their *guanxi*. All of these were indirect ties, accessed through parents (6.1 percent) and friends or acquaintances (1.3 percent). Men were more likely than women to use male contacts (76.0 percent versus 56.6 percent), and less likely than women to use female contacts (16.1 percent versus 36.5 percent). Note that female respondents still used more male contacts (56.6 percent) than female contacts (36.5 percent).

Three role relationships between the respondent and his or her personal contact can be identified: relatives, or strong ties (43.3 percent), friends, or medium ties (17.6 percent), and acquaintances, or weak ties (36.8 percent). A small number of the respondents failed to answer this question, and most of them did not know who their contacts were. When used as a dependent variable, the three responses constitute an ordinal scale of the strength of tie to the contact. Relatives are coded 3, friends 2, and acquaintances 1. When the strength of tie is used as an independent variable, the two weaker ties are used as dummy variables, with relatives being the omitted category. This strategy is useful to obtain more nearly accurate estimates of the effects of strength of tie on dependent variables.[3]

The percentage of respondents using relatives as *guanxi* decreased from the incidence for first job (43.3 percent) to that for job mobility (21.4 percent). This trend was stronger for males. As can be seen in Table 5.1, this occurs because of a reduction in the use of parents as contacts and increased use of friends and acquaintances. Similar trends were observed in the 1985 Tianjin study (Lin and Bian 1989) and in American studies (Ensel 1979; Lin, Ensel, and Vaughn 1981). These data indicate that people tend to develop their own social networks after entering the labor force, but females are less likely to do so than males.[4]

Status characteristics of the contact are measured by six variables. The first four (state sector, work-unit rank, occupation, and cadre status) were found to be useful predictors of the respondent's first job statuses.[5] Measurements for these variables are the same as for the respondents, and are also shown in Appendix C. The contacts for males and females are comparable; there is virtually no difference by sex in the social resources accessed. Contacts used in the job-mobility process had higher status (except for work-unit measures) than those used in the first-job process. This occurs because of the greater use of acquaintances and friends in acquiring job mobility.

Estimating Use of a Contact

Who is more likely to use personal contacts in the employment process? The first column of Table 5.2 presents a logistic model predicting this use of personal contacts in attaining the first job. Four predictors prove to be statistically significant. People who entered work earlier are less likely to use social ties than those who entered work in more recent years. This period effect indicates the relative openness of labor markets in the 1980s. Second, respondents whose fathers' work units had a higher bureaucratic rank were more likely to use *guanxi* than those whose fathers had a lower rank. By working in high-ranking organizations, their fathers are more able to find useful contacts. The effect of education on one's use of contacts is of a different nature: college and vocational-school graduates were allowed to search for jobs by themselves in the 1980s, which created a legitimate reason for them to use personal contacts.

Individuals who were assigned jobs directly by the state were less likely to use personal contacts than those who applied for jobs through an individual search (the omitted category in method of job placement). Although the use of personal contacts in direct state assignment was against party regulations, 26.9 percent of the jobs assigned by the state were channeled through social networks. A much higher percentage of contacts were utilized for indirect state assignments (88.7 percent) and individual application (76.2 percent). *Guanxi* prevailed when bureaucratic control of the labor market was relaxed.

The use of personal contacts in the employment process was also biased in favor of certain groups. Our solution to this selectivity bias (Berk 1983) was to include all significant predictors in the models used to estimate the strength of tie to the contact, status characteristics of the contact, and the respondent's first-job statuses (Marsden and Hurlbert 1988; Lin and Bian 1989).[6]

Estimating the Strength of Tie to a Contact

The strength of the tie to a contact is analyzed for respondents who have used personal contacts. All three variables for the father are significant predictors: the father's work-unit sector, work-unit rank, and occupation. The negative effects of each of these variables on the strength of tie indicate that the higher the status of the father, the weaker the tie with one's contact. Again, this demonstrates the ability of fathers with a higher work-unit or occupational status to search out weaker ties for more effective influence. I expected negative effect of direct state assignment and a positive effect of indirect state assignment on the strength of tie. In the former case, various levels of government authority control job assignments, and a wider network is required to access people with authority. In contrast, indirect state assignment is implemented by using *dingti* and *neizhao* practices, in which one finds a job through parents or relatives.

Estimating Status Characteristics of a Contact

In this section, I present the statistical results obtained to estimate statuses of contacts from strength of ties and personal and father's characteristics. Four statuses of the contact are estimated. As can be seen in columns three to six in Table 5.2, the use of acquaintances and that of friends generated results consistent with the strength of tie hypothesis. Acquaintances and friends tend to be found in the privileged state sector, and in organizations with higher bureaucratic ranks. Compared with relatives, acquaintances and friends are likely to be cadres and those with a higher-status occupation. The difference in the magnitude of coefficients for acquaintances as weak ties and friends as medium ties is not so great: friends tend to have slightly higher statuses than acquaintances. Thus, the strength of tie is not always linearly associated with social resources in our Tianjin sample. Substantively, these results indicate that in China, friendship as a long-term investment is just as effective in accessing the power or influence of the contact as a utility-driven orientation, expressed by the use of acquaintances.

The father's variables are associated with status characteristics of the contact on a variable-by-variable basis. That is, the father's sector is related to the contact's sector, the father's work-unit rank to the contact's work-unit rank, and the father's occupation to the contact's occupation. There are two causes for this pattern. First, one-fourth of the contacts mentioned by respondents are their own

TABLE 5.2

Predicting Use of the Contact, Strength of Tie to the Contact, and Statuses of the Contact

Independent Variables	Use of the Contact (1)	Strength of Tie to Contact (2)	Statuses of the Contact			
			State Sector (3)	Work-Unit Rank (4)	Occupation Status (5)	Being Cadre (6)
Predictors						
Acquaintances	—	—	.11*	.12*	6.93***	.15**
	—	—	.14*	.16*	.22***	.15**
Friends	—	—	.15*	.26*	6.30**	.22**
	—	—	.16*	.11*	.16**	.18**
Father's state sector	.03	-.10**	.16***	.20	1.73	.01
	.03	-.12**	.22***	.09	.06	.01
Father's work-unit rank	.04**	-.07**	.01	.46***	.98	.21**
	.14**	-.23**	.04	.66***	.10	.15**
Father's occupation	-.01	-.01**	.001	.002	.18***	.09*
	-.01	-.24**	.01	.07	.41***	.11*
Education	.08*	-.05	.06*	.21**	4.41***	.14*
	.12*	-.06	.16*	.19**	.31***	.12*
Communist party membership	.06	.18	.12*	.61*	7.36*	.25*
	.03	.04	.11*	.13*	.11*	.12*

Youth league membership	.02 / .01	−.06 / −.03	.01 / .02	.04 / .02	2.36 / .06	.03 / .02
Control Variables						
Sex (male = 1)	.03 / .03	.06 / .04	−.05 / −.07	.03 / .02	1.33 / .04	.07 / .07
Birth place (Tianjin = 1)	.04 / .04	.06 / .03	.04 / .05	.20 / .09	.57 / .04	.02 / .02
Year of entering work (×10)	.16*** / .24***	.01 / .04	.02 / .06	−.02 / −.03	−.04 / −.03	−.01 / −.01
Direct state assignment	−.53*** / −.49***	−.67*** / −.37***	.03 / .04	.12 / .06	.25 / .07	.01 / .01
Indirect state assignment	.09 / .06	.18** / .26**	−.07 / −.08	.11 / .04	1.64 / .04	.03 / .03
Constant	.56	2.27	.51	2.90	49.40	−.15
R squared	.27	.28	.26	.22	.32	.19
Number of cases	920	385	304	242	322	304

Notes:
(1) Entries are unstandardized coefficients followed by standardized coefficients.
(2) Significant levels are $*p < .05$, $**p < .01$, and $***p < .001$.
(3) Dependent variables 1, 3, and 6 used dichotomous measures. Linear regressions are obtained in order to compare standardized coefficients of predictors in these equations with the same predictors in other equations. Logistic regressions of the dichotomous measures revealed the same patterns.

parents (mainly fathers). For this group of respondents, one expects autocorrelations between the variables of the fathers and those of the contacts, which created a biased estimation. Second, nearly 20 percent of the contacts are contacts of respondents' parents (friends and acquaintances). High correlations exist between the father's and the contact's work-unit and occupation variables; very likely the fathers and their contacts were work colleagues. This is not uniquely Chinese; the practice of looking to colleagues for help is common in both China and the United States (Blau, Ruan, and Ardelt 1991).

A respondent's education and party membership prove to be significant and consistent predictors of the status characteristics of his or her contact.[7] Respondents with more education use social ties with higher statuses, and respondents who are party members also use contacts with higher statuses. These effects exist after the strength of tie variables and the father's variables are controlled. Thus, one's own initial position does have an independent influence on the social resources accessed through one's social ties.[8]

Social Resources as Predictors of First-Job Statuses

I present the statistical results obtained to predict a respondent's first job status from the status variables of the contact. In Chapter 4, three dependent variables of first-job status (work-unit sector, work-unit rank, and occupation) were predicted from characteristics of the respondent and his or her father. Here, status variables of the contact are incorporated as additional predictors, with the original variables being statistically controlled for. The results are presented in Table 5.3.

Three key points emerge. First, the effect of cadres on status attainment in the first-job process is consistent across all three dependent variables. Second, the influence of other contacts on the status-attainment process is status-specific. That is, one's contact's work-unit sector is highly associated with one's own sector, one's contact's work-unit rank is highly associated with one's own rank, and one's contact's occupation is highly associated with one's own occupation. This measure-specific pattern of influence reflects the fact that the contact helps the user get a job in the same occupational category, or in the exact same work unit. Third, as shown by the beta coefficients in Table 5.3, the contact's status is a more important predictor of first-job status than even the status of the father or the respondent.

The strength of tie variables have no direct effect on any dependent variable. Their influence on attained status, as demonstrated in American and Chinese studies (Lin, Ensel, and Vaughn 1981; Lin and Bian 1989), is indirect, via status characteristics of the contact. As shown in Table 5.2, acquaintances and friends are more likely to provide greater status privileges than relatives, suggesting that weaker ties lead to better social resources. And in Table 5.3, the strength of a weak tie has finally shown its outcome: status characteristics of the contact lead to better first-job outcomes.

Unexplained variances in all three dependent variables are considerably reduced after the contact's status is taken into account. The reduction of unexplained variance was 14 percent (.31 − .17) for work-unit sector, 13 percent (.40 − .27) for work-unit rank, and 8 percent (.43 − .35) for occupation. These show the importance of the contact's status as a predictor of status attainment. The concepts of *guanxi* and social resources are powerful theoretical constructs for understanding the process of job placement in China.

Guanxi and Job Mobility

I now turn to job mobility between one's first job and one's current job. The most important theoretical issue concerns the inequality of opportunities. In order to evaluate the potential for inequality, it is instructive to examine two extreme cases. First, if no Chinese workers are given the opportunity to change jobs after entering the work force, this immobility sustains any inequalities of opportunity associated solely with first jobs. Second, if opportunity for job mobility is equally provided to all Chinese workers, meaning that chances for and direction of job changes are uncorrelated with an individual's characteristics, this egalitarianism would also have the effect of maintaining the existing structure. To be sure, neither of these two patterns is a reflection of reality. The question is, therefore, how opportunities for job mobility are actually provided and who receive them.

Opportunities for job mobility are generally provided to people who have social and personal power. Social power refers to *guanxi;* one can mobilize his or her social networks to change jobs. Personal power is defined here as the ability of individuals to battle against the bureaucratic control of job switching; cadre status, party membership, and expertise and skills are included as types of political power. In addition to opportunity, I am also concerned with discovering the degree to which a current job is affected by one's first job. Has the first job provided greater or fewer opportunities for mobility,

TABLE 5.3

Regression Analysis: Social Resources and First-Job Status, Tianjin, 1988

Dependent Variables: First Job's

Predictors	State Sector	Work-Unit Rank	Occupational Status
Variables of the Contact			
Cadre	.10**	.14**	1.82**
	.15**	.16**	.15**
State sector	.46***	.20*	1.00
	.47***	.10*	.04
Work-unit rank	.14**	.44***	.27
	.17**	.68***	.03
Occupational status	−.00	.00	.18***
	−.03	.02	.51***
Acquaintances	.06	−.01	2.04
	.06	−.01	.08
Friends	−.06	.05	1.53
	−.05	.02	.05
Variables of the Respondent			
Father's status[1]	.19**	.58***	−.03
	.20**	.26***	−.09
Education	.11***	.10*	6.26***
	.25***	.10*	.53***
Communist party membership	.30**	.22	6.58**
	.13**	.04	.11**

continued

and does one's first-job status determine the social class position of an individual? I begin by describing practices related to job mobility in urban China.

Practices of Job Transfers

Mobility from first to current job involves two kinds of changes in status: change of workplace and change of occupation. Typically, occupational mobility has been at the center of studies of social mobility in Western societies. Because of the importance of work-unit structure in urban China, however, both occupational and work-unit mobility are examined. I use the term *job change* or *job mobility* to mean either workplace change, occupational change, or both. I distinguish occupational mobility from work-unit mobility

TABLE 5.3 *continued*

| | Dependent Variables: First Job's | | |
Predictors	State Sector	Work-Unit Rank	Occupational Status
Variables of the Respondent			
Youth league membership	.15**	.02	−2.58
	.12**	.01	−.08
Male	.03	.12	−.48
	.03	.05	−.09
Year of entering work (×10)	−.05**	−.06*	−.25***
	−.16**	−.08*	−.27***
First work-unit sector	—	.55***	1.73*
	—	.24***	.12*
First work-unit rank	—	—	1.06
	—	—	.09
Constant	.14	.93	55.28
R squared	.31	.40	.43
R squared without the contact's variables	.17	.27	.35
Number of cases	395	374	374

Entries are unstandardized coefficients followed by standardized coefficients.

*p < .05, **p < .01, ***p < .001.

[1]Father's work-unit sector for the sector equation, father's work-unit rank for the rank equation, and father's occupation for the occupation equation.

and describe the differences and correlation between these two types of movement.

In urban China, change of occupation is known as *gai bian gong zhong* (change in the type of work), and change of workplace is known as *diao dong gong zuo* (job transfer); each is implemented by a different process. Change of occupation is usually not an individual's choice, but subject to leadership decisions. Minor changes involving temporary switching of work responsibilities are determined by shop-floor managers or team leaders. Major changes, which include switching between manual and nonmanual jobs, or between occupations that are regulated by different technical and salary ranking systems,[9] are decided by the director of one's work unit and must be approved by the government office that has jurisdiction over that unit. Promotions along job ranks, which are on a quota system, are based primarily on seniority, educational achievement during employment, and performance (which is subject to evaluation by leadership).

Job transfers (movement between workplaces) may also signal a change of occupation during the process of reassignment after professional training.[10] Typically, with permission from one's current employer, an individual may go to college or vocational school for further training. While full-time students, such workers continue to receive regular salaries from their work units. Upon graduation, some of them will return to their workplaces with a different job title or a higher rank. Others may move up to the headquarters of the bureaus or companies that manage their former work unit. Still others may shift to a completely different industry or administrative system into jobs that fit their professional training.

Job transfers are generally a separate process from occupational change, and they fall into two formal categories. One is transfers of cadres. Successful cadres are transferred to take on more important positions in larger or higher-ranked organizations. If cadres are unsuccessful, cannot get along with their colleagues, or make personal or political mistakes, they are likely to be transferred to new places into new jobs. According to party personnel policy, these people are being given the opportunity for a "new life." A more extensive transfer is the reassignment of staff members and workers to new firms, or to support the expansion of an existing firm. This transfer may or may not involve relocation. This policy is quite unpopular with the Chinese people, however, since they traditionally are not used to leaving their hometown to work elsewhere (e.g., transfers of urban youths to the countryside during the Cultural Revolution: see Bernstein [1977]). Very often, such massive transfers are organized within a locality and, even more typically, within an industry, bureau, or company. Any transfers that result in upward mobility are attractive to staff members and workers; movement from the collective sector to state enterprises, for example, usually mean that one will have better working conditions, a higher salary and pension, a greater opportunity to receive a public apartment, and better insurance and benefits. In the industrial sector, these massive organized transfers are usually targeted to skilled workers, technicians, and engineers.

Job transfers by individual applications are similar to "job turnovers" in the West. A "one-way transfer" (*dan diao*) is one in which a person finds a work unit willing to hire him or her. A "two-way transfer" (*shuang diao*) is when two (or three) workers exchange work units. Career advancement is usually not a reason for such a job transfer, although it can be the case for some managers, party cadres, and professional people. These job exchanges reflect a different set of factors taken into account in the cost-benefit calculations of Chinese workers. Some prefer to leave their current work unit because they cannot get along with the office management. Others want to change jobs for lighter work, to work closer to home, to work together with a spouse, to have a greater chance of receiving a public apartment, or for higher bonuses, pensions, and benefits.

Factors in Job Transfers by Individual Applications

Chinese workers face serious organizational barriers for transferring jobs. But social and personal power is important in helping "movers" to overcome these organizational difficulties.

Guanxi as a Social Power. A first difficulty is in locating work units that may be hiring new workers. There are no employment services and advertising; consequently, social networks are the only means available for doing so. Second, transfers are dealt with on a case-by-case basis, without formal screening or examination. Although one's skills and expertise may be desirable, an individual must use social networks to obtain a successful transfer. In a two-way transfer, the individual must also convince the current employer to hire the person with whom he or she wants to exchange work units. Third and most important, in all types of transfers one has to fight prolonged battles to secure a "release" from the current employer. This often involves administrative interventions from one's work unit, as well as the bureau that manages the unit. An individual's relationship with his or her current leaders is a decisive factor in job transfers. With a good relationship, the leader is more likely to do "a favor" to release someone from current employment. Additionally, one's *guanxi* to higher levels of authority can provide support for this release.

Personal Power of Individuals. This personal power is the ability of individuals to convince a leadership that may be quite unwilling to release them from current employment. Although employers find it is relatively easy to release low-profile, less desirable workers, employers at the other end of the transfer may be equally unwilling to hire these workers. The best-trained and most ambitious workers are in short supply and therefore have more difficulties in getting released, but they also acquire greater personal and political power, such as cadre status, party membership, or special skills, to press for a successful transfer. Cadres can directly pressure party secretaries and executive managers to influence decisions favorably. Party members can contact party secretaries and direct supervisors to influence decision makers. And staff members and workers who have expertise or exceptional skills can coerce decision makers by intimating that they will not perform work responsibilities.

Recent Trends in Job Transfers

Most recent trends in job transfers include the implementation of "talent-exchange centers" (rencai jiaoliu zhongxin) and a labor-contact system. In the early 1980s, talent-exchange centers were established to help engineers and technicians in state industry to change jobs in order to use their expertise and skills (Davis 1990). Those wishing to switch jobs registered at the center for a job transfer. State and collective enterprises in need of technical staff could then use this center to identify good prospects and initiate a transfer of staff for their unit. Despite this effort, however, overall rates of turnover remained low, because few individuals could successfully get released from their employers. Davis cited studies that fewer than two percent of those who had registered succeeded in changing jobs. She also noted that the longer the centers were open, the lower the overall rate of mobility among technical applicants. These data suggest that, despite the development of talent-exchange centers, an individual's social and personal power was still the primary factor in job transfers during reforms in the 1980s.

The major reason the talent-exchange centers failed to fulfill their initial promise was ownership of labor by the work unit. In 1986, the government began to dismantle this work-unit ownership by instituting a nationwide labor-contract system. Under this labor-contract system, workers sign contacts with employers to work for a set length of time (usually 2–5 years); when the contact expires, either side can elect to terminate the relationship. However, this labor-contract system has affected only new workers who sign a contact with their employer when entering the work force for the first time. Staff members and workers already in the work force are not required to sign these labor contracts and are virtually unaffected by this policy (White 1987; Li 1991)

This labor-contract system had virtually no effect on respondents in our 1988 Tianjin survey. In this survey, seven respondents entered the labor force after the labor-contract system was implemented. Although there is no information about the labor contracts these seven individuals had, none of them had changed their work units. The effects of the labor-contract system for job mobility are beyond the scope of the statistical analyses I present in the paragraphs that follow.

Descriptive Data on Job Mobility

In the Tianjin survey, the respondents were asked whether they had changed jobs *or* work units since originally entering the labor force. This question involves two separate issues about changes in occupation and workplace. Because of this measurement error, I cannot determine specifically how many respondents moved between particular work units and how many moved between occupations. I can only describe movements between and within work-unit sectors (state versus nonstate), work-unit ranks (five ranks), and occupations (nineteen categories), based on the information for first and current jobs, and whether the respondents used personal contacts in changing their jobs. The descriptive data are presented in Table 5.4.

Nearly 63 percent of the respondents have changed jobs since entering the labor force. Within this group, 50.3 percent changed jobs by using personal contacts. I do not have information on the particular types of job change, and how each type is related to use of personal contacts. My guess is that personal contacts are more heavily used in job changes through individual applications rather than through organized job transfers. One evidence is the greater use of personal contacts in job changes in the 1977–88 period (82.3 percent), in which job changes through individual applications prevailed. Also, most job changes did occur in this period (70 percent), stimulated by a more open labor policy.

About 60 percent of the respondents in the state sector have changed jobs, compared with 55.5 percent in nonstate sectors. Thus, this survey does not confirm an earlier study that stated that job turnover was lower in the state sector than in the nonstate sector (Walder 1986, pp. 69–70). The difference lies, I believe, in intersector mobility. Only 5.7 percent of the respondents moved out of the state sector, compared with 36.3 percent of nonstate workers moving to state sector jobs. *Guanxi* is more heavily used for job changes from nonstate to the state sector than the other way around. Within-sector mobility predominates in both.

Job mobility in terms of work-unit rank reveals a similar pattern: more respondents experienced within-rank mobility (72.8 percent) than upward (15.6 percent) and downward (11.6 percent) mobilities combined. Occupational mobility reveals a different pattern: a high 43.7 percent of the respondents changed their jobs to a higher

TABLE 5.4

Job Mobility Between First and Current Jobs

Variable	Total	Job Changes Through Contact
Number of respondents who ever changed jobs	589	296
% job changes	62.8	50.3
% job changes in the 1977–1988 period	72.2	57.4
% job changes within labor cohort		
1977–88	50.9	56.4
1966–76	61.7	50.0
1949–65	76.8	49.2
<1949	65.2	35.6
Mobility between and within sectors		
from nonstate to state	9.6	52.8
from state to nonstate	4.2	47.2
within sector	86.2	51.2
Mobility across work-unit ranks		
from lower to higher	15.6	51.9
from higher to lower	11.6	46.6
within rank	72.8	52.0
Mobility in occupational status		
from lower to higher	43.7	51.4
from higher to lower	14.5	44.3
within occupation	41.8	51.6
% total upward mobility	54.2	50.5

Notes:
(1) Total respondents = 938.
(2) Percent total upward mobility = the respondents who were involved in upward mobility in work-unit sector, work-unit rank, or occupation.

status, and 41.8 percent did not change occupational categories. Nearly 15 percent involved downward mobility. Altogether, 54.2 percent of the respondents who changed jobs experienced upward mobility: from a nonstate sector to a state sector, from a lower-ranked to a higher-ranked organization, or from a lower- to a higher-status job. Half of this group used personal contacts to make job changes.

TABLE 5.5

Logistic Regressions of Job Mobility, Tianjin, 1988

Dependent Variables

Predictors	Job Change	Upward Mobility
Use of contacts (=1)	.37***	.36***
	(.08)	(.10)
Cadre (=1)	.50**	.44**
	(.16)	(.19)
Party membership (=1)	.33**	.16**
	(.13)	(.06)
First occupation (×10)	.14***	.30***
	(.03)	(.05)
Year of entering work (×10)	−.13**	.06
	(.04)	(.06)
Sex (male = 1)	.04	.45***
	(.08)	(.11)
First work-unit rank	−.03	.14*
	(.04)	(.06)
First state sector (=1)	−.03	.01
	(.10)	(.16)
Education	−.04	−.04
	(.05)	(.08)
Intercept	4.91	2.44
Goodness-of-fit chi square	855.76	464.55
Degree of freedom	848	482

Notes:
(1) Entries are logit coefficients followed by standard errors in parentheses.
(2) *$p < .05$, **$p < .01$, ***$p < .001$.

Patterns of Job Change and Upward Mobility

Table 5.5 presents logistic regressions predicting job change and upward mobility from nine independent variables. The use of contacts has a strong effect on both job change and upward mobility. Its effects hold after characteristics of individuals are controlled for. Clearly, opportunities for job mobility are available to people if channeled through their social networks.

Cadre status, party membership, and first occupation also strongly affect the odds of changing jobs, and the odds of pursuing upward mobility. These results suggest that individuals who have greater political power are successful not only in changing jobs but also in guiding the job change in a desirable direction. The year of entrance into the work force is negatively associated with job change, suggesting that the earlier a respondent entered the labor force, the more possibilities he or she has had in changing jobs. This seniority variable does not affect one's chances for upward mobility, however. Males and females have an equal chance of changing jobs, but males do enjoy greater upward mobility. Respondents in state and nonstate sectors, and in work units with different bureaucratic ranks have an equal opportunity to change jobs. But work-unit rank affects upward mobility, indicating that employees whose work units are located near the top of the bureaucratic hierarchy have greater ability to move up. Education has no effect on either dependent variable. This indicates that opportunities for job change and upward mobility are equally provided to employees with different levels of education.

Patterns of Current Job Statuses

Table 5.6 presents regression estimations for current work-unit sector, work-unit rank, and occupation, with first-job status and other variables as predictors. Two models are estimated for each dependent variable. Model I is estimated for total respondents, and Model II for respondents who have changed jobs. In each model, two coefficients of determination (R squared) are presented. The first measures the variance that is explained solely by first-job status, which shows the degree of "immobility." Unexplained variance indicates the degree of mobility. The second coefficient of determination measures the variance explained by all model estimators including first job-status. The difference between these two explained variances shows how much of mobility has been explained by predictors other than first-job status. In addition, beta coefficients provide information about the relative contribution of each predictor to the model estimation.

There is a high degree of immobility in terms of work-unit sector and work-unit rank. According to Model I, 60 percent of the variance in current work-unit sector is attributed to first work-unit sector. Although a 40-percent unexplained variance indicates that there is a good deal of cross-sector mobility, only 3 percent can be accounted for by predictors other than first work-unit sector; in other words, there is a considerable degree of mobility left unexplained by the model. Statistically significant predictors are sex, year of entering the work force, and first occupation. Cross-sector mobility favors males, those who entered the work force in earlier years, and those who have high-status occupations. Job change does not necessarily generate a movement from a nonstate to the state sector, or the other way around.

Immobility is even stronger for work-unit rank; 79 percent of the variance in current work-unit rank is attributed to first work-unit rank. Party membership and first work-unit sectors proved to be statistically significant in accounting for cross-rank mobility. Party members are favored in mobility to high-ranking work units, and mobility from a nonstate to the state sector is also accompanied by a movement to a high-ranking organization. But these two predictors make very small contributions to the model estimation (1 percent deduction of unexplained variance, and the beta coefficients are small).

Current occupational status is highly associated with first occupational status. The beta coefficient for first occupation is .57, which is double that for Americans (Blau and Duncan 1967, p. 170). In this American study, education had a beta coefficient of .39, which is considerably higher than the .27 in the 1988 Tianjin sample. Whereas mobility through educational achievement is the principal factor of current occupational status in the United States, it plays a secondary role in relocating individuals in the occupational structure in China. *In China, the primary and decisive factor is where individuals were allocated on initial job assignments.*

There is a lower degree of immobility in occupation (R squared of .57) than in work-unit sector and work-unit rank. Also, a good deal of occupational mobility (12 percent) is attributed to education, party membership, and year of entering the work force. Job change is associated with current occupational status; those who changed jobs have higher occupational statuses than those who did not change jobs. First work-unit rank has a moderate effect on current occupational status, suggesting that those who started careers in organizations with higher bureaucratic ranks have greater chances for promotion than those who started careers in organizations with lower bureaucratic ranks.

A common predictor of mobility patterns for all three dependent variables is party membership (see Table 5.6). This demonstrates the importance of political power in job mobility. There is a large difference in the effects of *guanxi* and education. Whereas work-unit mobility is largely affected by one's contact's work-unit status, occupational mobility is accounted for by education. This

TABLE 5.6

Regression Estimates of Current Job Statuses, Tianjin, 1988

Dependent Variables: Current Job Statuses

Predictors	Work-Unit Sector [I]	Work-Unit Sector [II]	Work-Unit Rank [I]	Work-Unit Rank [II]	Occupation [I]	Occupation [II]
First state sector (=1)	.70***	.48***	−.09*	−.12*	1.16	1.26
	.74***	.53***	−.04*	−.05*	.03	.04
First work-unit rank	.01	.02	.86***	.77***	.53*	.97*
	.01	.05	.89***	.81***	.04*	.07*
First occupation (×10)	.02	.02	−.00	−.00	6.57***	5.37***
	.07	.07	−.00	−.00	.57***	.43***
Sex (male = 1)	.05**	.06*	.01	.00	1.12*	1.74*
	.06**	.08*	.01	.00	.04*	.06*
Year of entering work (×10)	−.03***	−.05***	−.00	−.00	−1.34***	−1.83***
	−.09***	−.17***	−.00	−.02	−.11***	−.14***
Education	−.01	−.01	−.01	.00	3.76***	5.18***
	−.03	−.01	−.01	.00	.27***	.36***
Party membership	.07*	.08*	.14**	.21**	3.66***	3.53***
	.06*	.08*	.05**	.09**	.10***	.10**
Job change (yes = 1)	.03	—	.09	—	4.69***	—
	.04	—	.04	—	.15***	—
No use of contacts	.02	.05	.03	.03	−1.07	.46
	.02	.01	.01	.01	−.03	.01

Characteristics of the Contact

	Model I	Model II	Model I	Model II	Model I	Model II
Cadre (=1)	—	.11**, .12*	—	.11*, .09*	—	.88, .02
Work-unit sector (state = 1)	—	.24**, .24**	—	.11*, .07*	—	−.92, −.02
Work-unit rank	—	.09*, .08*	—	.09*, .12*	—	−.15, .01
Occupation	—	.01, .02	—	.01, .04	—	.01, .03
Constant	.28***	.53***	.46***	.79***	19.27***	30.01***
R squared for immobility	.60	.36	.79	.65	.57	.43
R squared for the model	.63	.44	.80	.67	.69	.59
Number of cases	855	494	852	491	880	519

Notes:
(1) Model I is for total respondents, and Model II for respondents who had changed jobs by the time of the survey.
(2) Entries are metric coefficients followed by beta coefficients.
(3) Significant levels: *p < .05, **p < .01, ***p < .001.
(4) "R² for immobility" is the R squared between first and current job measures of the same variable.

implies that whereas occupational promotions are based on human and political capital (education and party membership, respectively), job transfers between employers are sociopolitically oriented. To leave or enter a workplace in China depends on one's *guanxi* with decision makers and one's political strength, more consistently than educational credentials.

Summary

In China's bureaucratically controlled labor market, labor is a sociopolitical commodity. Its value is determined by the ability of individuals to access power and influence embedded in their social networks. In the employment and job-mobility processes, this power and influence can be measured by the status characteristics of personal contacts such as cadre status, work-unit sector, work-unit rank, and occupational status. These measures are significant predictors of first-job statuses and job-mobility outcomes. In terms of work-unit attainment associated with first job, statuses of personal contacts are more important determinants than family backgrounds or educational and political achievements. These findings challenge the current assumption that the allocation of labor under state socialism is predominantly, if not solely, a bureaucratic process. Social forces mobilized through individuals' networks have largely eroded the bureaucratic regime in the urban Chinese workplace.

The effects of these social forces are sustained in the labor market, in which cross-boundary mobility is extremely low. When this mobility is possible, *guanxi* appears to be important as a factor in breaking through once more. However, these patterns are not applicable to occupational mobility, which appear to be affected by a different set of factors, measuring individuals' personal characteristics. *Whereas work-unit mobility appears to be a sociopolitical process, occupational mobility is largely a process of individual attainment.*

Party membership has shown consistent effects on status attainment associated with both first and current jobs. It is also a significant predictor of job change and upward mobility. Party membership also affects the ability of individuals to access the power and influence of social contacts. In this chapter, I have referred to party membership as a personal power. But how do individuals acquire this power? How is the process of attaining party membership associated with an individual's work unit and other characteristics? These questions are examined in the next chapter.

6

PARTY MEMBERSHIP

Those engaged in the study of state socialist societies have little dispute with Djilas's (1957) long-held assertion that the Communist parties in Soviet-type countries had become a privileged class since their consolidation of power. Unlike a democratic state in which political party membership is a matter of personal choice, membership in the Communist party in the socialist state is a political status or privilege. The Communist party uses membership as a way to select loyalists who will safeguard the party's ideologies, interests, and political power. Recruitment of party members therefore becomes a key element in the study of political stratification and mobility in Communist states.

Who is likely to become a Communist party member? Studies of Eastern Europe have stressed class differences in their recruitment. Djilas (1957) argues in his "new class theory" that the interests of the Communist party are maintained in the government bureaucracies it controls. Thus, party memberships are provided to intellectuals who are trained for administrative and managerial positions, and the working class is subsequently deprived of political privileges. Research from Hungary lends support to this class analysis (S. Szelenyi 1986).

What has been neglected in this class analysis is an investigation into the organizational basis by which party membership recruitment takes place. In China, as documented in Chapter 2, the hierarchy of the party apparatus is created through government administrative and work organizations, and workers apply for and acquire party memberships in the workplace. As I elaborate in this chapter, the recruitment of party members is regulated and controlled by the hierarchy of the party apparatus. Work organizations whose party apparatus has a lower standing in the hierarchy are granted fewer party memberships than those whose party apparatus has a higher standing. This is a part of the interorganizational process of party membership recruitment, which is controlled by party branch secretaries. Formal and informal procedures have evolved to select loyalists, not necessarily in terms of their principles but in terms of the existing political structure in the workplace.[1]

The Road to the Communist Party in China

The Chinese Communist Party (CCP) was founded in 1921. It took twenty-eight years for the CCP to take over the country. On China's First National Day, October 1, 1949, a 28-gun salute, instead of the standard 21-gun salute, was fired off in Beijing's Tiananmen Square to commemorate the founding of the new People's Republic by the Communist party.

The transition from a party fighting a revolution to a ruling organization altered the nature of party membership. Membership in the party before the Communist revolution meant personal sacrifice. A revolutionary was willing to be devoted to the liberation of the Chinese people, ready to fight to the death whenever the party needed him or her. Party membership became one of the highest honors. After the revolution, party membership came to mean power, privilege, and upward mobility. Government posts were offered to party members, who were also chosen to govern civilian organizations. Workers were granted party memberships in order for them to be promoted to administrative and managerial positions. Party members even had greater abilities to develop social networks and greater access to social resources (Chapter 5).

The CCP has used its tremendous organizational resources to train and select its party loyalists. Recruitment of party members is a highly structured institution, and it is a path many choose in attaining high status in the workplace.

The Hierarchy of the CCP Organization

The organization of the CCP coincides with that of the government administration and work organizations. The central committee of the CCP resides within the central government. From this level down there are CCP committees in each division of the central administration and in various levels of local governments. Finally, the CCP system extends into all work organizations, where the rank of a party apparatus will parallel those of the work organization in the administrative system. High-ranking enterprises and institutions have party committees, middle-ranked ones have general party branches, and lower-ranked ones have party branches. Within each workplace, party branches and smaller party groups are formed within the existing internal work organizations. The command and communication system of the CCP organization is therefore established alongside the hierarchy of government administration and work organizations.[2]

Usually, party committee or branch secretaries are appointed by the next-higher level of party authority. So are the heads of party groups. A meeting for party members may be held to confirm appointed candidates for party secretary positions, although in some cases, party secretaries are elected by party members in an open race. But this is very rare for high-ranking or large organizations. Each party committee or branch has an executive committee led by the secretary. Usually, candidates for committee membership are named by the secretary and elected by party members.

One example of the operation of the CCP apparatus can be observed in the academic setting. "N" University in Tianjin is one of the country's leading educational institutions. Administratively, the university is subject to the central government's education commission, which is responsible for the university's budget. The university's CCP party committee reports to the party committees of the central and municipal education commissions. This dual party leadership applies generally to institutions and enterprises managed by central ministries. The party committee of a local university or business will report only to the party committee at the level of government that has jurisdiction over it. N University's party committee has nine standing members, each of whom holds an office in the party or administrative branches of the university. There are also lower levels of party committees in four colleges and a branch school of the university. General party branches exist also in departments, institutes, administrative and service divisions, a high school, an elementary school, a day-care center, and a chemical factory.

In one academic department of N University, for example, there exists a general party branch committee, consisting of a secretary who is appointed by the university's party committee, the department's chairman as the general party branch vice secretary, and three members (one being the director of the department office, one an assistant to the general party branch secretary for student affairs, and one the secretary of the faculty and staff's party branch). Several party branches are also formed in the department. One is for the faculty and staff, one for graduate students, and one for each of the four classes (cohorts) of undergraduate students. Within each party branch, small and workable party groups are formed along with the existing work groups. For example, within the faculty and staff's party branch, one party group is for the department staff, and several for the faculty according to their teaching and research interests. The party branches and party groups form the basic organizational structures through which party members have their weekly and special meetings. Initial evaluations of membership applications are also conducted in party branches and groups.

Recruitment Planning and Organizational Barriers

The CCP central committee establishes and evaluates its general requirements for recruitment, and priorities can change according to current policies. Party committees in local governments also evaluate local recruitment policies in the same fashion. According to these policies, party committees or branches in work organizations make annual plans for recruitment. They project the total number of members to be recruited, and determine recruitment priorities. Each work organization's recruitment plan needs to be approved by and included in the plan of the party apparatus of the government jurisdiction. Plans of party committees in lower levels of government are approved by and included in the plans of the party committee of the next-higher level of government.

All recruitment plans are "soft," subject to the hierarchy of the party organization. The party committee of a certain level of government plans recruitment for all work organizations under its direct jurisdiction, and for all lower levels of government, which in turn plan recruitment for all organizations under them. Because a higher level of government jurisdiction has greater authority in planning recruitment, it tends to have greater flexibility in granting membership to employees in its headquarter and its immediate subordinate enterprises than a lower level of government jurisdiction. This means that workers in enterprises managed by a municipal bureau, for example, tend to have a greater chance of joining the party than those in enterprises managed by a company, whose party committee is lower than that of the bureau in the hierarchy of party organizations. Such tendency is replicated at higher and lower levels of the hierarchy. In general, therefore, a work organization under a higher level of government jurisdiction tends to be granted more party memberships than another organization under a lower level of jurisdiction.

Recruitment plans are also affected by the personal relationships between party secretaries who submit these plans and the authorities who evaluate and approve them. When party secretaries have an enthusiastic relationship with authorities, their plans easily receive approval. Furthermore, if their organizations are more important to the government, they tend to have greater influence on party decision makers, and also can get their recruitment plans approved more easily.

Mr. Tang (personal interview 14), a party secretary of the party committee of a railroad manufacturer, said

> Our factory is managed by the Railroad Ministry of the central government. Our factory's party recruitment plan is evaluated by both the party committee of the ministry and the industrial commission of the municipal party committee of the city of Tianjin. I always receive positive evaluations and quick approval for our recruitment plan from leaders of both jurisdictions in part because our factory is a high-ranking enterprise; the party committees of the ministry and the municipal industrial commission regard our factory as an essential work unit for the state. In addition, many party leaders in the ministry and the industrial commission are old comrades, who are my *zhanyou* (comrades-in-arms). They know me, and are supportive of my work.

The number of party memberships to be granted in each organization is not based on the number of applicants it has. The reverse is often the case. When a party committee or branch plans to grant a large number of party memberships as the result of policy directives from "above," or because of some local decision to reward employees with political incentives, the party committee or branch encourages employees to apply by organizing many activities for applicants. When a small number of party memberships is projected, there is little incentive to organize activities, and people are discouraged from applying. In most situations, organizations have more applicants than available party memberships, and the selection is competitive.

The Application and Recruitment Process

From an employee's perspective, application for party membership begins at the party branch level. Because party membership is an effective path to promotion, many employees desire to join the party. Although this desirability was weakened by a material orientation toward bonuses during market reforms of the 1980s, it still existed among a large body of office workers, as well as manual workers because of the stability of CCP leadership. Nevertheless, a person who wishes to join the party applies to the party branch of his or her work unit, workshop, or work team. The applicant must declare that he or she is committed to the party's goals, loyal to the party, and ready to devote his or her life to the party. A personal history as well as demographic and political characteristics of relatives are usually included in the application.

The applicant is expected to participate in open lectures by the party branch secretary, to attend classes held for studying the party constitution and current policies, and to do voluntary work organized by the party. He or she is expected to provide frequent self-evaluations regarding work and nonwork activities, offering judgments on whether he or she has met the requirements of party membership. In many work organizations, the applicant may be assigned one or two party members as sponsors (lian xi ren). Their job is to help the party secretary and members to become acquainted with the applicant. When an individual has shown significant progress, according to the sponsor and the party secretary, he or she then receives a full evaluation by the party branch for the consideration of recruitment into the party.

Party Branch Meetings. The full evaluation begins with a party branch meeting in which applicants are recommended and evaluated. Such meetings are held several times a year, and applicants are not allowed to participate. At the meetings, party members report on the applicants they have sponsored, and other party members are expected to express their opinions regarding any recommendations, bringing in personal observations and evaluations of the applicant. After deliberations, the meeting ends with a vote on whether or not the party branch should proceed with further evaluation of each applicant.

Political and Historical Evaluations. When the party branch meeting approves a recommendation, a political and historical examination of the recommended applicant is conducted by the party branch secretary and his or her staff. The examination focuses on (1) the applicant's history, (2) the political background of the applicant's parents, and (3) the political background of the applicant's grandparents and other relatives (optional).

The purpose of evaluating the applicant's history is to search for the consistency of an individual's political commitments. Early political memberships are particularly relevant, such as those in the Communist Young Pioneer League (CYPL), an organization for children aged six to fourteen. A more important one is the Chinese Communist Youth League (CCYL), for young people aged fifteen to twenty-five, which is a "training camp" for young Communists. Because of their positions and unique contributions to the league, some CCYL members are allowed to transfer directly into the CCP as soon as they turn eighteen, the minimum age for party membership.[3]

In China, every citizen has a personnel dossier on file at his or her work unit's party office, and it is here that party officials go to evaluate an applicant's history. The personnel dossier consists of various files transferred from one's schools or previous work units. These files record information about political affiliations, prizes and criticisms received, and evaluations by earlier party authorities. The dossier for a CCYL member also contains results of evaluations received during Youth League recruitment.

Personnel dossiers also contain evaluations of the applicant's parents and other relatives. If the applicant had joined the CCYL, this information will already be available in the applicant's personnel dossier. Ms. Qian (personal interview 11), a party office staff member who managed personnel dossiers at a textile factory, commented:

> Usually, CCYL members have more files than nonmembers. When they joined the league, they had everything checked: the family's class origin (jiating chushen), parents' political background, and even those of relatives and grandparents. Those who have had clean and positive records are considered good applicants.

A negative record on relatives may include "bad" family origins (parents or grandparents were landlords, business owners, or Nationalist government officials before 1949), participation in the Nationalist armed forces and work in the Nationalist government before 1949, or anti-Communist party thoughts or behaviors. In such cases, confirmation is sought by contacting party offices of the relatives' work organizations. Personnel dossiers of these relatives are examined, and additional information about their current political performances (biaoxian) is collected. During the Cultural Revolution, if an applicant's relatives had negative political backgrounds, he or she would not be considered for party recruitment. Since the Cultural Revolution, however, the evaluation of an applicant's kin is more often used as a test of whether the applicant honestly reports to the party branch about his or her family ties.

Any information collected about the applicant is passed on to the applicant's party contacts, who are briefed by the party secretary's staff. The party branch secretary then holds a meeting with branch committee members so that they can collectively decide whether the applicant should be allowed to proceed to the final step in the evaluation process.

Recruitment Meetings. The final step in the evaluation is a recruitment meeting, where it is decided whether applicants will be chosen as party members. This meeting is not held without approval from the next-higher level of party authority.

The party branch secretary calls the meeting, and all party members of the branch are obligated to participate. Applicants and nonmember activists are encouraged to sit in on the meeting. The applicant being evaluated reads a prepared statement about why he or she desires to join the party, adding personal experiences and thoughts. Afterwards, the sponsors (usually two) report on the applicant's personal history and the political background of parents and other relatives. At this point, both party members and nonmembers are encouraged to contribute to an open discussion about whether the applicant has truly met the requirements for party membership. The applicant then responds to questions from the floor. During this entire process, the applicant's sponsors offer support and encouragement.

The meeting ends with a vote by the party members, who have generally reached a consensus before the meeting is ever held. Thus, most applicants are expected to receive enough votes. Otherwise, if the majority of party members were to vote against an applicant, it would be perceived by the general public as an inability of the secretary to do adequate research before the meeting. The expectation is that a recruitment meeting is held only when the party branch secretary is sure that the applicant will receive a majority of votes.

Behind the Scene: Social Factors in Party Recruitment

Applicants for party membership can make a verbal statement during the application process expressing sincerity and loyalty to the party. They also make every effort to participate in organized political activities. Of course, personal and family history are elements that the applicant cannot control. Verbal statements, political participation, and background information are each considered important in the application and recruitment process. But it is the party branch secretary and the party members who interpret these things. What is most important, therefore, is *how* all these constituent elements are interpreted. What, then, are the social factors at work that influence decisions? Of greatest interest are those factors which affect an applicant's relations to the party branch secretary—the key decision maker in party recruitment.

Occupation and Party Membership

Jobs are not just technical duties. Nor do they merely represent socioeconomic status. In a Communist workplace, there is a specific political dimension to occupational groups, varying with their significance to the party branch. First and foremost are the administrators and managers. These power elites are the political cornerstone of the work unit. Party membership is a prerequisite for high-ranking positions, and young people recruited into low-ranking positions are encouraged to apply for party membership in order to be promoted. A second group consists of office staff. This includes assistants to various managers, file and document management staff, staff in accounting and personnel offices, labor union office, youth league office, and women's associations. The party branch secretaries pay particular attention to these people during recruitment, since they tend to be involved in the decision making process in their organizations. Ms. Zhai (personal interview 20) was a youth league member when she joined the worker's union office staff:

> I did not want to apply for the party in the first place. It would be a waste of a lot of time to attend party classes and party meetings. I was about to be married and I needed time. But the party branch secretary of our work unit asked a friend of mine on his staff to talk to me. "You should apply, you know. Trust me. If you are not a party member, how could you do the union work in the administrative building here? Do you want to keep this job?" What she said made sense to me. So, I applied and became a party member several months later.

Yet a third group consists of professionals and technicians. The party branch secretary and his or her staff often will have a mixed attitude toward this group. On the one hand, they value their expertise and skills, and some members of this group consequently will be promoted to managerial positions. Thus, the party is in favor of recruiting these members. On the other hand, the group of "party people" who are politically oriented often do not get along with professionals and technicians, who generally do not like politics.

Because of these conflicting sentiments, professionals and technicians are given fewer opportunities to join the party than administrative office staff. A final group includes skilled and unskilled manual workers. These workers are considered the least important to
the party branch secretary. According to Ms. Qian (personal interview 11), who is a staff member in her factor's party branch office,
activists from this group may be recruited into the party as "a factor
to connect the party to the masses."

My analysis of occupation and its relations to party membership differs from both orthodox Marxism-Leninism and Djilas's new
class theory. Marxism-Leninism states that the working class is the
foundation of all Communist parties (Lenin 1965 [1916]). This view
favors recruiting manual workers into the Communist parties (S.
Szelenyi 1986). I argue that the working class has never been in a
favorable position in the political relationships that govern the
Communist workplace. The party branch secretary gains political
control of manual workers, but does not use them as a means to
control the workplace. As Djilas (1957) pointed out, the Communist
party is "in the name of the working class," but its interest in working classes is maintained only in the necessity of developing rebel-
lious social forces against the old system.

Djilas (1957) contends that Soviet-type Communist parties
have created a new class that consists of individuals controlling
political bureaucracies or collective property, as well as those own-
ing significant amounts of cultural capital. Thus, the highly educated and those in administrative, professional, and technical positions would enjoy greater political privilege than the working
classes. I would extend Djilas's argument by further distinguishing
between technical and political positions. I see administrative office
staff as more useful to the party branch secretary in the exercise of
political authority. Although professionals and technicians have
more resources (expertise, skills, knowledge), the politically oriented party secretary is less interested in these resources than in
loyalty to the party.

Personal Relations to Party Leaders

As just described, the party branch secretary controls the recruitment process. An applicant's loyalty to the party therefore is
shifted to his or her loyalty to the party branch secretary. During
party classes or meetings, applicants are often prepared to praise the
lectures given by their party secretary, the work done by the party
branch, and even personal traits of the secretary. Those who do not

wish to do so would limit their opportunities for recruitment, and those who have displeased the secretary would never be given a chance to join the party. Ms. Fang (personal interview 2) was the CCYL secretary in a factory of eight hundred employees for three years before being transferred to its labor and wage office at the factory. She would have been a party member if her relationship with the party branch secretary of her factory had been more positive:

> I had a bad relationship with our party branch secretary. I did not like her, and she did not like me either. We were different kinds of people. As a CCYL secretary, I reported to her. From work contacts, I learned that she was an empty-minded cadre. She knew little about the history of the Communist movements and Communist parties. Her lectures in party class were nothing more than propaganda and slogans. She earned her party membership because of her relationship with a party branch secretary in her former work unit. She took it for granted that everybody should be like her. I could not accept that. Once she knew I had a negative opinion of her, she retaliated by removing me as the Youth League secretary. I would have been a party member and would have been promoted to a higher position if I had gotten along with our party branch secretary.

My argument for the importance of personal relationships to the party leadership in the recruitment of members is similar to Walder's (1986). In this "party clientalism" model of authority structure in the Communist workplace, personal relationships are viewed as the key to understanding the distribution of rewards. "It is no longer the conformity to ideals of political virtue itself that is rewarded, but the concrete loyalty of workers to the party branch and shop management. . . . It is the relationship, not the moral quality that is rewarded in fact, [because] party branch secretaries care little for political virtue in the abstract: they need workers who will obey orders, side with management against the other workers, actively cooperate in production and political campaigns, and stay after the shift voluntarily to help leaders prepare posters, statistics, and carry out inspections" (p. 131).

I have portrayed how individual preferences and personal loyalties affect a worker's ability to succeed in application for party membership in the workplace, in spite of the procedures of an elabo-

rate party apparatus. Next, I propose hypotheses of party membership attainment.

Party Membership Attainment: Hypotheses

The process of attaining party membership occurs at two levels. At the interorganizational level, work organizations have different ways of acquiring approval for their recruitment plans from the
party authorities. At the individual level, the membership application and evaluation process is affected by a web of political interests
and relations in the workplace. Hypotheses about the effective attainment of party membership are proposed at both levels.

Bureaucratic Rank of the Work Unit

Recruitment plans are affected by the hierarchy of the government administration and that of the work organizations. The higher
the level of government, the more organizations are involved, and
the larger number of party memberships projected. Thus, a higher
level of government has greater ability to grant party memberships
than does a lower level. Accordingly, work organizations under a
higher level of government jurisdiction benefit by being granted a
larger number of party memberships.

Economic and Industrial Sectors of the Work Unit

The work organization's ability to grant party memberships
also varies according to the economic and industrial sectors to
which they belong. Educational and noneducational institutions,
which to the Chinese authorities are "superstructures" to control
ideologies, may claim a greater need for party loyalists than more
production-oriented enterprises, which are characterized as "economic bases." Thus, these institutions may more easily acquire
permission from the higher party authority to grant party memberships. The "economic bases," or industrial enterprises, may be allocated more party memberships than work organizations in the commercial and service sectors because of their significance to the
nation's industrialization. Finally, work organizations in the state
sector, because of their political significance for the party-state, may
be preferred in acquiring party memberships to those in the nonstate
sector.

Occupational Groups

The opportunity to attain party membership for different occupational groups is a function of their degree of involvement in the

decision-making process in the workplace. Specifically, administrators and managers are directly involved in the decision-making process, and thus have the greatest opportunity to join the party. Office staff participate in the decision-making process in varying degrees, and they have fewer opportunities. Professionals and technicians are given limited opportunities to participate in the decision-making process or join the party, even though as human resources they are valuable to the workplace. Finally, manual workers are expected to have the least opportunity to join the party, because they are totally excluded from the decision-making process. In addition, manual workers are not considered as valuable a resource as professionals, technicians, and office staff.

Personal Relations to Party Leadership

The better the personal relationship one has to party leadership, the greater chance of entering the party. We can assume that the better one's relationship is, the more satisfied one is with the leadership. Thus, satisfaction with party leadership is positively related to the chances of entering the party.

Virtuocracy versus Meritocracy

The political and historical evaluations of applicants suggest that party recruitment has been strongly oriented toward a reward system of virtuocracy (Shirk 1982, 1984). A key variable of political virtue is membership in the Chinese Communist Youth League. One competing system is that of meritocracy, in which an individual's ability and credentials are rewarded. Education, for example, is a good indicator of credentials. Although I do not suggest that people with higher education should or should not be awarded party membership, it is interesting to test whether youth league membership or education is the more important criterion.

Effects of Market Reforms

Nee (1989, 1991) has argued that the "market transition" that has occurred in China has altered the basis of social stratification: power and privilege will be more strongly associated with human capital resources, and political positions will give way to entrepreneurship as a route for upward mobility. Shirk (1984) argues also that in light of market reforms, there will be a shift from virtuocratic principles of political morality to a system of meritocracy. These arguments have two implications for the study of party membership attainment. First, party membership may still remain a valuable

TABLE 6.1

Logistic Estimates of Party Membership Attainment
in the Workplace, Tianjin, 1988

	Model I		Model II	
Predictors	Pre-1978	Post-1978	Pre-1978	Post-1978
State-owned work	.13	.56*	−.18	.46
unit	(.17)	(.25)	(.20)	(.35)
Rank of the work	.11*	.15*	.10*	.15*
unit	(.04)	(.07)	(.05)	(.07)
Industrial enterprise	.56**	1.26*	.13	.78
	(.19)	(.51)	(.21)	(.53)
Educational	.33	1.60**	.21	1.24*
institution	(.25)	(.53)	(.31)	(.57)
Noneducational	.72***	1.70**	.53*	1.31**
institution	(.22)	(.52)	(.26)	(.55)
Government agency	1.67***	2.07***	1.10**	1.46*
	(.32)	(.63)	(.37)	(.70)
Fathers who were			.04	.57**
cadres (cadre =			(.25)	(.21)
1)				
CCYL membership			.41*	−.42
before joining			(.19)	(.22)
the party				
Middle school			−.14	.30
			(.19)	(.44)

continued

political status during the period of market reform. What may have changed are recruitment criteria: there would be a transition from virtuocracy to meritocracy, from party clientalism to a theory of human capital. Second and conversely, party membership may have in fact lost its significance as a political status. As a consequence, party membership attainment would become an unpredictable process because no one even cares about acquiring it any more. In this case, the predictors cited will not be associated with party memberships granted since the introduction of market reforms.

Analysis of Party Membership in Tianjin

Slightly more than 19 percent (19.3 percent) of the respondents in the 1988 Tianjin survey were Communist party members. This

TABLE 6.1 *continued*

Predictors	Model I		Model II	
	Pre-1978	Post-1978	Pre-1978	Post-1978
High/vocational			−.18	.63*
school			(.20)	(.23)
College and above			−.36	.97**
			(.23)	(.33)
Administrative and			1.33***	.97***
managerial			(.21)	(.19)
Office staff			.62***	.46*
			(.18)	(.21)
Professional and			.22	.25
technical			(.32)	(.27)
Satisfaction with			.18*	.01
the leader of the			(.08)	(.10)
work unit				
Sex (male = 1)			.35**	.62***
			(.14)	(.18)
Years of work			.01	−.01
			(.01)	(.01)
Intercept	3.32***	1.56**	2.89***	1.12
Goodness-of-fit				
chi square	623.25	835.98	585.72	590.10
Degree of freedom	608	766	596	752

Those who became party members before joining the labor force were excluded. *p < .05, **p < .01, ***p < .001.

percentage is nearly three times the percentage obtained from a sample of rural households in South China (Nee 1989, 7 percent), but close to the 18.9 percent obtained from a sample of urban workers in Tianjin in 1985 (Lin and Bian 1991).[4] S. Szelenyi (1986) reported that 18 percent of Hungarian urban workers were Socialist Worker party members.

To assess party membership attainment, two logistic regression models are established (Table 6.1). Model I predicts party membership attainment from work-unit variables,[5] and Model II incorporates individual-level predictors. These models are assessed for two subsamples: party memberships that were granted before the end of 1978 and party memberships that were granted after 1978. The comparison of these two periods allows us to test whether the market reforms have had any impact on party membership attainment.[6] Respondents who entered the party before joining the labor force are excluded from the analysis to satisfy a causal sequence between workplace variables and party membership attainment.

Results and Interpretations for Model I

State ownership has an effect on post-1978 party membership, but not on party membership granted before 1978 (Table 6.1). The significant logit coefficient of .56 for the post-1978 equation reveals an odds of 1.75, suggesting that, with bureaucratic rank and industrial sector being held constant, work units in the state sector would grant 17.5 party memberships for every ten memberships granted by work units in the collective sector. The insignificant coefficient of state ownership for pre-1978 party membership means that work units in the two sectors granted about the same number of party memberships before 1978.

The difference in the effects of state ownership on party membership between the two periods indicates that there has been a decline of party membership as a political reward in the collective sector. This decline can be traced to current policies of market reform. Along with the abolition of economic quotas for collective businesses, party control in collective work units was relaxed. In small collective businesses established after 1978, such controls never even existed, and employees in the collective enterprises were income-oriented. Under these circumstances, party membership became relatively meaningless to both the leadership and employees. The situation in the state sector, however, was different. Work units in the state sector continued to receive state production quotas, though largely through guidance plans rather than mandatory plans, and party organizations in the state work units remained effective. Although income orientation was strong in the state sector, job promotion and political mobility (from a work unit to a cadre, and movement from low to high cadre rank) favored party members, and were as important.

Work-unit rank and industrial sectors are significant predictors of party membership both before and after 1978. The effect of work-unit rank on party membership was greater after 1978 than before. Such a trend is even clearer when looking at the effects of the industrial sector on party membership. For every ten memberships in the commerce/service sector (omitted category), industrial enterprises showed 17.5 memberships before 1978 (antilog of .56) and 35.3 memberships after 1978 (antilog of 1.26). In educational institutions, there were about the same number of memberships as in the commerce/service sector before 1978 and 39.0 memberships after 1978; in noneducational institutions, there were 20.5 memberships before 1978 and 54.7 memberships after 1978; and in government agencies, there were 53.1 memberships before 1978 and 79.2 memberships after 1978.

Results and Interpretation for Model II

Model I assesses the total effects of work-unit variables on party membership. When individual-level variables are incorporated in Model II (also Table 6.1), reduced direct effects of these work-unit variables on party membership were expected. The variable of state sector did not survive the statistical test, as other work-unit variables did. As shown in Model II, individuals with the same qualifications but working in high-ranking organizations, nonprofit institutions, or government agencies have better chances of joining the party. Party membership attainment is clearly not merely a process of individual achievement or credentials.

One's father's cadre status had an effect on party memberships after 1978 but not before 1978.[7] The data show that 56 percent of party memberships before 1978 were granted during the Cultural Revolution. In this period, party cadres were punished, and their children were deprived of political and social privileges (Parish 1984). After 1978, this practice was reversed. The difference in the effect of the father's cadre status on party membership is perhaps associated with this historical trend.

The effects of CCYL membership and education on party membership differ between the pre-1978 and post-1978 periods. Before 1978, those who acquired CCYL memberships before entering the work unit were likely to become party members. Education did not make a difference in party membership attainment. After 1978, respondents with higher education have tended to have better chances of becoming party members, and previous CCYL membership had a *negative* (though statistically insignificant) effect on one's joining the party. This suggests that market reforms did alter the basis of political mobility. Whereas in the past the party favored those who had relatively fewer educational credentials or who had greater political virtue (CCYL), the party now is interested in those with greater human capital (education) and less focused on criteria of ideological commitment.

Nonmanual staff have been favored over manual workers (omitted) in party recruitment both before and after 1978. This find-

TABLE 6.2

Logistic Coefficients of Workplace and Individual Variables
on Being Cadres, Tianjin, 1988

Cadre Status Obtained

Predictors	Before 1978		Before 1988	
	(I)	(II)	(I)	(II)
Communist party	1.82***	1.80***	2.35***	2.44***
member	(.27)	(.30)	(.23)	(.26)
First-Job Occupation				
Administrative and	1.85**	1.48*	1.58**	1.45*
managerial	(.64)	(.71)	(.59)	(.62)
Office staff	.91*	.83*	.73*	.62*
	(.39)	(.42)	(.33)	(.38)
Professional and	.58	.24	.63	.83
technical	(.65)	(.71)	(.56)	(.60)
Skilled worker	.50	.51	.32	.10
	(.38)	(.44)	(.30)	(.33)
Other Individual Variables				
Sex (male = 1)	.70*	.67*	.71**	.66*
	(.31)	(.33)	(.26)	(.27)
Years of work	.06***	.07***	.06***	.07***
	(.01)	(.01)	(.01)	(.01)
Middle school	.38	.38	1.37**	1.14**
	(.41)	(.47)	(.41)	(.44)
High/technical	.71	.65	1.57***	1.34**
school	(.45)	(.51)	(.42)	(.45)
College and higher	.77	.75	1.89***	1.72***
	(.49)	(.56)	(.46)	(.49)

continued

ing confirms Djilas's (1957) assertion that a Communist party operates merely in the name of the working class but does not serve in
the interest of the working class. But Djilas's new class theory is
only partially supported by the Chinese data. Whereas administrative and managerial cadres and office staff have the privilege of becoming party members, as is implied by Djilas's new class theory,
Chinese professionals do not have better chances of joining the party
than manual workers, contrary to Djilas's expectation. The data support my view of occupation as a relational term: people in some

TABLE 6.2 *continued*

Cadre Status Obtained

Predictors	Before 1978		Before 1988	
	(I)	(II)	(I)	(II)
Workplace Variables				
State-owned		.33		.38
		(.45)		(.36)
Bureaucratic rank		.38**		.37**
		(.14)		(.12)
Industrial enterprise		1.15**		1.09*
		(.55)		(.48)
Educational institu-		.47		.69
tions		(.78)		(.68)
Noneducational		1.61*		1.19*
institutions		(.66)		(.56)
Government agen-		1.81**		2.39***
cies		(.72)		(.71)
Intercept	−4.62***	−4.56***	−6.05***	−6.14***
−2 Log likelihood chi square	390.25	349.80	542.03	503.90
Degree of freedom	10	17	10	17
Number of cases	650	611	947	940

*p < .05, **p < .01, ***p < .001. Standard errors in parentheses.

occupational groups are more important than others to party branch secretaries not because of their skills or expertise, but because their positions are politically significant to party control over the workplace.

To test whether one's relationship with the party leadership promotes one's chances of joining the party, one variable is used: satisfaction with the leader of one's work unit. The assumption here is that the more satisfied one is with his or her leader, the better the relationship with that person. "The leader of the work unit" (*danwei lingdao*) refers to the party secretary *or* director of the work unit. Although some respondents may have referred to their leaders as directors rather than party secretaries, in the Chinese workplace, most work-unit directors are party secretaries or vice-secretaries. As it turned out, one's satisfaction with one's work unit leader increased one's likelihood of joining the party before 1978. Such an effect disappeared after 1978. This indicates that party clientalism might have been on the decline since the introduction of market reforms.

Party Membership as a Path to Power Elites

To confirm whether one's party membership is a strong indicator of one's political mobility, I analyze here party membership as a predictor of one's being a cadre.

The term *cadre* has various meanings in China. Cadre as an occupation refers to nonmanual staff. It includes (1) party, administrative, and enterprise or institution leaders (*dang, zheng, qishiye danwei fuzeren*); (2) technical cadre (*jishu ganbu*); and (3) ordinary cadre (*yiban ganbu*), which are clerical or office staff. The term also refers to the distinction between cadres and the masses. "Cadres" here mean only the primary group—leaders of various organizations, whereas all other nonmanual staff and manual workers belong to the masses. Because I am interested in whether party membership provides a path to the class of power elites, this second definition of cadres is adopted in the analysis that follows.

Eighteen percent of the respondents in the 1988 Tianjin survey reported that they had administrative or managerial positions in the workplace. Small-group leaders (*shao zu zhang*) are not considered as administrative and managerial cadres for two reasons. First, although they are leaders of small groups of six or seven people, these group leaders themselves are classified as ordinary staff or workers in labor-personnel files and not yet "officials." Second, they have little access to the decision-making process on the shop floor or in the work unit. Their principal tasks are to transfer information between their supervisors and members of their groups.[8]

Sixty-seven percent of the party members in our Tianjin survey were cadres. Table 6.2 presents logistic models to estimate the independent effect of party membership on the cadre status, with work-unit and individual-level variables as statistical controls. As expected, party membership exerts a strong influence on the likelihood of one's being a cadre, both before and after 1978. Its effect is greater after 1978 than before 1978, suggesting that the decade of market reforms tightened the link between party affiliation and authority. The finding implies that although party intervention into economic operations may have been partly relaxed, the party's control of authoritative positions in the work unit has been strengthened.

Several individual-level variables reveal interesting results. The effect of education on the likelihood of being a cadre was not significant, though positive, before 1978. But after 1978, education had a strong effect on the odds of becoming a cadre. Thus, educational credentials have been a criterion for the selection of cadres since the market reforms. Those people who were manual workers, professionals, and technicians in their first jobs have had significantly fewer chances of becoming cadres than people who had administrative, managerial, and office jobs in their early careers. Not surprisingly, males have been more likely to occupy administrative and managerial positions than females before and after the reforms. In addition, older employees tended to be cadres both before and after market reforms, which means that people have better chances of being promoted the longer they stay in the work force.

Summary

In the Communist party-state, membership in the Communist party is a status or privilege rather than a choice according to one's political orientation. The allocation of this status or privilege is essential in understanding the distribution of power and authority. I have described and analyzed how one's work unit influences one's entry into the Communist party. The data from the 1988 Tianjin survey have shown that the distribution of party memberships is indeed a function of the work-unit structure. Despite formally announced criteria, individuals with the same qualifications but in work units with different characteristics have unequal chances of joining the party. Specifically, the recruitment process favors those work organizations with a higher bureaucratic rank and organizations whose strategic functions are to safeguard the Communist party's authority (government agencies) or ideologies (educational and noneducational institutions). Workers in these organizations are more likely to become party members, even when their individual characteristics are held constant.

Within the workplace, I examined job positions in relation to the existing political structure. I found that people who entered the work force with job assignments (administrative, managerial, or office work) associated with the decision-making process have better chances of joining the party than those who joined the labor force as professionals, technicians, or manual workers. Although professionals and technicians have human or cultural resources that Djilas believed would be valued by the new bureaucratic class, and working classes are claimed by orthodox Marxism-Leninism to be the foundation of the Communist party, neither group has a privileged position in the existing political structure in the workplace.

Following Walder's party clientalism perspective, I explored personal relationships with the party branch secretary as a path to party membership. Interview data suggest that one's relationship with the party secretary is a decisive factor for party membership attainment. Because of lack of a direct measure, I used an indirect measure to test this observation in the analysis of the Tianjin data. I found that one's satisfaction with the leader of one's work unit significantly increased the odds of joining the party before 1978 but not after 1978. Interestingly, education had no effect on party membership before 1978 but did after 1978; membership in the Communist Youth League had an effect on party membership before 1978, but its effect disappeared after 1978. These findings indicate that market reforms have indeed altered the basis of political stratification in China: virtuocracy has given way to meritocracy, and party clientalism has given way to a theory of human capital. Although party membership has been a path to the elite class of cadres both before and after market reforms, the meaning of party membership for the Chinese worker appears to have changed.

7

WAGES

In this chapter I focus on the relationship between wages and the work-unit structure. Beginning with an overview of the different types of wages, I next describe three wage reforms and corresponding wage systems. I then analyze official statistics to explore wage differentials by workplace variables at the national level. Finally, I turn to the 1988 Tianjin survey to estimate a series of individual-level regression models in which salaries and bonuses are predicted from workplace, human resource, political, and occupational variables.

Types of Wages

The Chinese official wage bills report six types of wages: (1) basic wages, (2) bonuses, (3) compensations and subsidies, (4) supplementary wages, (5) wages for extra work, and (6) other wages.[1] Table 7.1 shows national wage bills for *state industrial employees* from 1978 to 1985. Industrial labor accounts for 45 percent of China's nonagricultural labor force, and its wages reveal the same percentage in the national wage bills. Although wage structures in nonindustrial sectors can be somewhat different, national statistics for wages in other industries were not available for this study.

Basic wages or salaries, which accounted for 67.7 percent of the total wages of state industrial labor in 1985 (Yuan 1990, p. 190), are further divided into time-rates and piece-rates. Both types may coexist in a single enterprise. Time-rates decreased from 83.5 percent of the total wages in 1978 to 56.9 percent in 1985, and piece-rates increased from 0.4 percent to 10.8 percent during the same period. These changes reflected reform initiatives that called for wages to be linked to the quantity and quality of outputs produced by workers, rather than to the workers' presence at work settings. But these initiatives did not affect the entire structure of wage bills, since time-rates were still the major source of workers' wages.

TABLE 7.1

Types of Wages and their Percentage Distribution
in Chinese State Industry: 1978–1985

| Year | Total | 1 | | 2 | 3 | 4 | 5 | 6 |
		a	b					
1978	100	83.5	0.4	3.5	6.0	3.5	2.6	0.5
1979	100	70.8	3.0	9.9	9.1	3.2	2.6	1.4
1980	100	65.7	4.0	11.1	14.3	2.0	2.2	0.7
1981	100	63.4	6.9	11.6	14.1	1.3	2.2	0.5
1982	100	59.9	9.8	12.3	14.4	1.1	2.0	0.5
1983	100	58.8	10.9	12.5	14.5	1.0	1.9	0.5
1984	100	55.9	10.8	15.2	14.0		2.2	1.9
1985	100	56.9	10.8	14.9	14.3		2.3	0.8

1. Salaries: a. time-rate   b. piece-rate
2. Bonuses
3. Supplementary wages
4. Subsidies and compensations
5. Extra-hours wages
6. Other wages

Bonuses (and piece-rate wages), which were common before being eliminated during the decade of the Cultural Revolution (1966–76), quickly reemerged as a major incentive wage after 1978. Bonuses were 14.9 percent of the total wages in 1985, up from 3.5 percent in 1978. A 1985 representative sample of Tianjin wage earners showed 13.7 percent bonuses for workers in state enterprises (Lin and Bian 1991, Table 1). The bonus rate increased to 25.1 percent in 1986, according to a different Tianjin sample of wage earners (Walder 1990, p. 140). The 1988 Tianjin survey analyzed in this study reveals 22.9 percent bonuses.

Work-related compensations and consumer-related subsidies accounted for 14.3 percent of total wages in state industry in 1985 (column IV, Table 7.1). Both are centrally regulated and made available through workplaces. Compensations are provided to those working underground, outdoors, at sea, under high temperatures, in conditions that may affect their health, and with high-prestige but low-pay jobs, such as elementary-school teachers and nurses. Price and housing subsidies are common and have always been important to an urban worker's earnings.[2] Compensations and subsidies also are provided to encourage people to work in regions where there is economic hardship.[3]

Supplementary wages (*fujia gongzi*) are token payments to compensate low-paid workers who started working before the Great Leap Forward in 1958. Since 1984, supplementary wages became a part of regular salaries. Extra-hour wages are paid for work done outside regular work hours and on national holidays. Finally, "other wages" include allowances and compensations that are paid on a case-by-case basis. On average, the last two categories accounted for only about three percent of the total wages in 1985.

Typically, workers receive cash payments for wages on a monthly basis. Each category of wages except for bonuses is shown on an accompanying pay slip. Bonuses may be given more than once a month, and usually on days other than payday. The amount varies from one workplace to another. According to the 1988 survey, it ranged from five *yuan* (about ninety cents) a month to more than the monthly salary. Year-end bonuses, which are paid at the end of either the fiscal or lunar-calendar year, have become common since the market reforms. In the 1988 Tianjin survey, year-end bonuses averaged the equivalent of one month's salary. Because salaries and bonuses are the main sources for wage differentials, I will focus on these two types of cash incomes in the remainder of the chapter.

Wage Reforms and Corresponding Salary Systems

The Chinese wage system has experienced three systematic reforms over the last forty-three years. The first was launched in 1950, one year after the Communist Revolution. It was aimed at transforming the food supply system of wartime communism to a wage system. Previously, military and nonmilitary personnel did not earn wages but received food, supplies, and cash allowances according to their positions in the Communist forces. Under the new wage system, government and military officials and employees in the newly established state-owned industries began to receive cash salaries and compensation according to their job titles and ranks.

The second wage reform in 1956 was part of an overall plan to nationalize the economy. The aim was to regulate wages for an expanded work force in both the state and collective sectors. Workers in the state sector increased from 32.0 percent of the total urban labor force in 1949 to 63.6 percent in 1952 and finally to 81.4 percent in 1956. The collective sector absorbed 18.5 percent of the urban labor force in 1956 (State Statistical Bureau of China 1988, p. 123).

Salary standards in the refined wage system, which was patterned after the Soviet model, were centrally regulated along regions, occupations, industries, sectors (state versus collective), level of management of enterprises (central versus local), and characteristics of workplace (e.g., technology and size). The core of this wage system was a complex structure of salary standards for more than three hundred occupational classifications (Li 1991, p. 68). Under this system, salary increases were determined by the annual budget of the central government, and state-fixed quotas for salary increases were distributed from various levels of government bureaucracies to baseline enterprises and institutions. Characteristics and consequences of this wage system have been documented in an English-language research literature (Howe 1973; Korzec and Whyte 1981; Whyte and Parish 1984; Walder 1986).

Economic policy changes since 1978 stimulated the third wage reform, launched in 1985. This latest reform differentiated between business enterprises on the one hand and government agencies and not-for-profit institutions on the other. The blueprint for wage reform in business enterprises is the State Council's document "Circular of Wage Reform Problems in State Enterprises" (State Council 1985a), and that for agencies and institutions is "A Plan for the Reform of the Wage System for Personnel in Government Agencies and Institutions" (State Council 1985b).

The Wage System in Enterprises

The central directive of wage reform in enterprises is to provide them with profit-producing incentives. In the previous wage system, state enterprises turned all profits over to the state and paid their workers with wages redistributed by the state. Except for a small amount of bonus funds (linked to limited above-quota outputs), these enterprises had no incentive to produce profits for the state. Under the new wage system, however, wage budgets are linked to an enterprise's profitability and performance. Basic wages and profit quotas are projected from the enterprise's economic indicators over the past three years, and they are allowed to retain, after taxes, above-quota profits for investment in plant capacity, employee welfare programs, "floating" salaries (bonus-type, temporary salary increases), salary raises, and bonuses. These incentives, particularly cash income-related measures, have stimulated profit- and wage-oriented behavior from enterprises and their managers and workers.

Despite formally announced regulations, case-by-case bargaining between government authorities and enterprises has determined wage budgets and profits retained by enterprises. Enterprises utilize their political and organizational powers to influence government authorities to obtain larger wage budgets, higher rates of retained profits, low-priced resources, price subsidies, tax benefits, and special funding (Walder 1989; Li 1990). Because the "father-son" relationship still characterizes the socialist state and its production units (see Chapter 2), enterprises with government priorities in the past continue to be favored in these vertical relations of profit determination.

The Wage System in Agencies and Institutions

A different wage system applies to government agencies and not-for-profit institutions. Under the previous system, these organizations received fixed, itemized wage budgets as well as other budgets from government authorities. Employees's basic salaries were fixed, compensations and subsidies were fixed, and bonuses, if any, were fixed. After wage reform in 1985, these organizations received fixed total budgets from government authority. They were given some flexibility to manipulate wage budgets within their total budgets. For example, wage budgets may be raised by reducing other expenses, and money created may be used in the form of year-end bonuses or floating salaries. Not-for-profit institutions were given even more flexibility. Upon completion of contracted missions with the government, these institutions were allowed to organize their staff members to engage in income-oriented activities, and earnings made through these activities were retained and distributed in the form of bonuses (Han, Ren, and Tian 1991). Government agencies were not provided with these incentives. Salary increases in both government agencies and institutions were subject to the wage budget of the central government. In short, compared with enterprises, wage distributions for government agencies and not-for-profit institutions remained basically redistributive.

Salary Standards

A significant change made in the 1985 wage reform was the integration of more than three hundred systems of salary standards into four broad classifications: (1) manual workers in enterprises, (2) nonmanual staff in enterprises, (3) nonmanual staff in government agencies and not-for-profit institutions, and (4) manual workers in government agencies and not-for-profit institutions.

Manual Workers in Enterprises

Salary standards for state workers in large and medium-size enterprises were published by the Labor and Personnel Ministry of the central government in 1985. Table 7.2 presents these salary standards. Columns indicate eleven salary standards reflecting differences in wage regions, work-unit characteristics, and occupations. A wage earner is tied to one of these eleven standards because of the region in which he or she lives, the type of work unit in which he or she works, and the occupational category that he or she belongs to. The salary for the highest standard is 30 percent higher than that for the lowest.

Regional differences in wages are regulated along eleven salary standards. In the earlier wage system, there were eleven wage regions. In the current structure, there are seven regions. The fifth region uses salary standards 1–5 (see Table 7.2); the sixth region, 2–6; the seventh region, 3–7; the eighth region, 4–8; the ninth region, 5–9; the tenth region, 6–10; and the eleventh region, 7–11.

Industry and occupations account for intraregional differentials. In a sixth-ranked region (second to seventh standards), such as Beijing and Tianjin, primary industries (and related occupations) such as mining, steel and iron smelting, and fishing on the sea use fourth, fifth, and sixth salary standards; secondary industries (and related occupations) such as manufacturing, construction, railway, transportation, textile, electricity, and chemical production use third, fourth, and fifth salary standards; and third industries (and related occupations) such as agriculture, commercial, and food processing use second, third, and fourth salary standards.

Rows in Table 7.2 show fifteen pay ranks that stratify individual workers within region, type of workplace, and occupation. The fifteen ranks are obtained by creating and integrating seven additional ranks into the previous eight-rank system. Monthly salary for the highest fifteenth rank is three times as much as that for the lowest first rank, which is entry-level pay. Although these government-regulated salary standards are relatively fixed, enterprises are allowed to add up to 1.5 yuan per month to each pay rank using retained capital. This amount is less than 2 percent of the average monthly salary in Tianjin in 1988. The additional wages are termed "floating salary" (liudong gongzi), in contrast to the standard

TABLE 7.2

Salary Standards for Manual Workers
in Large and Medium-Size State Enterprises
(unit = *yuan*/month)

Salary Standards Reflecting Differences in Regions,
Workplaces, and Occupations

Pay Rank	1	2	3	4	5	6	7	8	9	10	11
1 (lowest)	33	34	35	36	37	38	39	40	41	42	43
2	36	37	38	39	40	41	43	44	45	46	47
3	40	41	42	43	44	45	47	48	49	50	51
4	44	45	46	47	48	49	52	53	54	55	56
5	48	49	50	51	52	54	57	58	59	60	61
6	52	53	54	55	56	59	62	63	64	65	66
7	56	58	59	60	61	64	67	68	69	70	72
8	61	63	64	65	66	69	72	73	75	76	78
9	66	68	69	70	72	75	78	79	81	82	84
10	71	73	74	76	78	81	84	85	87	89	91
11	76	78	80	82	84	87	90	91	94	96	98
12	81	84	86	88	90	93	96	98	101	103	105
13	87	90	92	94	97	100	103	105	108	110	113
14	93	96	98	101	104	107	110	112	115	118	121
15 (highest)	99	102	105	108	111	114	117	120	123	126	129

Source: Li (1991), p. 117.

salaries shown in Table 7.2. Floating salaries may be taken off workers' monthly pay slips if enterprises' retained capital is shortened.

It should be noted here that these salary standards are for large and medium-size state enterprises. Small state enterprises and enterprises in the collective sector are excluded. Historically, their salary standards are lower. As recommended by the Department of Labor and Personnel Affairs (Li 1991, p. 117), local governments should use salary standards for large and medium-size enterprises "as a reference" to regulate wages for small state enterprises and all collective enterprises. This means that the wage structure shown in Table 7.2 is applicable to small state enterprises and enterprises in the collective sector, but a greater number of low pay ranks and low salary standards are expected.

TABLE 7.3

Salary Standards for Nonmanual Staff
in Large and Medium-Size State Enterprises
(unit = *yuan*/month)

Salary Standards Reflecting Differences in Regions,
Workplaces, and Occupations

Pay Rank	1	2	3	4	5	6	7	8	9
1 (highest)	248	255	263	270	277	285	292	299	306
2	224	230	236	243	250	256	263	269	276
3	202	208	214	220	226	231	237	243	249
4	185	190	196	201	207	212	217	222	227
5	170	175	180	185	190	195	199	204	209
6	155	160	165	169	173	178	182	187	192
7	141	145	150	154	158	162	166	170	175
8	128	131	136	139	143	147	150	154	158
9	115	118	122	125	128	132	135	138	142
10	102	105	108	111	114	117	120	123	126
10.5	96	98	101	104	107	110	112	115	118
11	90	92	94	97	100	103	105	108	110
11.5	84	86	88	90	93	96	98	101	103
12	78	80	82	84	87	90	91	94	96
12.5	73	74	76	78	81	84	85	87	89
13	68	69	70	72	75	78	79	81	82
13.5	63	64	65	66	69	72	73	75	76
14	58	59	60	61	64	67	68	69	70
14.5	53	54	55	56	59	62	63	64	65
15	49	50	51	52	54	57	58	59	60
15.5	45	46	47	48	49	52	53	54	55
16	41	42	43	44	45	47	48	49	50
16.5	37	38	39	40	41	43	44	45	46
17 (lowest)	34	35	36	37	38	39	40	41	42

Source: Li (1991), pp. 118–9.

Nonmanual Staff in Enterprises

Table 7.3 presents salary standards for nonmanual staff in large
and medium-size state enterprises, which also were published by
the Labor and Personnel Ministry of the central government in 1985
(Li 1991, p. 118–19). "Nonmanual staff" refers to all employees ex-

cluding manual workers. Here there are nine salary standards for each pay rank. Monthly salary for the highest standard is 23.5 percent higher than that for the lowest salary standard. This differential is lower than the 30 percent for manual workers. The fifth region uses salary standards 1–3 (see Table 7.3); the sixth region, 2–4; the seventh region, 3–5; the eighth region, 4–6; the ninth region, 5–7; the tenth region, 6–8; and the eleventh region, 7–9. It is unclear in the government document what specifically determines which of the three alternative salary standards should be used for a particular workplace, industry, or occupation within each region.

Within each salary standard, individual staff are ranked on a scale of seventeen full ranks and seven half ranks. Monthly salary for the highest rank is 7.29 times as much as that for the lowest rank. This differential, which is much greater than the 3.0 for manual workers, results largely from salary discrepancies between officials of enterprises and the ordinary staff. For this reason, the range of standard salaries for nonmanual staff for the entire nation, which is 272 *yuan* (about $50) per month, or 8.0 times more than the lowest pay, is much greater than the 92 *yuan* per month, or only 2.9 times more than lowest pay, for manual workers in enterprises.

Nonmanual Staff in Government Agencies
and Not-for-Profit Institutions

A "structural wage system" was established to regulate salaries for nonmanual staff in government agencies and not-for-profit institutions. In this system, a staff's total salary is the sum of four components: basic wage, wage for position, seniority wage, and bonus wage. The basic wage is a fixed wage to support an above-poverty living standard. The basic wage in the sixth wage region, which includes Beijing and Tianjin, is forty *yuan* a month. Wage for position is the main component of the structural wage. "Position" here refers to the administrative, managerial, and technical positions that a staff member currently holds. When a person holds more than one position, the highest-paying position determines the wage. A wage for position will also change when the wage earner moves to another position. Seniority wage is a wage for one's accumulated years of work. It is set at a half *yuan* per month for every year of work accumulated, with a maximum of twenty *yuan* per month for a person with forty years of work or more. And finally, the fourth component is the bonus wage, which is distributed by Chinese authorities to praise and recognize staff for outstanding

TABLE 7.4

Salary Standards for Nonmanual Staff
in Government Agencies and Institutions
(unit = *yuan*/month)

Pay Rank	Basic Salary	Positional Salaries					
		1	2	3	4	5	6
*Executive Staff in Central and Provincial Governments**							
President, vice-president, Premier	40	490	410	340			
Vice-premier, member of state council	40	340	300	270			
Minister, governor	40	270	240	215	190	165	
Vice-minister, vice-governor	40	215	190	165	150	140	
Bureau chief	40	165	150	140	130	120	
Deputy bureau chief	40	140	130	120	110	100	
Department chief	40	130	120	110	100	91	82
Deputy department chief	40	110	100	91	82	73	65
Section chief, chief staff member	40	91	82	73	65	57	49
Deputy section chief	40	73	65	57	49	42	36
Staff member	40	57	49	42	36	30	24
Clerk	40	42	36	30	24	18	12
*Technical Staff in Central and Provincial Governments**							
Chief engineer, ministry	40	215	190	165	150	140	
Associate chief engineer, ministry	40	165	150	140	130	120	
Chief engineer, bureau	40	140	130	120	110	100	
Associate chief engineer, bureau	40	130	120	110	100	91	82
Engineer	40	100	91	82	73	65	57
Assistant engineer	40	57	49	42	36	30	
Technician	40	42	36	30	24	18	

continued

achievements. Usually this is a fixed payment, ranging five to ten *yuan* a month in Tianjin.

Table 7.4 presents designed differentials for position wages in the sixth wage region. Six salary standards are set for administrative and technical positions ranging from central government posts to office clerks in municipalities and provincial cities. Wage differentials between the adjacent pay standards range from 10 to 50 percent. Except for organizations in the sports sector, not-for-profit institutions use this structural wage system. The sports sector uses a more flexible, wage-as-compensation system for athletes.

TABLE 7.4 *continued*

	Basic	Positional Salaries					
Pay Rank	Salary	1	2	3	4	5	6
*Executive Staff in Eight Municipal Governments***							
Mayor	40	215	190	165	150	140	
Deputy mayor	40	165	150	140	130	120	
Bureau chief	40	140	130	120	110	100	
Deputy bureau chief	40	130	120	110	100	91	82
Department chief	40	120	110	100	91	82	73
Deputy department chief	40	100	91	82	73	65	57
Section chief	40	91	82	73	65	57	49
Deputy section chief	40	73	65	57	49	42	36
Staff member	40	57	49	42	36	30	24
Clerk	40	42	36	30	24	18	12

*Beijing, Tianjin, and Shanghai are included.
**Guangzhou, Wuhan, Dalian, Nanjing, Chengdu, Shenyang, Haerbin, Xian.
Source: Li (1991), pp. 153–4.

Manual Workers in Government Agencies and Not-for-Profit Institutions

Like nonmanual staff in government agencies and not-for-profit institutions, skilled and unskilled manual workers in these organizations receive a fixed basic wage (Table 7.5). An additional "occupational wage," which is similar in type to the positional wage for staff personnel, is also used. Ten wage levels are set for skilled workers, with a high-low ratio of 2.2. Eight wage levels are used for unskilled workers, with a high-low ratio of nearly 2.0. Within each pay rank, a skilled worker earns 28 percent more basic and occupational wages combined than an unskilled worker.

The Bonus System

Bonuses as an incentive wage had a variable history before 1978. Between 1949 and 1957, bonuses were common in profit-making enterprises and nonexistent in government agencies and not-for-profit institutions. According to a 1952 central government regulation (FECCG 1952), bonuses were considered to be a material

TABLE 7.5

Salary Standards for Manual Workers in Central
and Provincial Government Agencies
(unit = *yuan*/month)

Rank	Basic Salary	Rank Salary Standards									
		1	2	3	4	5	6	7	8	9	10
Skilled	40	73	65	57	49	42	36	30	24	18	12
Unskilled	40	49	42	36	30	24	18	12	6		

Note: Municipal governments of Beijing, Tianjin, and Shanghai are included.

Source: Li (1991), p. 155.

incentive to promote quantity and quality of production, reduce production costs, and improve living standards of workers. Centrally imposed bonus rates were less than 15 percent of total basic wages. According to a survey conducted in forty-eight enterprises in 1956 (Li 1991, p. 240), however, actual bonus rates were much higher than planned.

The Great Leap Forward year of 1958 witnessed the decline of bonuses. Bonuses were said to be the "new opium of socialist workers"[4] (Li 1991, p. 241), and it was claimed that quality work and high productivity should be stimulated by a pro-Communism spirit, rather than a bourgeois orientation toward money. This leftist movement was partially revised in 1959. A low bonus rate of about 4 percent of annual salaries was resumed for enterprise workers, but not for party secretaries, managers, union officers, and youth-league leaders in enterprises. Nonenterprise workplaces were prohibited from using bonuses.

Several central government documents were published from 1962 to early 1964 to regulate bonus rates and promote a more egalitarian orientation in the distribution of bonuses within enterprises (Li 1990, pp. 243–45). But bonuses were once again criticized as incorrect management strategy as a means to stimulate work performance in the Socialist Education Campaign (also known as "Four Clean-ups Campaign") from late 1964 to early 1966. This leftist critique dominated and was reinforced during the subsequent Cultural Revolution decade (1966–76). Bonuses were finally eliminated entirely from urban workplaces until the market-oriented reform launched in 1978.

In March 1978, Deng Xiaoping, then the vice-chairman of the CCP, in his conversation with reform-minded officials demanded that "the bonus system be restored" (Deng 1983, p. 99). In May of that year, the State Council's "Circular of the Reward and Piece-Rate Wage System" laid out principles for a new bonus system, and was sent to all organizations. This system took shape along with reform initiatives for a profit-retention system, a tax system, a new salary system launched after the 1985 wage reform, an enterprise contract responsibility system, and price reforms. By 1988, the bonus systems established in profit-making enterprises, government agencies, and not-for-profit institutions can be summarized as in the following paragraphs.

Profit-Making Enterprises

Between 1978 and the first half of 1984, bonuses in profit-making enterprises were regulated within a new profit-retention system. Under this system, enterprises were allowed to retain a certain percentage of annual profits to invest in (1) improvement of facilities, (2) collective welfare programs, and (3) bonuses, with 60 percent of retained profits for the first type of funding and no more than 40 percent for the latter two funds combined. When retained profits were generated from above-projection profits, percentages for the three types of funds were 50, 30, and 20 percent, respectively. In addition, an enterprise's annual bonus funds could not exceed two months' worth of wages. Enterprises that made "outstanding contributions" could be allowed annual bonus funding in the amount of three months' basic wages.

Despite these centrally imposed regulations, bonus funds were not effectively controlled, and increases in bonus funds were considerably higher than overall profitability or productivity (Walder 1987), and were three times higher than required (Li 1991, p. 249). In addition, economic egalitarianism affected the distribution of bonuses, and bonuses failed to generate either profitability or productivity (Walder 1987). By April 1984, the profit-retention system was replaced by a tax system, in which profit quotas were abolished and enterprises retained after-tax profits. To control bonus funds, a standard bonus rate was projected at two and a half months' basic wages, and "above standard" bonuses were taxed. The bonus standard was rejustified in 1987 and 1988 (Li 1991, p. 250).

Differentials in retained profits did exist among enterprises. In 1985, selected manufacturing industries were ranked in terms of per capita retained profits as follows: petroleum chemicals (1598 *yuan*, or about $290), electric power (966 *yuan*, or $176), tobacco (944 *yuan*, or $172), iron and steel (820 *yuan*, or $149), automobiles (748 *yuan*, or $136), medicine (705 *yuan*, or $128), machinery (602 *yuan*, or $109), nonferrous metal (565 *yuan*, or $103), petroleum (553 *yuan*, or $101), chemicals (487 *yuan*, or $89), textile (373 *yuan*, or $68), light industries (367 *yuan*, or $67), construction materials (304 *yuan*, or $55), and coal (73 *yuan*, or $13) (Liu and Xu 1991, p. 359). Because retained profits determine bonus funds, it is not surprising that bonus rates differ among industries and enterprises.

Government Agencies

Bonuses entered the economic system of government agencies as a completely new phenomenon in 1978. Bonus rates, types of bonuses, and distributive strategies for all levels of government agencies are subject to centrally imposed regulations. A year-end bonus was implemented by the central government in 1978. Bonuses ranged from five to ten *yuan* a month, or about 1–2 percent of the annual wage of an average government employee in that year. Officials with a civil-service rank of 17 (i.e., a department chair) and higher were denied the year-end bonus because they earned higher salaries. Since 1985, bonuses have become a component of the "structural wage" for employees in government agencies and not-for-profit institutions. By 1986, an annual bonus rate equivalent to no more than one month's average salary was set by the central government. This bonus rate increased to one and a half month's average salary in 1988.

Not-for-Profit Institutions

These institutions, like government agencies, began to use bonuses in 1978. In 1979, a new "total budget system" was implemented, in which institutions negotiated with government authorities for total budgets for wages and expenditures on a yearly basis. Surplus obtained from monthly and year-end balance sheets are retained by institutions and can be used in the form of bonuses. Institutions are also allowed to organize their employees to engage in income-oriented activities upon completion of contracted missions with the government. Earnings made through these activities are additional bonus funds. Despite centrally imposed regulations for the maximum annual bonuses (e.g., equivalent to one month's basic wage for hospitals and schools, one and a half month's basic wage for scientific research institutes), bonuses tend to be higher for institutions that are able to generate bonus funds.[5]

Determinants of Salary and Bonus Distributions: Hypotheses

Salaries are income distributed to support the basic living standard of wage earners. The nature of salary distribution is bureaucratic or redistributive; salary standards and differentials are centrally
imposed, and salary increases are subject either to central regulations (for enterprises) or to the budget of the central government (for
other types of organizations). Bonuses, in contrast, are an incentive
wage. Enterprises and institutions have gained a great deal of autonomy by generating and distributing bonuses. How different are salary and bonus determinations because of the effects of workplace
and individual-level variables?

State Ownership Effects

Both salaries and bonuses are expected to be higher for state
workers than for collective workers. Salary discrepancies between
workers in the two sectors occur because of a government bias in
favor of the state sector. The basic mechanism for this bias is that
salary standards are higher for state workers than for collective
workers, even within the same occupation and industry (Li 1990, p.
117). Bonus disparities between the two sectors, however, are associated with the state sector's penetration of commodity markets.
State enterprises continue to base a certain portion of their production on mandatory state quotas (Walder 1989), and receive more
supplies from the government at low state-fixed prices than do collective enterprises. State enterprises also generate bonus funds by
selling surplus supplies, transferring state projects, and providing
technology and skills to less powerful collective enterprises at higher market negotiated prices (Walder 1987). As a result, there may be
greater variations in bonuses than in salaries between state and collective enterprises.

Bureaucratic Rank Effects

The higher rank a work unit has, the stronger influence the
unit has on government decisions. Since vertical relations with the
government have remained important both before and after reform,
workplaces with a higher bureaucratic rank have been favored during both periods. Salary standards are higher for organizations with
higher ranks (Li 1990). Even during the third wage reform in 1985,
the central government demanded that wage differentials be maintained among enterprises that are managed by different levels of
governments. This suggests that salaries may be higher for workers

in organizations with higher bureaucratic ranks. Intensified bargaining over profit retention, price subsidies, and special state funding (Liu and Xu 1991, p. 366) have signified the importance of a workplace's bureaucratic rank in generating bonus funds. Therefore, the rank variable is expected to have greater effects on bonuses than on salaries.

Industry Effects

Although vertical relations with government bureaucracy affect the level of retained profits for those enterprises in industrial, commercial, and service sectors, the enterprises themselves decide how to distribute bonuses. The direct relationship between retained profits and bonus funds stimulate these enterprises to produce more bonuses than not-for-profit institutions in educational and non-educational sectors, whose bonus funds are generated in part from the redistribution of state-retained profits and in part from earnings made through their noncontractual activities. Government agencies are prohibited from organizing their employees (government bureaucrats) to engage in income-oriented activities, and thus rely on state-retained profits for bonuses. The distribution of bonuses in these agencies remains exclusively redistributive (Liu and Xu 1991, p. 358). This industry variable is expected to have a reverse effect on salaries: government bureaucrats would have the highest salaries, followed by employees in not-for-profit institutions, and workers in enterprises would have the lowest average salaries. However, the industry-salary relation may be spurious because of the strong association between the strategic functions of industries and occupations (the primary criteria for salary distribution).

Size Effects

A positive association is expected between workplace size and salaries. The effect of workplace size on bonuses appears mixed, however. Small enterprises, because they obtain fewer projects within the state plan, make greater use of markets. According to market-transition theory (Nee 1989), this would imply more opportunities to generate bonus funds. But then large enterprises are more likely to receive state projects and supplies at a low state-fixed price. When, as observed by Walder (1987), they sell surplus supplies at a market price or transfer state projects to small enterprises and receive high "processing fees," large enterprises are able to penetrate the market and generate more bonuses.

Human Resource Effects

Human resource variables play a significant role in the distribution of bonuses and salaries. Because a worker's performance is more important for bonus increases than for salary raises, educational credentials (a determinant of ability and performance) should generate higher returns for bonuses than for salaries. In addition, despite the overall reduction of income inequality during market reforms in urban China (Walder 1990), gender inequalities may have been sustained and perhaps even increased after central control of the labor structure was partially relaxed (Honig and Hershatter 1988; Bian 1990; Lin and Bian 1991). If this is true, male-female gaps will be greater in bonuses than in salaries.

The destratification hypothesis, which has been proposed for Eastern Europe (Szelenyi 1978) and for rural-urban discrepancies in China (Whyte 1986),[6] may be useful in explaining the reduced income gaps between more experienced and less experienced workers. The seniority rule has been used as a predominant determinant of basic wages (Davis-Friedmann 1985; Hu, Li, and Shi 1988; Walder 1990), but this rule is challenged by data on the distribution of bonuses during reform in China (Walder 1987). The relation between work experience and bonuses may not be as positive as it is between work experience and salaries.

Social-Political Status Effects

Party membership is a political resource that would be expected to generate bonuses and salaries. "Party clientelism" theory (Walder 1986) would imply a stronger relation between party membership and bonuses than that between party membership and salaries, provided that workplace party cadres have power to distribute bonuses directly to their political loyalists. If, however, technical managers who are less politically oriented hold the power to distribute bonuses, as documented in Walder's (1989) recent study, party members may not be specially favored. Occupation, which has been a primary criterion of the Chinese wage system both before and after reform (Korzec and Whyte 1981; Li 1991), will be used as a control variable in the analysis of salaries. Occupation may be considered an indicator of worker power in the analysis of bonuses. This would be particularly true for managerial and administrative cadres who are redistributors of bonuses, and, to a lesser degree, for clerical workers who have day-to-day contacts with these cadres.

Interaction Effects

The management-as-redistributor thesis (see Chapter 1) predicts that in industries in which bonuses are generated from retained profits, workplace party cadres and managers become redistributors of bonuses. Such an interactive effect would be significantly reduced if bonus funds were made available through a centrally imposed redistributive process. Therefore, administrative and managerial cadres in government agencies and not-for-profit institutions are expected to have lower bonuses than their counterparts in industrial, commercial, and service sectors. Such cadre-workplace interactive effects may not exist for salaries when the distribution is a function of central control.

Wage Differentials: Aggregate Data

A 1985 Chinese industry census provides a fruitful source of aggregate data on wage differentials by industry, ownership, bureaucratic hierarchy, and establishment size. This is the most up-to-date and comprehensive data set on the Chinese industrial structure. The analysis here is based only on the available reported official statistics rather than the original data set. Salaries and bonuses were not separated in these reports, nor were individual-level variables such as sex, years of work, education, occupation, and party membership included. Nevertheless, these official statistics do provide a valuable opportunity to analyze the wage structure as a function of workplace segmentation at the national level.

Wage Differentials by Industry

The first section of Table 7.6 presents average wages and differential indexes by industrial sectors for 1980 and 1985.[7] For both years, the top-paid sectors were industries of construction, resources exploration, transportation, postage service, and electricity. Not surprisingly, the lowest-paid sector was the agricultural industry. Commerce and service sectors combined were the second-lowest paid industries. Government agencies, industrial enterprises, and science, culture, education, and health are in the middle. Within the industrial sector, significant wage differentials existed between heavy industries and light industries, and these differentials were consistent in both 1980 and 1985. These data lend support to our analysis about wage policies.

A considerable increase in the overall discrepancy in wage differentials was observed, however. The range of wage differential indexes increased from 32 percentage points in 1980 to 40 percentage points in 1985. A comparison between light industries and heavy industries reveals an increase of wage differentials from 1:1.16 in 1980 to 1:1.22 in 1985. At the industry level, therefore, economic and wage reforms in the first half of the 1980s did not decrease wage inequalities but, on the contrary, reinforced them. The hypothesis that market reforms reduce social inequalities in state socialism (Szelenyi 1983, 1989; Whyte 1986) is not supported by the aggregate data from China, although it has been confirmed by individual-level data (Nee 1989; Walder 1990). The findings shown here lend support to my argument that industrial sectors with government priorities in the pre-reform periods continued to do well during the course of partial reforms.

Wage Differentials by Ownership

Sections 2 to 5 in Table 7.6 are based on data from a national industrial census conducted by the State Council in 1986. This census covered all industrial enterprises, providing a valid and reliable data base on labor, wages, and other aspects of the industrial system. Unfortunately, labor and wage statistics of the same quality are not available for nonindustrial sectors. Thus, the analysis to be presented in the rest of the "aggregate data" section will focus on industrial enterprises only.

The second section of Table 7.6 presents average wages and differential indexes across five types of ownership in industry for 1980 and 1985. In 1980, state enterprises showed the highest average wage, followed by foreign-capital enterprises, the joint state-collective enterprises, collective enterprises, and other types of ownership (such as private, family businesses). The rank-order between the first two types of enterprises was reversed in 1985, but the rest remained unchanged. Wages of employees in foreign enterprises increased by 17 percent per year, and the average wage was nearly twice the total average in 1985. The number of employees increased from 6600 in 1980 to 78,100 in 1985, which was about 0.01 percent of the total industrial labor force. Higher wages in foreign-capital enterprises reflect the strategy of foreign capitalists to use wages to attract qualified workers.

The overall wage differential was larger in 1985 than in 1980. This was due largely to wage increases in foreign capital enterprises. The wage differential between state and collective enterprises, which absorbed 99 percent of the industrial labor force and accounted for the same percentage of the total wages in industry (Li

TABLE 7.6

Average Annual Wages by Structural Variables: 1980 and 1985
(unit = *yuan*)

	1985		1980	
	Average Annual Wage	Differential Index*	Average Annual Wage	Differential Index*
(1) By Industry*				
Total	974	100.0	762	100.0
Construction and re-sources expenditures	1173	120.4	871	114.3
Transportation and postal service	1092	112.1	841	110.4
Management agencies	988	101.4	801	105.1
Industrial enterprises	988	101.4	787	103.3
Heavy industries	1032	106.0	820	107.6
Light industries	846	86.9	708	92.9
Science, culture, education, and health	941	96.6	717	94.1
Commerce and service	864	88.7	690	90.6
Agriculture, forestry, water, weather	788	80.9	627	82.3
Others	989	101.5	749	98.3
Below: Industrial System Only***				
(2) By Ownership				
Total	1076	100.0	779	100.0
Foreign capital	2135	198.4	789	101.3
enterprises	1195	111.1	859	110.3
State enterprises	1091	101.4	748	96.0
State-collective joint ventures				
Collective enterprises	900	83.6	629	80.7
Other types	843	78.3	505	64.8
(3) By Bureaucratic Hierarchy (state and collective only)				
Total	1040	100.0	754	100.0
Central ministry	1358	130.6	942	124.9
Local governments	1147	110.3	834	110.6
County government	978	94.0	729	96.7
County collective	874	84.0	638	84.6
Urban street collective	915	88.0	592	78.5
Township collective	835	80.3	570	75.6

continued

TABLE 7.6 *continued*

	1985		1980	
	Average Annual Wage	Differential Index*	Average Annual Wage	Differential Index*
(4) *By Size of Constant Capital (in ten thousand yuan)*				
Total	1076	100.0	—	—
More than 100,000	1469	136.5	—	—
50,000–100,000	1449	134.7	—	—
10,000–50,000	1341	124.6	—	—
5000–10,000	1281	119.1	—	—
1000–5000	1193	110.9	—	—
500–1000	1120	104.1	—	—
400–500	1100	102.2	—	—
300–400	1077	100.1	—	—
200–300	1061	98.6	—	—
100–200	1015	94.3	—	—
50–100	948	88.1	—	—
10–50	837	77.8	—	—
Less than 10	724	67.3	—	—
(5) *By Number of Employees*				
Total	1076	100.0	—	—
More than 100,000	1463	136.0	—	—
50,000–100,000	1469	136.5	—	—
30,000–50,000	1406	130.7	—	—
10,000–30,000	1364	126.8	—	—
5000–10,000	1271	118.1	—	—
3000–5000	1218	113.2	—	—
1000–3000	1163	108.1	—	—
500–1000	1085	100.8	—	—
300–500	1028	95.5	—	—
100–300	928	86.2	—	—
Fewer than 100	799	74.3	—	—

*Calculated by dividing the average wage for the category by total average wage, multiplied by 100.
**Figures in the 1985 column are for 1984. Data for 1985 are not available.

Source: Yuan (1990), pp. 177–89.

1991, p. 152 and p. 168), revealed a 5 percentage-point decrease from 1:1.15 in 1980 to 1:1.10 in 1985. During this period, collective enterprises grew both in terms of labor (54 percent) and total wages (120 percent). The growth in the state sector was relatively moderate in labor (19 percent) and in wages (65 percent). The decrease of wage inequalities between the two ownership types within industry contrasts with the increase of overall wage differentials among the industrial sectors of the country (see the previous section). If market reforms sustain and increase wage differentials among industries, which has been shown in the first section of Table 7.6, they reduce wage differentials between state and collective enterprises. It is worth noting here that state employees still earned more than their collective counterparts after seven years of urban reform. Whether the relation of earnings between the two types of ownership will eventually be reversed remains to be seen in the 1990s.

Wage Differentials by Bureaucratic Hierarchy

The third section of Table 7.6 presents average wages and differential indexes by bureaucratic hierarchy. The bureaucratic hierarchy of an enterprise is determined by the level of the government that manages it. The data are limited to state and collective enterprises only. Foreign-capital enterprises and those in other economic sectors (private, family businesses) are considered by the Chinese leadership to be independent business entities, and do not fall under any level of government bureaucracy. It is unclear, however, why joint state-collective enterprises were not considered as an independent category in the official statistics. In reality, all the state-collective joint ventures are subject to a certain level of bureaucratic hierarchy in the government bureaucracy (Li 1991, p. 513).

Two broad levels of management are identified for state enterprises: central ministry and local government. Within the local government level, state enterprises can be managed by provincial/municipal government, city government, urban district government, or rural county government. Separate statistics on this last type were provided in the data. In addition, three levels of management are identified for collective enterprises from highest to lowest: county, urban street, and township.

In the state sector, the higher the rank in the hierarchy, the higher the average wage. This positive relationship was maintained and reinforced in the first half of the 1980s. Wage differential between local and central state enterprises increased from 1:1.13 in 1980 to 1:1.18 in 1985, gaining a 5 percentage-point increase. In the collective sector, the overall wage dispersion across levels of management remained unchanged over the six years. One change, however, was that urban street collectives, although ranked lower, were ahead of rural county collectives. This was the result of unequal production opportunities provided to benefit urban rather than rural areas.

Wage Differentials by Establishment Size

Sections 4 and 5 of Table 7.6 present average wages and differential indexes by two indicators of workplace size: constant capital and number of employees. Both indicators measure the size of inputs and not of outputs. Measures of outputs such as profits, output values, or productivity are not included in the official statistics. In addition, the data are limited to 1985 only, which prevents us from pursuing an historical comparison of size effects on wage differentials.

Overall, average wages were positively associated with both constant capital and number of employees. The average wage in enterprises with more than 1 billion *yuan* (about $180 million) of constant capital is twice that of enterprises with less than 100,000 *yuan* of constant capital. The average wage in enterprises of more than 100,000 employees is 83 percent higher than in enterprises of fewer than one hundred employees.

Wage Attainment: Individual Data

Official government statistics analyzed in the previous section have shown wage differentials along all workplace variables under examination. How strongly do these variables affect the wage attainment of individuals? I contend here that individuals with the same qualifications but tied to different work settings will earn different levels of salaries and bonuses. We can now turn to the 1988 Tianjin survey for this type of analysis.

The two dependent variables are bonuses per month and monthly salary in a natural logarithm form. The average monthly salary is about eighty-five *yuan* ($15), which is higher than the seventy-five *yuan* obtained from a 1985 Tianjin sample (Lin and Bian 1991) and eighty *yuan* ($14) from another Tianjin sample in 1986 (Walder 1990). These figures reveal an average 4.4 percent annual increase in Tianjin workers' salaries from 1985 to 1988. The average bonuses per month, a measure obtained by adding the monthly bonuses and year-end bonuses divided by twelve months, is 25.3 *yuan*

TABLE 7.7

Metric Regression Coefficients of Workplace and Individual Variables on Bonuses and Salaries (N = 877)

Predictors	Bonuses			Salaries		
	(I)	(II)	(III)	(I)	(II)	(III)
Workplace Variables						
State-owned	.50***	.45***	.48***	.17***	.08***	.08***
	(.13)	(.13)	(.13)	(.03)	(.02)	(.02)
Bureaucratic rank	.13**	.10*	.10*	.03**	.02*	.02*
	(.05)	(.05)	(.05)	(.01)	(.01)	(.01)
Industrial enterprise	.31**	.25*	.24*	.11***	.05*	.03
	(.12)	(.12)	(.12)	(.03)	(.02)	(.04)
Noneducational institutions	.19	.06	-.01	.19***	.09***	.03
	(.17)	(.18)	(.24)	(.04)	(.03)	(.04)
Educational institutions	.06	-.21	-.06	.24***	.11**	.08
	(.20)	(.21)	(.29)	(.04)	(.04)	(.05)
Government agencies	-.74*	-.83*	-1.03**	.33***	.17**	.07
	(.33)	(.33)	(.38)	(.07)	(.06)	(.06)
Size	-.01	-.01	-.01	.01	.01	.01
	(.04)	(.04)	(.04)	(.01)	(.01)	(.01)

Individual Characteristics

Sex (male = 1)	.54***	.49***	.09***	.04*
	(.10)	(.10)	(.02)	(.02)
Years of work	-.02***	-.03***	.01***	.01***
	(.00)	(.00)	(.00)	(.00)
Middle school	.39*	.32*	.08**	.07**
	(.15)	(.15)	(.03)	(.03)
High/technical school	.53***	.36*	.07*	.06*
	(.16)	(.17)	(.03)	(.03)
College and higher	.62***	.41*	.23***	.12***
	(.19)	(.20)	(.03)	(.04)
Communist party member		-.05		.04*
		(.15)		(.02)
Skilled worker		.19		.02
		(.23)		(.02)
Clerical and technical		.17		.07*
		(.15)		(.03)
Professional		.20		.18***
		(.22)		(.04)
Administrative and managerial		.78***		.12***
		(.17)		(.03)
Constant	1.66	4.05	3.76	3.80
R squared	.05	.15	.45	.48

*p < .05, **p < .01, ***p < .001. Standard errors in parentheses. Both bonuses and salaries are in a natural logarithm form.

($4.60), or less than one-third of regular monthly salary. This ratio is consistent with those reported for other Tianjin samples (Walder 1990; Lin and Bian 1991). Overall, there is greater inequality in bonuses, whose coefficient of variation is over one (26.7/25.3 = 1.06), than for salaries (31.6/84.6 = 0.37). This was not predicted by the equalization hypothesis, which refers to market reforms in state socialism (Szelenyi 1978; Whyte 1986).

Individual-level predictors include sex (55.6 percent males), years of work (average is 21.2 years), education (elementary school or lower, 14.9 percent; junior-high school, 31.1 percent; high school or technical school, 33.9 percent; college and above, 20.1 percent), occupation (unskilled manual, 24.4 percent; skilled manual, 32.3 percent; clerical and technical, 21.1 percent; professionals, 8.0 percent; and administrative and managerial cadres, 14.3 percent), and party membership (20.9 percent).[8]

Four variables are used for work-unit status. Ownership is a dichotomous variable, with state-owned work unit being coded "1" (78.1 percent) and others "0" (21.9 percent). Bureaucratic rank is an ordinal measure, with five ranks ranging from lower to higher: section (15.7 percent), department (27.4 percent), division (26.7 percent), bureau (27.0 percent), and higher (3.2 percent).[9] Four dummy variables are used for industry. These dummy variables are: industrial enterprises (50.5 percent), educational institutions (9.8 percent), noneducational institutions (14.9 percent), and government agencies (2.7 percent). The omitted category is commerce and service sectors (22.0 percent). Workplace size is measured by the number of employees, with seven categories: 50 or fewer employees (5.1 percent), 51 to 100 (4.6 percent), 101 to 500 (30.3 percent), 501 to 1000 (21.9 percent), 1001 to 3000 (26.2 percent), 3001 to 5000 (5.2 percent), and more than 5000 employees (6.6 percent).[10]

Three ordinary-least-squared regression equations are estimated for (ln) bonuses and (ln) salaries each. The results are presented in Table 7.7. The three-step analysis begins with Equation I, in which only work-unit predictors are used. From this "organizational" model, I gained information about the total effects of each of the work-unit variables on bonuses and salaries, respectively. The independent and direct effects of work-unit variables on the dependent variables are further estimated in Equation II, in which sex, years of work, and education are incorporated, and still further estimated in Equation III, in which party membership and occupational status are finally considered.[11]

Effects of State Ownership and Bureaucratic Rank

State ownership and bureaucratic rank are significant predictors of both bonuses and salaries. This is so even after individual-level variables are statistically controlled for. As hypothesized, the magnitudes of the coefficients of the two work-unit variables are considerably larger in the bonus model than in the salary model, suggesting that state ownership and bureaucratic rank generate greater monetary values for one's bonuses than for one's salary. For example, based on results from the third equation, a natural log difference of .48 for state-owned work units means that, with other things being held constant, a state worker would have 1.62 (the antinatural log) times as much bonus pay as a collective worker has; if a collective worker receives the sample average of 25.3 *yuan* ($4.60) bonus pay per month, a state worker would earn a bonus pay of 41.0 *yuan* ($7.50) per month, yielding a 15.7 *yuan* ($2.90) difference. In contrast, the same state worker would increase his or her monthly salary by only 1.08 times as much as the collective worker would earn; if the collective worker earns the sample average salary of 84.6 *yuan* ($15.40) a month, the state worker would earn a monthly salary of 91.4 *yuan* ($16.60), yielding a 6.8 *yuan* ($1.20) difference. Clearly, sector discrepancy in bonuses is substantially greater than in salaries. Similar calculations could be provided here to show differential effects of the rank variable on bonuses and salaries.

The Industry and Size Effects

The dummy variables for industry produce both expected and unexpected findings. Salaries are associated with strategic functions of industries, as shown by the first equation. The strong associations diminish after party membership and occupational status are added to the estimation (the third equation). This means that the effects of industries on salaries are only indirect, especially for clerical, technical, professional, and administrative/managerial occupations, which are concentrated in government agencies and in educational and noneducational institutions. This is not surprising. But it is unexpected that industrial workers do not have significantly higher wages than workers in the commercial and service sectors, as has been previously documented (Li 1990, p. 255). Findings on bonuses, however, are as expected. Compared with the commerce and service sectors (omitted category), bonuses are significantly higher in industrial enterprises and lower in government agencies. Bonuses in educational and non-educational institutions are comparable to the commerce and service sectors, implying that there are higher bonuses in the not-for-profit institutions than in government agencies. These expected relations remain significant after individual-level variables are added to the model. Clearly, segmentation by industry in relation to bonuses favors the direct producers and does not favor government bureaucracies.

Neither bonuses nor salaries are affected by workplace size. This is an unexpected finding.[12] A strong size effect on total earnings was reported for Polish urban workers (Domanski 1988, 1990). Size variable is also a significant predictor of earnings in all studies in the United States cited in this paper. This reduced or noneffect of workplace size on salaries and bonuses in China needs to be examined in future research.

Effects of Gender and Human Resource Variables

Males earn both higher salaries and higher bonuses than females. As hypothesized, bonus discrepancy between the sexes is considerably greater in bonuses than in salaries (.49 versus .04). To illustrate the point, a male worker would earn 1.63 times as much bonus pay as a female worker earns, with other qualifications being held constant, but the same male worker would earn only 1.02 times as much salary as the female worker would earn. Gender inequalities have indeed been enlarged in bonuses as compared to salaries.

Work experience affects salaries positively and bonuses negatively. This is an expected finding. Just as seniority is a favorable rule in the redistributive process of salary determination, younger workers are motivated to perform better in order to receive bonuses.

Bonus returns for education are greater than salary returns. Based on the results from the third equation, if workers with an education lower than middle school (the omitted category) earn the sample average bonus per month of 25.3 yuan ($4.60) and the sample average monthly salary of 84.6 yuan ($15.40), middle schoolers would earn 34.7 yuan ($6.30) bonus pay and 90.5 yuan ($16.50) salaries, which yield 37 and 7 percentage point differences, respectively (anti-logarithm of 1.37 for b = .32 for bonuses and anti-ln of 1.07 for b = .07 for salaries). College graduates would earn 38.2 yuan ($6.90) in bonuses and 95.4 yuan ($17.30) salaries, which yield 51 percentage points and 13 percentage points difference, respectively (anti-ln of 1.51 for b = .41 for bonuses and anti-ln of 1.13 for b = .12 for

TABLE 7.8

Metric Regression Coefficients of Interaction Terms
on Bonuses and Salaries

Predictors	Bonuses	Salaries
Industrial enterprise	.23*	.03
	(.12)	(.05)
Noneducational institutions	−.09	.03
	(.24)	(.05)
Educational institutions	−.26	.08
	(.31)	(.06)
Government agency	−1.19*	−.01
	(.49)	(.08)
Administrative and managerial cadre	.83***	.11**
	(.20)	(.04)
Cadre × Industrial enterprise	.01	.02
	(.10)	(.08)
Cadre × Noneducational institution	−.59*	.01
	(.30)	(.06)
Cadre × Educational institution	−.95*	.02
	(.47)	(.11)
Cadre × Government agency	−1.23*	.08
	(.63)	(.12)
Constant	1.83	3.08
R squared	.16	.48

*p < .05, **p < .01, ***p < .001. Standard errors in parentheses. Both bonuses and salaries are in a natural logarithm form. Results that are not related to the interaction terms are not displayed.

salaries). These are substantial differences, even in absolute *yuan* terms.

Effects of Political and Occupational Variables

Party membership is not as closely associated with bonuses as it is with salaries. This is an unexpected finding for the "party clientelism" theory. The noneffect of party membership on bonuses may indicate the decline of party membership as a political power that can generate economic interests, because party members are no longer favored by technical managers who control the redistribution of bonuses within the workplace.[13] But party membership is a significant predictor of career promotions and political mobility (see

Chap. 6). As expected, clerical/technical workers and professionals have higher salaries than unskilled workers (omitted category), but, unexpectedly, do not earn substantially higher bonuses. In fact, bonus discrepancies occur primarily between cadres and noncadres.

There is greater return for cadre status in bonuses than in salaries. For example, if a worker earns the sample average bonus of 25.3 yuan ($4.60) and the sample average salary of 84.6 yuan ($15.40), a cadre would earn 55.2 yuan ($10.00) for bonuses (anti-ln of 2.18 for b = .78) and 95.6 yuan ($17.40) for salaries (anti-ln of 1.13 for b = .13), which yields about a 30-yuan ($5.50) difference for bonuses and 11 yuan ($2) difference for salaries. These results show that cadre-worker inequality has indeed been increased because of greater managerial power in the distribution of bonuses. To further confirm the cadre-as-redistributor hypothesis, interaction terms between cadre status and industry variables are incorporated in the model (Table 7.8). With the original independent predictors remaining significant, interaction terms produce expected findings. Whereas in general, government employees have significantly lower bonuses and industrial enterprise workers have significantly higher earnings than workers in the commerce and service sectors (omitted category), cadres in government agencies and educational and non-educational institutions reveal *additional* decreases in bonuses than cadres in the industrial, commercial, and service sectors. As expected, no interactive effects are found in the salary model.

Summary

The Chinese official statistics have shown wage differentials among workplaces in different industries, ownership sectors, levels of management, and establishment sizes at the national level. Wage differentials by industry increased from 1980 to 1985, whereas little change was revealed in wage discrepancies between workplaces in the state and collective sectors and at different levels of management.

The 1988 Tianjin survey has shown that wage reforms do indeed signify the effects of workplaces on the wage attainment of individuals. Specifically, both state ownership and bureaucratic rank of workplaces have greater effects on bonuses than on salaries, confirming that workplace segmentation on the basis of political and organizational criteria has clearly been strengthened in the context of market reform. The shift from central control to enterprise autonomy, moreover, has altered the effects of strategic functions of workplaces on bonuses and salaries. Bureaucratic agencies that are favored in salary distribution have negative impacts on bonuses, and the direct producers that are not favored in salary determination show strong positive impacts on bonuses. This finding suggests a growth of economic rationalization in the distribution of labor rewards in China.

There is a greater gender difference in bonuses than in salaries. The mechanisms for this new source of gender inequality need to be examined. As expected, education is more strongly associated with bonuses than with salaries, suggesting that educational credentials, which are assumed to promote performance, have become a source of worker power in demanding rewards from shop-floor managers. Also, work experience is associated negatively with bonuses and positively with salaries. Although mechanisms that explain the reverse relationship need to be explored, I interpret this as a new pattern of labor-reward distribution that discounts traditional seniority rule.

The most interesting findings have been the greater inequality between cadres and ordinary workers in bonuses than in salaries, and the division between shop-floor managers and government bureaucrats. These unexpected findings from the perspective of the destratification hypothesis (Szelenyi 1978; Whyte 1986) can be explained by the management-as-redistributor thesis: the shift of redistributive power from a few government bureaucrats to a greater number of shop-floor party cadres and technical managers has resulted in a greater inequality between cadres and workers. Further, the shift of the redistributive process from the societal level to the workplace level has resulted in shop-floor management gaining redistributive power while government bureaucrats lose it.

Workplace size has no direct effect on wage attainment of individuals, even though the aggregate data show that it is associated with average wages. Research has shown that the size-wage relation exists in other state socialist societies, such as Poland (Domanski 1988), as well as in market capitalist countries, such as the United States (Kalleberg, Wallace, and Althauser 1981). Why workplace size has no effect on wage attainment of individuals in China needs to be studied.

8

COLLECTIVE CONSUMPTION

There is a popular expression in China, "*qiyie ban shehui,*" which can be translated as "enterprises run the society." It especially refers to the tendency of workplaces to offer a wide range of benefits, goods, and services to their employees and their families. These include housing, pension, medical insurance, medical facilities and services, nurseries, day-care centers, schools, technical training, libraries, recreational facilities, meal halls, barber shops, bath houses, and nursing homes. In a 1986 Tianjin survey, Walder (1990) found that almost 90 percent of his respondents worked in organizations that provided a health clinic, meal hall, and shower facilities, and almost all the respondents reported using these facilities. Two-thirds of the workplaces also provided infant nurseries and libraries, and close to half provided holiday travel, auditoriums, retail stores, and kindergartens. Except for those facilities that are used primarily by employees of a restricted age group (sports teams, nurseries, kindergartens), all facilities, when available, were used by a large majority of the respondents. The Chinese workplace can certainly be viewed as a microcosm of an urban community and welfare organization.

There are important social consequences for urban workplaces serving as urban communities or welfare organizations. One consequence is a structured dependence: the dependence of individuals on their workplaces for satisfaction of social needs, and the dependence of the socialist state on work organizations to control workers (Walder 1986, chap. 2). Another consequence is that workplace managers are oriented not only to being managers of economic enterprises but also leaders of urban communities; a factory director, for example, is responsible not only for employees' incomes, but also for their general welfare and the welfare of their dependents (Walder 1989). Still another result is its structured inequality of collective consumption: access to collective benefits, goods, and services is determined by one's place of employment. This last issue is the focus of the present chapter.

In the following pages I examine three forms of collective consumption: (1) employee insurance and benefits, (2) collective welfare programs, and (3) housing and community resources. The basic theoretical question here is to define the relationship between work-unit structure and collective consumption in planned economies. Because mechanisms that explain this relationship differ for different forms of collective consumption, I will describe and analyze these three forms of collective consumption separately.

Labor Insurance and Benefits

The labor insurance and welfare system is a national program that was established after the 1949 revolution. Under the former Nationalist government, workers were provided with very little insurance. Communists perceived this as a form of class exploitation (Li 1991). Thus, their new government announced its first version of the "Labor Insurance Regulation of the People's Republic of China" in 1951, and tried it out in several key industries. In January 1953, the regulation was revised to cover more industries, and insurance standards were raised. This 1953 version of labor insurance regulation was a comprehensive program, offering a wide range of insurance and welfare benefits to staff and workers in state-owned organizations. The regulation became a reference for nonstate organizations. Since 1953, only minor revisions have been made to raise the standard of insured benefits.

The regulation requires work organizations to provide insured benefits to their employees. Funding for insured benefits is a fixed portion of each work unit's wage budget. There is little difference in the insured benefits among organizations in the state sector. A greater variation exists between the state and nonstate organizations, and among work units within the nonstate sectors. Although detailed and complete statistics on labor insurance and benefits are not available at the national level, there exists an official estimate of insurance coverage in China's industrial (i.e., manufacturing and excavating) sector. In 1985, forty million employees in the industrial sector received benefits from the labor insurance regulation, which was 45 percent of the total industrial labor force (Yuan 1989, p. 196 and p. 528).

Chinese industrial workers who received benefits from the national insurance regulation included all the state employees (38.6

million) and 15 percent of the collective employees. This relatively smaller segment of the collective employees consisted of those who worked almost exclusively in enterprises managed by county or city district governments, or by higher levels of government. Most of the collective employees (a total of 13.6 million as of 1985), who worked in street and township collectives, joined another 27.9 million uninsured workers who worked in village workshops, cooperative businesses in the countryside, or as individual laborers in urban and nonurbanized areas.

In 1959, insured benefits were 15 percent of the total wage bill for China's urban labor force; this percentage increased to 25 percent in 1985, and is still on the rise (Yuan 1989, p. 197). Apparently, these nonwage incomes are important dimensions of workers' economic well-being. In order to understand these nonwage incomes, I summarize them into six types, as follows.

1. Health Insurance

Before 1984, state employees were provided full coverage for medical costs without premium charges. These employees' dependents (spouses and children who do not work) were provided 80–90 percent coverage (varying by industry and enterprise). Only a token registration fee was required for outpatient services, and this fee was waived for employees who used the outpatient services at their work units' hospitals or clinics.

This system of free medical care prior to 1984 benefited state employees and their families, but it also caused problems. One was a decline in the quality of service, caused by an uncontrollable increase in the number of patients. People with minor illnesses demanded major treatments, and many people with no illness at all requested treatments for psychosomatic illnesses. Another problem was waste of medical supplies. "Family pharmacy," the practice of storing up-to-date medicine in one's home for the convenience of family members, became very popular. These practices were in part responsible for a constant shortage of medical services and conventional medications.

By 1984, an "individual responsibility system" was created to overcome these difficulties. A common practice in Tianjin has been for each insured worker to be guaranteed a medical remittance of about eight to ten *yuan* a month (about $1.20–1.80, which is about 10 percent of an average monthly salary in Tianjin) if he or she does not visit the clinic or has no medical bills during the month. Those who did make clinic visits or incurred medical bills would not be given this remittance. Also, work units reimbursed only 80–90 percent of medical expenses for employees and 50 percent of those for their dependents. This policy encourages insured workers to eliminate unnecessary clinic visits. It also has the effect of contributing to wage differentials between state workers, who have the privilege of receiving a medical remittance, and collective workers, most of whom do not.

2. Pension

There are three categories of retirement: *tuixu* (retirement at the official retirement age), *lixu* (retirement plan for senior cadres), and *tuizhi* (early retirement because of illness). Each type of retirement provides a different set of pensions and benefits. *Tuixu* is the standard form of retirement. In this category, males retire at the age of sixty and females at the age of fifty. A retiree with ten years of work receives a monthly pension equivalent to 70 percent of his or her last monthly salary until death. The pension rate is higher with years of work accumulated, up to 100 percent of the base salary for a retiree with forty years of service. Retirees with the category of *tuixu* are guaranteed medical benefits but denied minor compensations such as cash allowances for bath and barber services.

The category of *lixu* applies to aged officials who joined the revolutionary forces before October 1, 1949, China's National Day. Retirees in this category are guaranteed a pension of 100 percent of their salaries and full benefits as employees. Staff and workers who have made "great contributions to the society" may be granted this status of retirement, which is an honor and incentive.

The third category, *tuizhi*, applies to staff and workers who retire before normal retirement age because of long-term illnesses. Persons who apply for *tuizhi* are required to have evidence from doctors and hospital officials of their inability to work. If the applicants are manual workers, they must obtain additional approval from the Labor Evaluation Committees in their workplaces. Retirees with the *tuizhi* status receive a pension of no more than 70 percent of their basic wage, and they continue to receive medical benefits.

3. Insurance for Injury, Disability, and Death

A wage payment is given to workers who are injured while on duty. Full salary is guaranteed for the first six months after an accident, then reduced to 60 percent while on sick leave after the first six months. The days lost to work injuries are still counted toward years of employment. This policy protects injured or disabled workers so that they will still receive a retirement pension equivalent to that of other workers who entered the labor force in the same year. In addition, injured and disabled persons are given a 10–30 percent higher pension to compensate for any long-term costs of the accident.

Workers who die on the job are insured for full coverage of funeral and burial costs. A worker's dependents will receive monthly payments from the deceased person's work unit to maintain the previous living standard. These payments continue until they are no longer dependents. Both employees and retirees who die, but not on the job, are also insured for full coverage of funeral and burial costs. Their families usually receive a single payment from the work unit approximately equal to the deceased's monthly salary.

4. Benefits for Women Workers

There are a set of special benefits available to women workers in China. All women employees are granted a day off with full pay on Women's Day (March 8). Pregnant women are assigned moderate duties and given only light work beyond the sixth month of pregnancy. Full pay is guaranteed for three month's maternity leave after delivery. Longer maternity leaves of up to three years are granted, depending on work units, and grantees can maintain 65 percent or higher portions of their salaries while on leave. When they return to work, these women can send their babies to the work unit's nursery, free of charge, and are allowed to breast-feed their babies in the nursery during work hours. Children can stay in free day-care programs in their mothers' workplaces until they enter school. When the mothers prefer nurseries or day-care centers outside their workplaces, they themselves must pay the bill. If, however, the workplaces do not have nursery or day-care programs (as in fact many do not), mothers are reimbursed for up to 75 percent of expenses for infant or child care. Since the "one couple for one child family" policy was instituted in 1979, children-related benefits are granted to the mothers (as well as their husbands) who comply with the government birth-control policy. Those who chose to have a second child are deprived of all these benefits.

5. Holidays, Sick Leave, and Leave of Absence

The Chinese work week is forty-eight hours (six work days a week). There are seven national holidays.[1] Workers with more than eight years of service are guaranteed full pay for up to six months of sick leave. During the first eight years of employment, workers receive 60 percent of their base salaries for sick leave. Leave of absence for personal reasons generally incurs a loss of pay. But manual workers are given the option to take leaves of absence in exchange for credits they have earned from overtime work. Office workers and officials do not have this option, but are allowed to take two days off during the month without loss of pay.

6. Other Benefits

Transportation allowances are provided to employees who live a long distance from the workplace. Allowances for barber and bathing services are provided to employees whose work units do not already offer these services. (Some work units continue to provide these cash allowances as an added benefit even after they added barber and bathing services. This is against regulation, however.) Financial aid for employees whose families encounter economic hardships can be available to applicants on a case-by-case basis. Compensation for winter heating costs are also provided to employees in the North. Married people who comply with the government policy of one child for one couple receive a "one-child allowance" of five *yuan* a month for fourteen years (half this allowance is from the husband's work unit and the other half from the wife's). Finally, a provision for food and price subsidies by the central administration or local governments is available through work organizations, as part of employees' monthly wages.

Insurance and Benefits in Nonstate Sectors

There is no national regulation for labor insurance and benefits for workers in the nonstate sectors. Table 8.1 summarizes information collected from several local documents and interviews with officials of several nonstate organizations in Tianjin. This information is by no means representative of the overall situation in Tianjin. Regional differences are also expected to occur between Tianjin and other areas of China. Nevertheless, Table 8.1 clearly indicates the differences in insured benefits between work organizations under different levels of government jurisdiction.

In general, workers in collective enterprises managed by municipal bureaus, urban district governments, and rural county governments receive about the same benefits as state sector workers, with several minor items of limited benefits. Workers in collective enterprises managed by urban subdistrict governments receive significantly reduced medical benefits and pensions, and further reduced cash allowances for other fringe benefits. Collectives managed by rural township governments receive more limited benefits on almost every item included. Finally, workers in village businesses, cooperatives, and family businesses receive none of the benefits.

Collective Welfare Programs and Subsidies

Collective welfare programs that are offered in urban workplaces include medical facilities (hospitals, clinics, and health-care centers), meal halls, bathing facilities (because few homes have showers and public bath houses are not numerous), barber shops, nurseries, day-care centers, recreational facilities (sports, movie and opera theaters, music, and performing arts), and libraries. There are also industry-sponsored schools (elementary, high, and technical schools and even colleges, which are for employees' children), nursing homes, and sanitariums. These are subsidized commodities and services.[2]

Sources of Funding

These collective welfare programs are not benefits mandated by the national labor insurance regulation. They are optional benefits that must be funded by each organization's "soft budget money." This soft budget money comes from several sources. One is the organization's profits (after taxes). Profit retention as a financial policy existed periodically between 1953 and 1965, and became standard after 1979. Regulated by government jurisdiction, a profit-making enterprise sets aside a portion of its retained profits for the funding of collective welfare facilities and benefits. Another source of soft budget money is earnings made through activities engaged in outside the state's plan, such as subcontracting with other firms, selling materials to rural township industries, and investing in collective units under the enterprise's jurisdiction. Additionally, revenues and material resources may be diverted from other uses, but still counted as a cost of production. For example, construction materials for building production may be diverted to housing for day-care centers. Finally, the fourth source is special funding provided by the government jurisdiction that manages the work organization. Although common in all types of organizations, this special funding

TABLE 8.1

Labor Insurance and Benefits for Workers in Nonstate Sectors

Item	Collectives by Municipal Bureau	Collectives by Urban District or Rural County	Collectives by Subdistrict Government	Collectives by Township Government	Village, Cooperative, and Private Sectors
1. Health insurance					
Employees	Same as state	Same as state	up to 75% coverage	50–70% coverage	none
Dependents	up to 50% coverage	up to 50% coverage	limited amount	limited amount	none
2. Pension as % of salary	60–90%	60–90%	60% fixed	vary, up to 60%	none
3. Injury, disability, and death benefits					
Injury	same as state	same as state	one-time limited payment	one-time limited payment	ask help from government
Disability	same as state	same as state	limited amount	limited amount	
Death	limited amount for funeral	limited amount for funeral	for funeral	for funeral	none

4. Benefits for women workers

3-month maternity leave	same as state	same as state	same as state	50% of salary	none
Longer maternity leave	same as state	none	none	none	none
Infant nursery allowance	limited amount	none	none	none	none
Day-care allowance	limited amount	none	none	none	none

5. Holiday, sick leave, and leave of absence benefits

Holiday	same as state	same as state	same as state	same as state	none
Sick leave	same as state	same as state	50% pay	limited pay	none
Leave of absence	same as state	same as state	no pay	no pay	none

6. Other benefits: limited | limited | none | none | none

Source: (1) "Regulations of Wage and Benefits for Tianjin Financial and Trade Industries." (2) "Jinghai County Grain Bureau Documents on Wages and Benefits." (3) Interviews with officials of five collective organizations (personal interviews 7, 18, 22, 24, 36).

for enterprises has declined since 1979, and retained profits have become the main source of funds for collective welfare programs.

Soft budget money for collective welfare programs and subsidies has figured as a consistent proportion of the total insurance and welfare budget. According to official statistics (Yuan 1989, p. 197), such funding in China's manufacturing and mining industries was 15–17 percent of the total insurance and welfare bill between 1978 and 1985. (More than 60 percent of the budget goes to pension and health insurance and benefits.) The funding increased from 513 million *yuan* in 1978 to 1835 millon *yuan* in 1985, revealing an average annual growth of 36.8 percent. This is three times the 11.7 percent of the growth for total wages.

Past studies have explored variations in the collective welfare programs and subsidies in the state and collective sectors, and have suggested that larger organizations with higher bureaucratic rank are able to provide more and better programs and benefits than smaller, less important organizations (Davis-Friedmann 1985; Whyte and Parish 1984; Walder 1986, chap. 2; Davis 1988, 1990). In his recent work, Walder (1992) offers a "fiscal structure" theory to explain why there is variation in the funding of collective welfare programs and subsidies among organizations with different "budgetary rank" and of different sizes.

Variations in the Funding of Collective Welfare Programs

Walder began his analysis with a conceptualization of property rights. "The hallmark of 'redistributive' economies is that no clear legal or substantive standards exist for determining the rights of enterprises to the earnings from capital invested out of public funds" (Walder 1992, p. 525). In "redistributive" economies, property and income rights of an organization are subject to the government jurisdiction that "owns" and manages it. The revenue base for any government jurisdiction is composed of revenue remitted by the jurisdictions below it and by revenue generated from enterprises over which it has property and income rights. The higher the level of government, the more sources of revenue there are, and the larger the budget will be. As a result, a government jurisdiction with a large budget tends to have a greater capacity to allow work organizations to retain "slack" resources. This pattern of property rights and revenue flows is referred to by Walder as the fiscal structure of the state.

The taxation and investment processes are a result of this fiscal structure of government jurisdictions and their subordinate work organizations. In redistributive economies, tax rates are tailored to each enterprise, and fiscal solvency is the only constraint on the redistributive activity of a government jurisdiction. A government jurisdiction with a large budget and many sources of revenue tends to soften tax assessments, and enterprises under it will retain substantial slack in their budgets, allowing them to fund the discretionary construction of facilities and provision of benefits. A government jurisdiction with a small budget and few sources of revenue tends to impose higher taxes on its subordinate enterprises, who thus have little funding for developing collective welfare programs and providing subsidies.

Similarly, investment finance is also a function of the fiscal structure: more capital investments are available to enterprises whose government jurisdictions have large budgets and many sources of revenue. When these capital investments are granted in the form of loans, which has been common in China since 1985, most enterprises are allowed to exempt or deduct their annual repayments (both principal and interest) from the income subject to taxation. Tax exemptions and deductions are more likely to be available in a higher level of government jurisdiction, because its larger budget permits a greater financial flexibility.

Why are government jurisdictions that have the financial ability to fund some organizations willing to do so? Walder specifies two mechanisms at work here. The first concerns the fiscal structure of work organizations. A government jurisdiction with a large budget and many firms has less incentive to extract revenue from any single firm than does a jurisdiction with a small budget and few firms, because it receives a smaller proportion of its revenues from each single firm. In addition, monitoring many firms is more costly. These fiscal structural mechanisms determine that high-level jurisdictions will have less incentive to extract revenues from their subordinate enterprises, who will consequently have more soft budget money (or "slack resources" in Walder's wording) for the funding of collective welfare programs and subsidies. A second mechanism is the dependence of government jurisdictions on enterprises for products and tax revenues. Resourceful enterprises, because of their particular products or large revenue contributions, can be favored in the taxation and investment processes. This mechanism determines that certain industries and large enterprises tend to have more soft budget money (or slack resources) to support collective welfare programs and subsidies.

TABLE 8.2

Collective Welfare Programs in State-Owned Industrial Enterprises, 1985

| | | Enterprises Managed by | |
| | Central | Local Governments | |
Item	Government	Total	County
Number of employees (in ten thou-sands)	8689.8	29,892.1	6608.7
Number of enterprises	3825.0	66,517.0	35,263.0
Average size of enterprises	2271.8	449.4	187.4
Per ten thousand employees			
1. Library books	36,488.7	25,307.8	14,277.7
2. Club space (square meter)	4758.1	2723.3	1615.1
3. Medical staff	192.2	97.2	42.0
4. Hospital beds	138.3	49.7	3.5
5. Sanitarium beds	13.4	3.5	0.6
6. Children in nursery and day care	739.0	555.1	341.0
7. Elementary-school students	1746.4	678.4	181.0
8. Middle-school students	1379.6	430.8	44.1
9. Technical-school students	164.3	75.7	2.2
10. Middle-level professional-school students	39.2	14.3	1.4
11. College students	63.4	20.6	1.1

Source: Yuan (1989), pp. 202–3.

Aggregate Data on Enterprise Welfare Programs

Systematic data at the level of organizations were unavailable on collective welfare programs and subsidies until China's industrial census of 1985.[3] The census data set is not accessible to researchers outside China, however. My analysis is based on tabulations published by Chinese authorities from this data source, and Table 8.2 displays a summary of these results.

The data include 70,342 state industrial enterprises. These enterprises averaged 550 employees in 1985 (Yuan 1989, p. 528). "Industrial enterprises" as defined here are equivalent to manufacturing and mining industries in the United States. In 1985, China's industrial sector comprised 45 percent of the total urban labor force, and was responsible for 70 percent of both the gross output values and income in nonagricultural industries (State Statistical Bureau of China 1989, p. 32). The industrial sector is the core economic sector in terms of national revenues. Within this sector in 1985, state enterprises accounted for 41.1 percent of the industrial labor, 63.5 percent of the gross industrial output values, and 74.6 percent of the industrial capital. Collective industrial enterprises (by urban districts, rural counties, and townships), state-collective joint ventures, and firms with foreign capital investment are not included in the table. These nonstate establishments totaled 288,359. Numerous village, cooperative, and family businesses are also excluded. Few of these nonstate industrial enterprises have comprehensive collective welfare programs and subsidies as state industrial enterprises do.

Eleven collective welfare programs are listed in the summary. The higher the level of government, the more extensive and inclusive is the collective welfare program in the state enterprise. As shown in Table 8.2, enterprise size is positively correlated with the level of government that manages the enterprise. Enterprises managed by the central government averaged 2272 employees, those by local governments averaged about 449 employees, and those by county governments averaged 187 employees. Because of this relationship, the data presented in Table 8.2 also support Walder's resource dependence thesis: that enterprises with greater capacity (because of their larger size) will be able to develop more welfare programs. More definite conclusions could be drawn if a raw data set were analyzed, and a multivariate analysis would show the independent effects of bureaucratic position and size of enterprises on indicators of collective welfare programs.

Housing and Community Resources

The final form of collective consumption I examine in this chapter is housing and community resources. In market societies, home and living location are treated largely as commodities. Access to a particular kind of housing or community is predicted by an individual's demographic and social-class background. Past studies in Eastern Europe and China, on the other hand, have identified similar outcomes in socialist societies. Despite an egalitarian ideal that treats housing as welfare rather than a commodity, inequalities in housing and neighborhoods have been generated by their "redistributive" process of resource allocation, which favors government bureaucrats and high-ranking intellectuals who have the power to allocate resources and the privilege to enjoy them (for Eastern Europe, see Szelenyi 1978, 1983; Hegedus and Tosics 1983; Misztal and Misztal 1986; Ciechocinska 1987; Hegedus 1987; Musil 1987; for

China, see Howe 1968; Parish 1984; Whyte and Parish 1984; Lee 1988; Davis 1990).

A unique feature in the residential process in China, which has not yet been examined with sufficient attention, is that the funding for public housing is retained and invested by work organizations. Workers depend on their work units for public apartments. My analysis will focus on this organizational dimension of the residential process.

Private and Public Housing in Urban China

In urban China there are three general types of housing: (1) private housing, (2) work-unit housing, and (3) municipal public housing. The last two types are public. Proportions of the three types in Tianjin in the early 1980s were 16 percent, 38 percent, and 46 percent, respectively (Gu et al. 1984, pp. 374–75). The proportions for the last two public types were expected to grow through the late 1980s, because housing investment has become heavily public. Nationally, between 1949 and 1987, 95 percent of the housing investment was from public funding and only 5 percent was privately funded (Sun, Chen, and Li 1991, p. 7).

Private housing in China has experienced a dramatic decline since 1949. In the 1950s, at the time of the state's takeover of private firms, surplus private housing was turned over to the government (Whyte and Parish 1984, p. 77). Selling or leasing of houses by individuals was criticized as being capitalistic, and was therefore restricted, if not prohibited. The remaining privately owned houses were passed down from one generation to the next within a family (Howe 1968). The national policy on private housing finally changed during the reforms of the 1980s. Some housing units were built by the state for sale in the market place, in support of their goal toward commercialization of housing (Lee 1988). But few families are able to buy a house. In Tianjin, for example, an apartment of modest size and quality with sixty square meters of built area cost about 100,000 yuan (about $18,000) (Chaichian 1990), or about seventy-five years of income for an average wage earner in 1988 (Bian 1990).

Work-unit (public) housing compounds are built by work organizations, and units are distributed to employees. In Tianjin, enterprises with more than 1000 employees and high-ranking institutions and agencies usually own work-unit housing compounds. In these compounds, neighbors tend to be work colleagues. Middle-size and small enterprises and low-ranking institutions and agencies that lack the capacity to build these work-unit housing compounds can participate in municipal housing projects. Also, to avoid the problems associated with managing their own work-unit housing construction and management, many large enterprises and high-ranking organizations may participate in municipal housing projects. In the distribution of these units, work organizations are grouped according to the government jurisdictions that manage them, and organizations under the same government jurisdiction are expected to get housing units in the same building complex, the same block, or the same neighborhood, consisting of several adjacent blocks. Therefore, employees whose work units are under the same government jurisdiction tend to live nearby one another.

Most work units do not necessarily have housing units in a single location (neighborhood). Universities are the exception; many build housing compounds on their campuses. Other organizations must apply to local governments for land distribution, and will be allocated noncontinuous locations for housing projects if plans are submitted in different years. Similarly, if work organizations participate in municipal housing projects, they receive housing units in different locations from the projects carried out in different years. In Tianjin, work organizations have on average three locations in which they own housing units.

The Funding of Public Housing

In China, public housing has been considered an aspect of employee welfare rather than a commodity. Correspondingly, in state planning housing investment is considered funding for consumption rather than for production. As welfare, housing subsidies have been high and public rents have been extremely low. According to a national survey, public rent per month was 1.1 percent of an average household's monthly expenditure in 1985. Expenses on housing were less than 2 percent of the income of an average wage earner, which differs sharply from the United States (16 percent), Japan (16 percent), and industrial countries in western and northern Europe (11–18 percent). It is also lower than those in the former Soviet Union (4 percent), Hungary (5.5 percent), and Bulgaria (7.5 percent) (Sun, Chen, and Li 1991, p. 14).

Funding for Housing in Enterprises. Funding for housing in profit-making enterprises is raised by retaining a portion of profits (after taxes). In practice, an enterprise is likely to make a bank loan for housing investment and pay interest and principal from its profits. To do so, the enterprise must acquire permission from its government jurisdiction and apply to the local branch of the Construction Bank of China, which is designated as the bank that evaluates housing-loan applications for the government. Government permission is granted with deference to the preferences of state bureaucrats, whose interests will vary according to the importance of the enterprise in terms of its products and revenue contributions. Network relations between government decision makers and managers of the enterprise also play an important part, particularly when the government jurisdiction is likely to receive benefits from the enterprise. One direct benefit that occurs is the promise of some of the enterprise's new apartments to the government jurisdiction, or to government officials or staff who are in charge of evaluating the housing-loan application.

However, government permission does not guarantee a loan, unless it is for production within the state's plan. Loans are granted based on the ability to pay interest and principal to the bank within a short term (three to five years). Profitability and credit history are two critical indicators used by the bank to evaluate enterprises, but those criteria are not as "scientific" as may be supposed. "Social" factors are involved in the process. According to several factory directors I interviewed, they report on factors that contribute to their success: pressure from government officials, enterprise managers' personal connections with bank loan directors, correct treatment of bank loan officers during inspections, and willingness of the enterprise to provide "some" apartment units to the bank.

In addition to bank loans, enterprises also collect housing funds from earnings made through "off-book" activities, such as subcontracting with other firms, selling used equipment, and transferring production projects.

Funding for Housing in Nonprofit Institutions. The major housing funds for nonprofit institutions come from local governments' budgets. Several factors affect the distribution of these funds. A first consideration is what proportion of local budgets can be reserved for housing funds. These budgets, of course, are subject to central and local policies. Because of the policy of "production first and consumption second," the Chinese government's housing investment decreased from 10.6 percent of the total construction budget in the early 1950s to 5.7 percent in the late Cultural Revolution period (1971–76). Following policy changes, the rate increased to 20 percent in 1980 and stayed at about 20–25 percent in the first half of the 1980s (Sun, Chen, and Li 1991, p. 7). It was during this period that the government invested in large housing projects. A second factor is the size of the housing budgets available at the successive levels of government jurisdiction. The higher the level of government jurisdiction, the larger the housing budget, and the greater the amount of housing funds distributed to the institution.

Within each government jurisdiction, institutions report to authorities to specify their need for housing. The number of employees who need housing, or who live in hardship conditions, and the number of housing units currently maintained by the institution are all considered in funding decisions. How do the government bureaucrats who control these housing funds evaluate the general status of an institution relative to others? Mr. Feng (personal interview 26), a university official, said:

> Administratively, our university is subject to the central government's Education Commission. We were ranked among the top ten universities in the country consecutively from 1979 to 1988, several times ranking among the top five. I said to the deputy commissioner who was in charge of budgets, "Look at the facts. We are again in the top ten. Our intellectuals work hard to put our university ahead of others, but many of them live in hardship conditions. We need money to build apartments. We won't be able to keep our professors motivated to work hard unless the commission provides them with better apartments, higher bonuses, and better welfare benefits." Of course, other university presidents said the same thing. But we were ranked higher, and deserved more support.

Housing funds also are derived from incomes accumulated by activities outside the state's plan. Research institutes and universities subcontract with profit-making enterprises, colleges open summer and night schools, cultural clubs organize special programs, and schools establish income-oriented workshops, to name a few such activities.

Funding for Housing in Government Agencies. Funding for housing in government agencies comes from local governments' housing budgets, whose distribution is similar to that for institutions. The key factor here is the level of government involved. Because higher levels of government have large budgets and many sources of revenue, they also have larger housing budgets than do lower levels of government.

There is one unique way that government agencies acquire housing units. It has become common for government jurisdictions to "skim off" apartments from the housing units controlled by their subordinate enterprises and institutions. The "skimming" activity usually takes place when a government jurisdiction grants housing-loan permission to its enterprises, or when it distributes housing funds to its institutions. Mr. Su (personal interview 13), director of the union organization in a state manufacturing factory, said:

> Our factory proposed to build a fifty-unit housing complex in 1982. It was the only housing proposal we ever submitted. In order to get bank loans, we needed permission from our company and the municipal bureau that has the jurisdiction over it. As it turned out, the company "skimmed off" two units, and the bureau demanded three. They were all two-bedroom units, rather than one-bedroom ones. We had to satisfy their demands; otherwise we would never have gotten permission for a bank loan application. But we did not let the workers know about it. It had to be done this way.

In sum, enterprises retain sales profits for housing funds, and those with higher retained profits are likely to raise housing funds. Institutions and agencies, on the other hand, do not have sales profits but rely on the government for housing funding. In this circumstance, their relationships with government jurisdiction become important for them to raise housing funds. In general, organizations under a higher level of government jurisdiction tend to collect more housing funds than organizations under a lower level of government, because a higher level of government tends to have a larger budget. Government jurisdictions tend also to have unique ways to raise funds for government officials' housing: "skimming off" apartment units controlled by their subordinate enterprises.

Work Organizations as Actors in the Public Housing Market

Every work organization in China has a housing budget. Its housing investments are not just oriented toward capital returns. Instead, public housing in China is a form of welfare in which public rents are subsidized by the workplace to compensate for low incomes. But there is a housing market: in particular, construction is determined by the availability of funds. Construction costs will also vary according to the materials used, building style (apartment buildings cost more than flat houses), and built-in facilities (e.g., kitchens and toilets). Finally, land values vary with the availability of public infrastructures (e.g., piped gas) and public services (e.g., schools, shopping facilities, and public parks). Work units must confront various decisions such as whether to provide fewer, high-quality units with good services, or more, lower-quality units in less attractive neighborhoods. As investors, work units are legitimately concerned with the efficient use of their housing funds.

Work-Unit Housing Markets. City land is owned and managed by the municipal government, whose planning includes land development and housing projects. Work organizations may initiate independent projects to build housing compounds in their territories, but their projects have to be incorporated into municipal housing plans and are subject to government evaluation and approval for the supply of construction material, infrastructure, and public facilities and services. After approval, work organizations must negotiate with specific government offices to arrange for the supply of water and utilities, the provision of a household registration service, public schools, nursery and day-care services, retail stores (grain station, grocery, breakfast stops), and other public facilities and services (cultural clubs, street parks, and gardens). Although there are standard procedures, the bureaucratic process can be very slow. In some cases, construction can be delayed at any given time for an insufficient supply of materials; or, newly built apartments may not be usable because there is no water or electricity;[4] or, employees may not be able to move into new apartments if the local police are not cooperative with household registration; or, residents may need to travel long distances to buy groceries if retail services are not provided in the neighborhood. When work organizations are willing to offer some of their new apartment units to government offices, however, these problems rarely, if ever, occur. In addition, work organizations are expected to provide funds for building infrastructures.

Many large organizations initiate projects to build housing compounds on city land. In these cases, they buy land from the municipal government. Land values vary in quality and quantity of infrastructure and services provided, or to be provided, by the municipal government. With a larger budget, a work organization can buy more or better land. But this is only the economic side of the land-assignment process. On the political side, land is priced by government bureaucrats on a case-by-case basis. There is no standard method of assessing land values. Work organizations can influence government assessments in a number of ways. They can seek to influence municipal leaders or offer benefits to government land assessors in return for a low price. They also can claim to be a special case and ask the municipal government to provide additional aid to finance a deal. After the land assignment is completed, work organizations face more similar situations and must use their social and political networks to solve further difficulties in planning their housing construction.

Municipal Housing Markets. The majority of work organizations do not, in fact, have sufficient budgets to build their own housing compounds. Numerous small establishments (stores, service stations, schools, cultural clubs, city bus routes, bank branches, etc.) have their housing funds managed by their government jurisdictions, and participate in municipal housing projects. Their government jurisdictions can buy municipal apartments by group or block, and distribute them by unit to the participant organizations. Many large organizations also will participate independently in municipal housing projects.

Municipal housing projects have been a predominant force in housing development in China's largest cities, including Tianjin. An earthquake in Tianjin in 1976 destroyed several neighborhoods and caused many houses to be categorized as "housing at risk." Between 1977 and 1990, with the central government's support, about thirty large areas on the periphery of the city were developed into residential areas, and a large number of inner-city neighborhoods were also reconstructed. Apartment units built in these areas had from one to three bedrooms, with running water and individual kitchen and toilet facilities. Housing quality also varies with the provision of piped gas, hot water, and radiator heating systems. Variation in the quality of public infrastructures, public facilities and services, and retail supplies exists from one neighborhood to another.

The distribution of municipal apartment units is both economic and redistributive. On the one hand, apartment units are priced according to the cost of construction and availability of public facilities and services in the neighborhoods. Thus, work organizations that have larger budgets can buy more or better units in pleasant neighborhoods. However, demand generally exceeds supply, which results in greater competition. Prices are fixed by the government and cannot determine who wins or loses in the competition. The mechanism at work is the power of the work organizations to influence government housing decision makers. Mr. Jiang (personal interview 29), a government official, commented:

How "close" is your work unit to the municipal housing office? That's important. Equally important is how close your

work-unit managers or party secretaries are to municipal housing officials. And you must find ways to convince them that
your work units deserve it: are you state-owned, so that your
work unit is entitled to government resources? Does your work
unit belong to a bureau that has the potential to influence top
figures in the government? What resources can your work units
provide to the municipal office in exchange for housing units?

In sum, the economic and political powers of work organizations will determine their position and success in the public-
housing market. One's access to housing and community resources
is thus conditioned by one's work unit. How characteristics of individual workers affect the distribution of housing and home locations is discussed in the following section.

The Internal Housing Market Within the Workplace

An urban resident who desires to live in a public apartment,
whether through the work unit or in a municipal housing project,
will be allocated an apartment by his or her work unit. The work
unit functions as a real-estate agent, receiving housing applications
and distributing apartments from the stock that it controls. Married
couples are eligible to apply. To avoid duplicate applications, nor-
mally male employees are the only applicants. There are a few ex-
ceptions, however. Divorced women with children, married women
whose husbands' workplaces are not in the same town, and wives
whose husbands turn over the application rights to them may apply
to their workplaces for an apartment. The last situation is likely to
occur when the wife has a better chance of getting an apartment
than her husband, or the wife's work unit offers better apartments or
better locations.

From the individual's perspective, housing allocation is a
queuing process. Work units establish point systems based on marital status, seniority, and other criteria by which all employees are
ranked. Most people are always in the queue, waiting for a better
combination of size, quality, and location. As they near the top of
the list, complex calculations may come into play. Is now the time
to have a child or to bring a daughter-in-law into the household?
Should one accept the current offer or hold out for a better one next
year? Should the husband or the wife apply? Despite housing shortages, there is considerable flexibility in the system, because work
units are continually adding to their housing stock every year, and
because people without housing are in competition with those who

simply wish to improve their position. Newly built apartments tend to have more space, better layouts, modern equipment, and better neighborhoods. Therefore, people often seek to turn in their old apartments for a new home. Even those with private housing may decide to exchange their dwelling for one allocated by the work unit.

Although housing is provided partly according to need, it may also be used by the work unit as a reward to employees. Stated another way, after such need factors as marital status and family size are statistically controlled, independent effects of socioeconomic and political status are expected to exist on access to neighborhood-level resources.

Szelenyi (1978, 1983) has advanced a redistributive hypothesis to explain housing inequalities in Eastern Europe. He argues that the redistributive economy favors a bureaucratic and intellectual class has the power to allocate resources and the privilege to enjoy them. I would expect this process to hold true in the distribution of housing units in the context of Chinese work units. Housing applications are influenced by one's current administrative or occupational position and by political and work-related performance, all of which are formally reported criteria, in addition to marital status and family size. These criteria are officially justified, and favor those who are involved in or influence decision-making processes of housing distribution and those who are technically more valuable to their work units than others. As one municipal official (Mr. Jiang, personal interview 29) commented,

> Work units do not get a lot of apartment units; they know they cannot. But they work hard to get at least a couple of nice units for their party secretaries, managers, chief engineers, model workers, and other valuable persons.

Workplace Variations in Housing Quality: Aggregate Data

Table 8.3 displays housing statistics from Beijing. As can be seen in the first three rows, families who live in work-unit rather than municipal housing have more living space, live in better-equipped apartment buildings rather than flat houses, and pay lower rents (which means they receive more housing subsidies from their work units). As mentioned previously, larger organizations are likely to build work-unit housing because they have the financial ability to do so. Thus, the comparison between work-unit housing and municipal housing indicates that working for large organizations enables

TABLE 8.3

Housing Type, Space, and Rent by Work Organization, Beijing, 1986

Source of Housing	Number of Neighborhoods*	Square Meters per Household	% Households Living in Apartment Buildings	Monthly Rent (*yuan*/square meter)	
				Apartment Building	Flat House
Total	746,013	23.52	32.38	.112	.111
Municipal housing	501,180	22.09	22.41	.125	.121
Work-unit housing	244,833	26.46	52.79	.100	.083
Central Jurisdiction					
University and college	21,860	30.65	72.32	.111	.097
Enterprise	47,675	25.02	66.02	.111	.052
Municipal Jurisdiction					
Enterprise	150,783	26.34	49.49	.092	.083
Institution	9427	25.12	36.53	.120	.105
Urban District or Rural County					
Enterprises and institutions	15,088	26.96	25.79	.117	.103

*Based on reports from 145 organizations. Unreported organizations own about 70 percent of the total work-unit housing stock (in terms of construction space).

Source: Sun, Chen, and Li (1991), p. 20.

employees to live in better-quality public apartments and at a lower cost.

A more complex picture is revealed by the data on work-unit housing in Beijing. Except for universities and colleges, the average housing space per household is about the same among work organizations under different levels of government jurisdiction. Significantly more housing space exists for universities and colleges, but this is because special housing projects were granted by the central government to leading national universities and colleges in Beijing in the mid-1980s. Better-equipped apartment buildings with large units were built in these special projects, which were an incentive for compensating high-ranking professors.

The percentage of households living in apartment buildings (rather than flat houses) is a good indicator of housing quality. Usually, apartment buildings have facilities such as running water, toilets, and kitchens in each unit. Families living in flat houses have to share running water and toilet facilities with their neighbors, and use a shared neighborhood yard to place stoves for cooking. Also, housing space for an apartment unit tends to be larger. As the data indicate, the percentage of households living in apartment buildings increases with the level of bureaucratic rank. Institutions and enterprises under central jurisdiction have higher proportions of families who live in apartment buildings (72.32% and 66.02%). These are followed by enterprises and institutions under municipal jurisdictions (49.49% and 36.53%). The district/county-managed work units have the smallest proportion of families living in apartment buildings (26.96%). The data clearly reveal the advantages of higher-ranked organizations in the housing market.

Rent by square meter (m^2) is an indicator of housing subsidies provided by work organizations. The lower the per-unit rent, the higher the housing subsidies. There are two patterns revealed by the Beijing data. First, the higher the bureaucratic rank, the lower the per-unit rent (implying higher subsidies). Per-unit rent of apartment buildings for organizations under central jurisdiction averages .111 yuan per square meter, compared to .092–.120 yuan for organizations under municipal bureaus and .117 yuan for organizations under district/county level of government. Similarly, per-unit rents of flat houses are negatively associated with the bureaucratic rank of an organization. Second, within the same level of government, enterprises provide more subsidies and charge lower rent than institutions do. For example, the rent of a flat house in central enterprises is about half that of central universities and colleges. And rents for both apartment units and flat houses are significantly lower in municipal enterprises than in municipal institutions. These data suggest that profit-making enterprises do have greater financial ability to subsidize employee housing than nonprofit institutions.

Inequality in Access to Community Resources: Individual Data[5]

Table 8.4 presents logistic regression equations that estimate variations in the availability of five types of public facilities and services in neighborhoods: piped gas, leading elementary schools, grocery stores, breakfast stops, and street parks. This analysis is focused on the impact of work organizations on the distribution of home locations. Data presented are from the 1988 Tianjin survey.[6]

Measuring Community Resources. (1) Piped gas. Piped gas is available to 78 percent of the sampled neighborhoods. Gas was first used as a heating material in Tianjin in the early 1970s. Priority in providing piped gas has been given to (a) new neighborhoods, (b) work-unit housing compounds whose residents' work units are willing to invest in the construction of gas pipes, and (c) residential areas being reconstructed according to the municipal government's plan. Organizations with the financial resources can get housing with piped gas through (a) and (b), and those with greater bargaining power can influence government to include their employees' neighborhoods in municipal plans. Whatever the mechanism, the bureaucratic rank of an organization is expected to affect the availability of piped gas to its employees.

(2) Leading elementary schools. Although elementary education is compulsory, the quality of elementary schools varies between officially recognized "leading" schools and others. The government provides leading schools with better-qualified faculty, more modern equipment, a stronger curriculum, more classroom space, and more extracurricular programs. There are two ways in which work organizations affect the school system. First, they provide resources to support school programs in the areas in which their employees live. Second, in newly developed housing compounds in which powerful organizations have apartment units, these organizations can influence government decisions to build schools with modern equipment and develop them into leading schools. In the 1988 Tianjin sample, 34 percent of the neighborhoods included leading elementary schools.

(3) Grocery stores. Most grocery services are provided by the municipal commercial bureau. Because public transportation is not

TABLE 8.4

Logit Coefficients of Access to Neighborhood-Based Resources, Tianjin, 1988

Dependent Variables

	(1) Piped Gas	(2) Leading School	(3) Grocery Store	(4) Breakfast Stop	(5) Park or Garden
Work-unit rank	1.080***	.620***	.727***	.336***	.657***
	(.191)	(.167)	(.163)	(.156)	(.158)
State agency	.771**	.512*	-.149	.215	.310
	(.314)	(.274)	(.261)	(.250)	(.257)
State enterprise	.196	.233	-.083	.229	.104
	(.212)	(.239)	(.205)	(.198)	(.218)
1000+ workers	.105	-.200	-.221	-.129	-.002
	(.192)	(.167)	(.164)	(.157)	(.158)
SES	.210***	.207***	.116**	.115**	.141***
	(.061)	(.051)	(.051)	(.049)	(.049)
Cadre	.457*	.414***	.416**	.539***	.547***
	(.252)	(.175)	(.199)	(.188)	(.172)

Monthly salary	-.004	.001	-.002	-.002	-.0003
	(.002)	(.002)	(.002)	(.002)	(.002)
Married	.001	1.150***	.118	.510	.628
	(.512)	(.572)	(.430)	(.410)	(.468)
Household size	-.003	.014	.026	-.004	-.010
	(.062)	(.055)	(.054)	(.052)	(.053)
Intercept	-.027	-3.519***	.033	-.626	-2.198***
	(.628)	(.673)	(.536)	(.512)	(.569)
Log-likelihood	890.58	1101.33	1128.03	1203.00	1185.25
Chi square	108.97	106.14	47.78	42.16	85.18

Notes:
(1) Standard errors are in parentheses. Numbers of cases are 938 and degrees of freedom are 9 for all equations.
(2) SES is an index created by adding standard scores of education to those of occupation.
(3) *p < .05, **p < .01, ***p < .001 (one-tailed test).

made available to all residential zones, most residents in Tianjin prefer to have grocery stores that are within walking distance. A work organization can affect the grocery service network in three ways. First, it can build a grocery store in its housing compound and then "lend" it to public grocery providers. Second, grocery stores are part of the collective infrastructure of newly developed neighborhoods. Work organizations with the financial ability can buy apartment units in these more costly housing compounds. Third, powerful organizations can influence the municipal commercial bureau to establish grocery services in the neighborhoods in which their employees live. In the 1988 Tianjin sample, grocery stores were available to 69 percent of the neighborhoods.

(4) Breakfast stops. Breakfast stops are similar to small cafes in the United States. It has been traditional for Tianjinese to go to these stops for breakfast on weekends. Workers also prefer to have quick breakfasts in these stops on weekdays. Therefore, it is convenient if they are close to one's home. The ways in which work organizations affect the breakfast provider network are similar to the ways they affect grocery services. In some cases, work organizations may open breakfast stops in their own housing compounds. Sixty-three percent of the sampled neighborhoods included breakfast stops.

(5) Street parks and gardens. Neighborhoods that are close to or surrounded by parks and gardens are very much preferred. Green woods, lakes, and flowers produce fresh air and beautify the environment, which is often very stark in most urban zones. Street parks and gardens are part of the infrastructure of the newly developed compounds. Work organizations can buy apartment units in these compounds when funds are available. Street parks and gardens are also available in a few old neighborhoods in which foreigners once lived before the Communist revolution. Housing in these areas has since been turned over to municipal government agencies and high-ranking organizations in Tianjin. Forty percent of the sampled neighborhoods included such public areas.

Results and Discussion. What is the most important predictor of access to a quality neighborhood? The Tianjin data show that the primary predictor is a dummy variable of the bureaucratic rank of one's work organization (the division rank = 1, and otherwise = 0). This rank variable strongly increases access to each of the five neighborhood resources. Take its effect on piped gas as an example. The logit coefficient is 1.08. It implies that if a person in a low-ranked

work unit had the average 77-percent probability of living in a neighborhood with piped gas, another person with equivalent characteristics, but working in a high-ranked firm, would have a 91-percent
probability—an advantage of fourteen percentage points. Or, in another example, the logit difference for schools (logit b = .62) implies
that a person with the average probability of living in a neighborhood with a leading elementary school (about 34 percent) would
gain an advantage of another fifteen percentage points, to 49 percent,
if he or she worked for a high-ranked firm. Clearly, these are substantial effects, and are significant after other work-unit variables
and individual-level variables are statistically controlled for.

Working in a state agency also improves the odds of having
access to piped gas and leading schools. "State agencies" in this
study refer to government offices and nonprofit institutions such as
educational and other academic entities. It appears that working in
these agencies affects access to exactly those facilities whose availability has been determined by these same agencies. That is, piped
gas is assigned by the municipal government to the neighborhoods
where governmental officials live, and leading schools are assigned
by authorities of the municipal education bureau to the neighborhoods where employees of educational and other academic institutions have homes. This demonstrates the "segmented" influence of
work organizations on the distribution of community resources.

Two individual-level predictors generate interesting results. As
indexed by education level and occupational status, social status
(SES) consistently affects access to community resources. These effects are much smaller than those of work-unit rank, but they are
nevertheless substantial. Another significant predictor is whether or
not one is a cadre. Cadres, as documented in Chapter 6, are administrative and managerial officials. The class of cadres is involved in the
decision-making process in all work organizations. In the logit equations, the cadre status is significantly associated with access to all
facilities. The significance of social status and cadre status in predicting the neighborhood resources supports the class elite
argument—the redistributive system favors the bureaucratic class
and its functional practitioners (highly educated and those in certain occupational groups) who have the power to allocate resources
and the privilege to enjoy them (Szelenyi 1978, 1983).

Wage is not significant in any equation. This is a very interesting finding. Although urban residents have differential access to
community resources according to the rank of their work organizations, their incomes do not alter this access. Thus, at the individual

level, housing can be defined as a welfare program and not a commodity. In Hungary, Poland, and Czechoslovakia, where data on housing have been reported (Szelenyi 1983), housing is a semicommodity. Private housing constitutes about half the urban housing market, with a spatial distribution that might be associated with price. Thus, income is associated with housing quality in Eastern Europe (Szelenyi 1983; Hegedus 1987; Ciechocinska 1987; Musil 1987). These comparisons seem to suggest that market forces had not emerged to coordinate urban housing in Tianjin by 1988, after a decade of economic reforms, because income simply could not "buy" residential locations in Tianjin.

Summary

In this chapter, I have examined three forms of collective consumption: employee insurance and benefits, collective welfare programs, and housing and community resources. I demonstrate that an individual's access to collective resources in China is *conditioned* by his or her work unit.

Differences in employee insurance and benefits exist primarily between economic sectors. The Chinese government has established national regulations to protect the welfare of the work force in the state sector. A minority of collective workers, who work in enterprises with high bureaucratic ranks and who are treated as semistate workers, are eligible to benefit partially from this national program. The majority of the urban work force—or, to be precise, the industrial labor force for which data are available for this study—has been left unprotected. Although the government's lack of financial resources explains to some extent why not all workers can be covered by the national insurance program, this argument cannot explain why state workers ought to be protected and not others. Political rationalization provides an explanation here. That is, the socialist state is oriented to "all-people" ownership, and workers in this type of state ownership group form the class base for the Communist party. It is a political choice to protect state workers with national legislation.

The distribution of collective welfare programs shows a similar pattern, but with a different explanatory variable. It is true that collective welfare programs are largely available in state work units, and that few collective firms offer these programs. Yet, the mechanism that explains the variation in collective welfare programs is different. There is no national regulation on their provision, and there is no government restriction on their provision in the collective firms. Funds for these programs are "soft money." Thus, the financial capability of work organizations is the key to understanding why these welfare programs are likely to be offered in more resourceful enterprises. It is for this reason I have applied Walder's (1992) fiscal structure model to analyze official statistical tabulation data on collective welfare programs.

Although the limited official data on China's state industrial enterprises prevent us from pursuing a more sophisticated multivariate analysis (i.e., to assess the independent effects of "budgetary rank" and workplace size on the provision of collective welfare programs), it clearly shows that the status quo of these programs is strongly associated with the level of government that has jurisdiction over an enterprise. That is, the higher the level of government jurisdiction, the better the collective welfare programs available to enterprises. These data testify to the usefulness of Walder's fiscal structure model in explaining the availability of "soft budget money" in the redistributive economy.

The final form of collective consumption is housing and community resources. Again, the focus has been to show the effect of work organizations on the distribution of collective goods and benefits. Public housing is distributed through work organizations, and the distribution of community resources—public facilities and shopping services—is affected by work organizations in various ways. Official statistics on housing data from Beijing demonstrate that three work-unit variables explain variations in housing quality: workplace size increases the odds that the organization can build its own housing compounds; bureaucratic rank or level of government jurisdiction is strongly associated with the percentage of households living in high-quality apartment buildings rather than flat houses, and is also associated with a work organization's ability to provide housing subsidies; and the distinction between enterprises and institutions is associated with rent, controlling for housing quality.

The analysis of community resources has shown that the bureaucratic rank of one's work unit strongly affects one's access to neighborhoods with desirable public and shopping facilities, after one's social and political statuses are controlled for. Income, however, does not have an effect. These results reflect the government-controlled allocation processes of housing and living location in Tianjin. As central players in the urban market, work units compete intensely with one another. Their success depends primarily on financial resources and political influence based on their formal rank and, for state agencies, strategic position in the decision-making process relative to the distribution of community resources.

Unexpectedly, state enterprises are no more successful than collective enterprises in placing their employees in better locations. Further, large establishments, which are mainly state enterprises, appear to have no advantages despite the fact that they have more funds for housing construction than do collectives and smaller establishments in the state sector (Lee 1988). These results suggest various possibilities. For one, state enterprises, which have a large number of workers waiting for public apartments, are oriented toward investing in housing space rather than in better location. Additionally, state enterprises may manage their housing funds for the provision of housing subsidies (which the Beijing data have shown) rather than investment for home locations. Nonetheless, different mechanisms and organizational processes are involved in the inequality we can observe in access to housing and to community resources.

9

SEGMENTATION AND INEQUALITY: CONCLUSIONS AND DISCUSSION

Conclusions

In this book, I have examined workplace segmentation and its impacts on the social stratification of urban workers in China. I have argued that a lack of market capitalism should not eliminate consideration of the existence of a segmentation phenomenon in planned socialism. But the institutional processes in which work organizations are segmented differ between market and planned systems. With the Chinese case in mind, I have explained workplace segmentation in planned systems as having three types of government interests: the ideological interests of the Communist party in maintaining state ownership over the means of production and consumption, the national interests of state planners in the country's economic development, which favor certain industries, and the control interests of government bureaucracies in hoarding resources and incentives under their jurisdictions. The aggregate and individual data analyzed in Chapter 2 demonstrate that the well-being of workplaces and the labor market characteristics of workers indeed varied by sector, industry, and bureaucratic hierarchy. These findings have led to the first conclusion of this book: workplace segmentation in socialist planned economies is an institutional expression of government interests.

A second conclusion is that the socialist workplace represents an important social status. Chapters 3 to 5 provide supportive data for this conclusion: not only do the government intentionally allocate better qualified workers to work organizations in the state sector and in industries with government priorities or a higher bureaucratic rank, but individuals also use their social and political resources to enter or move into these favored organizations. Because the allocation of labor and incentives is associated primarily with workplaces and secondarily with occupations, work-unit status is a more important status criterion for social mobility than is one's occupation. Chapters 4 and 5 show that status transmission from one generation to the next is identified with one's work unit rather than with one's occupation; work-unit status is a determinant of one's occupation, but not vice versa; and job switching between economic sectors or between bureaucratic ranks is more difficult to achieve than mobility between occupational categories. These findings imply that the socialist workplace is not just an organizational condition under which status attainment occurs; just as do criteria such as education, occupation, and income, one's workplace (work unit) serves as a basic criterion for defining social-class position in the socialist society.

A third important conclusion is that inequalities under state socialism are structured by interfirm as well as intrafirm forces. In Chapter 6, I show how the distribution of political and organizational incentives is affected by the workplace, with an analysis of party membership and cadre status. Party memberships are more likely to be granted in work organizations in the state sector, those with a high bureaucratic rank, or in an industry with government priorities, and less likely to be granted in work organizations in the collective sector with a low bureaucratic rank, or in an industry without government priorities. Within the workplace, staff members and workers with a politically significant position in the work unit, or with a positive relationship with work-unit leadership, are more likely to join the party than others without these political and social powers. In Chapter 7, I show that employees whose workplaces are in the state sector, have a higher bureaucratic rank, or are in a favored industry also have higher salaries and/or bonuses than workers whose workplaces are not in these favored positions. This is so after individual characteristics are statistically controlled for. In Chapter 8, I show that workplace characteristics are a determinant in access to collective consumption. The aggregate data of collective welfare benefits and the quality of housing demonstrate that employees whose work units are operated by a higher level of government enjoyed more welfare benefits and better public housing. The individual data on home locations demonstrates that one's work-unit bureaucratic rank affects one's access to public and retail services.

These findings imply that despite the socialist ideal of equalization, the organizational structures created and maintained by the socialist government are a generic source of political, economic, and residential inequalities. In the remainder of this chapter, I discuss implications of these conclusions for the research of structural segmentation in market and planned systems, and the study of social inequalities in China during market reforms.

Structural Segmentation in Market and Planned Systems

The concept of structural segmentation involves two related questions: (1) why some organizations are favored in the distribution of scarce resources and opportunities, and (2) why organizational outcomes are translated into rewards for some workers and not others. The first concerns "economic segmentation," and the second, "labor market segmentation," as derived in part from economic segmentation.

Regarding the question of the distribution of scarce resources, theories of market capitalism have suggested that a firm's monopoly position in the economy is a key factor. The underlying force behind the segmentation process is the firm's profit motive: firms compete for a monopoly position in commodity and labor markets in order to obtain a higher level of profits. As a firm obtains this monopoly position and expands in size, nonmarket mechanisms, which Chandler (1977) refers to as "administrative coordination," and Edwards (1979) calls "bureaucratic control," become the primary coordinating mechanisms within the firm. Therefore, research on economic segmentation in market capitalism focuses on the concept of the firm's profit motive, its monopoly interests, and its internal bureaucratic coordination.

When I examined "workplace segmentation" in planned socialism, for China in particular, I also paid attention to these three features as they were manifest in the socialist economy: the profit motive, the monopoly interest, and the bureaucratic process. But I did not address these features at the level of the firm. Firms in planned socialism are not independent enterprises as they are in market capitalism; rather, they are dependent on the government. When firms are organized under the government's "umbrella," a firm's motives, interests, and coordinating mechanisms are redefined in terms of government interests. Therefore, the national interests of state planners have redefined the profit motive and determined which industries or firms are profitable; the ideological interests of the Communist party have redefined the monopoly of resources and determined which sector dominates the economy;

and government administration has redefined bureaucratic control or coordination at the societal level and determined how to allocate resources, opportunities, and incentives through an elaborate hierarchy of work organizations.

Reconceptualizing profit motives, monopoly interests, and coordination processes enables us to compare the origins and mechanisms of economic segmentation in both market capitalism and planned socialism. Differences in segmentation structures between these two distinctive systems can therefore be specified within this framework. Just as important as these differences are the common theoretical principles underlying them: profit motive, monopoly interest, and organizational structuring are the *elements* examined by researchers interested in comparative analysis of economic segmentation.

To answer my second question, regarding the allocation of rewards or labor market segmentation, explanations from the perspective of market capitalism point to three mechanisms: level of profits, worker power, and internal labor markets. These mechanisms are either absent or greatly altered in a traditional planned economy such as China's. Scholars of Eastern Europe have offered a labor shortage argument: incentives are provided by the socialist governments to stimulate workers to move into and stay in government-favored sectors or firms. The assumption is that labor is a commodity that can be "owned" and sold by individuals. This assumption, however, is not held in China, where labor is neither a commodity nor is it in short supply.

My analysis of labor market segmentation in China centers on labor as a national resource. When individuals are deprived of their private labor rights, the government can then implement public ownership of labor resources. At the societal level, the government allocates labor with job-assignment programs and restricts job switching between organizations. The consequence of this type of bureaucratic control is the hoarding of workers by individual workplaces. Work organizations have no formal means for targeting human resources, but instead hoard management staff, technicians, and skilled workers who are under their control. In order to do so, and to prevent negative behaviors and encourage positive commitments from the work force, work organizations provide ideological, material, and organizational incentives to their employees. Since economic reforms in the 1980s, material rewards, particularly in the form of cash bonuses, have become the most effective incentive.

The preceding chapters have shown how necessary and possible it is for labor market segmentation to emerge in China without so-called "labor markets." However, the comparative significance of this analysis remains to be addressed. Does a society lacking "labor markets" have greater or fewer labor-market inequalities than a society where labor-market mechanisms prevail? The Tianjin survey data show that segmentation variables reduce the unexplained variance in Chinese workers' salaries by 7 percent and their bonuses by 10 percent. An American study (Kalleberg, Wallace, and Althauser 1981, Table 2) shows a 44-percent reduction of the unexplained variance in wages by segmentation variables for American workers, and a Polish study (Domanski 1988, Table 2) shows a 40-percent reduction. Statistically, more wage inequalities are the result of structural segmentation in the United States (a market society) and Poland (a planned society as of 1982, when the data were collected), where labor-market mechanisms were and still are at work, than there are in China, where bureaucratic control of labor has largely replaced "market" mechanisms. Research in the future should be directed toward exploring the mechanisms that explain these statistical results.

Nevertheless, the findings in this study do imply that the bureaucratic allocation of labor has independent effects on labor market inequalities. Such a bureaucratic allocation characterizes not only the state socialist economies in China and in the former Soviet Union and Eastern European countries, but also in other nonmarket societies (see Kalleberg 1988). Even in market societies, the bureaucratic control of labor (Edwards 1979) has been identified as one of the key features of large corporations. To what extent does this bureaucratic control in a socialist society differ from that within a capitalist society, in terms of its implications for the working class? This type of comparative analysis has already been initiated, largely addressing processes and mechanisms within the socialist workplace (Stark 1986; Walder 1987, 1989). Future research should be directed toward exploring theoretical principles and comparing statistical patterns of labor market inequalities within bureaucratic settings, but also between different systems.

Market Reforms and Social Inequalities in China

The data analyzed in this study were collected before 1989. Since then, the Communist world has undergone dramatic changes. Economic and political reforms in Eastern European countries and in the former Soviet Union did not save their Communist regimes.

On the contrary, by 1991 all these regimes had collapsed. Further-more, Communist parties in many of these countries are now un-constitutional. Although it would be naive to predict that Commu-nism as a school of thought will vanish, and as a social movement it will never reemerge, it is clear that Communism as a decisive force in state power in Europe is over.

Changes in China have been of a different nature, and inconsis-tent with those in the former USSR and Eastern Europe. Unlike mass movements in Eastern Germany, Poland, and Russia, the Chi-nese students' prodemocratic movement in 1989 did not lead to the downfall of the Communist government. Shortly after the events in Tiananmen Square in May and June 1989, state control of the econ-omy and party control of the society were tightened. Yet political tensions did not cause a reversal of the market reforms. On the contrary, these reforms continued in effect at both national and, particularly, local levels. Equally significant is the fact that the pace of these reforms has been closely monitored and controlled by the central and local authorities.

A distinctive feature of China's reforms is the emphasis on both economic openness and political stability. Deng Xiaoping's philosophy has been to use economic capitalism in service of politi-cal Communism.[1] Economically, the first half of 1992 witnessed further large-scale reforms: the commercialization of urban hous-ing, the implementation of a stock system to transform state firms into "business" enterprises, the recognition of labor markets, and the opening of China's markets to foreign capital investment. In the political structure, however, the party still tightly controls all levels of government administration, party cadres still comprise the core of workplace managers, party authorities in government jurisdic-tions and in workplaces still play a decisive role in selecting these managers, and socialism rather than capitalism is still the label used to interpret all practices in both economic and political spheres.

The tensions between economic capitalism and political Com-munism have the effect of reshaping relationships between the state bureaucracy and work organizations, between state bureaucrats and workplace leadership, and between workplace leadership and ordi-nary workers.

The State Bureaucracy and Work Organizations. The state bu-reaucracy has been in a contradictory position during recent eco-nomic reforms. On the one hand, the reforms have been initiated to decrease the party-state's intervention in the economy and to transmit decision-making power to autonomous enterprises. On the other hand, the economic reforms are conducted by the party-state, which intends to strengthen its power through these reforms, not weaken it. This dual nature of the reform process explains two consistent trends between traditional and modified planned economies. First, the party-state's control of the macro economic process and structure will be maintained. Second, at the micro level, government's jurisdictions over work organizations will be protected. Changes are taking place largely in terms of the use of market mechanisms to coordinate the economic processes.

In the newly released blueprint of enterprise reforms in China (State Economic Reform Commission et al. 1992), the central government called for a stock system as a new mechanism to coordinate state and collective enterprises. In this stock system, enterprises will be transformed into business corporations in which stocks are shared by the state, organizations, and individuals. Yet, the state insists on a majority share of the stock in any previously state-owned enterprises (comprising 70 percent of the urban labor force and about the same percentage of capital and output values), and remains determined to prevent its share from being sold to any businesses, groups, or individuals. Government jurisdictions will be called upon to perform as stockholders for the state.

Exactly what will result from this stock system awaits empirical evidence. In principle, however, this blueprint of new reforms protects the ideological interests of the party by maintaining state domination over the means of production. Therefore, the patterns of workplace and labor market segmentation that I have analyzed in this book will largely be maintained. Specifically, the government allocation of economic resources, opportunities, and incentives will favor (a) enterprises in which the state has a lion's share, (b) industries with government priority for economic development, and (c) organizations that have favorable positions in the state bureaucratic hierarchy.

State Bureaucrats and Workplace Leadership. State bureaucrats and workplace leadership are distinctive elite groups whose interests are met through different sources. In Chapter 7, I noted the tension between these government bureaucrats and the workplace leadership in an analysis of bonuses. We have seen that the distribution of bonuses, which are a central material incentive used by the government to stimulate enterprise performance, favored workplace cadres over government bureaucrats. In the future, as more decision-making power is shifted from government bureaucrats to workplace leadership, we will very likely see more incentives shifted to favor workplace leadership. In short, workplace leaders will gain prerogatives while government bureaucrats lose theirs.

Reforms in China are fundamentally conducted as a political-economic campaign by the government. As I have already discussed, the Chinese government has maintained its control of the macro and micro economic processes. Consequently, the interests of government bureaucrats are still being met. Standard wages are still set higher for government bureaucrats than for workplace leaders. Even during the commercialization of urban housing, special housing compounds are being built and special housing subsidies and lower rents are provided for former and current government officials. Profit-making enterprises are being charged high management fees by government jurisdictions, and the money in part goes into the pockets of government bureaucrats. Government jurisdictions control and regulate the transaction of imported and exported goods in favor of their employees (government officials and staff members). And government bureaucrats use their power, influence, and interpersonal networks (*guanxi*) to acquire material compensation.

Szelenyi (1978, 1983, 1989) has argued that economic reforms in state socialist societies will transfer power and privileges from government bureaucrats to direct producers. Although it is uncertain that ordinary workers and peasants in China, who are "direct producers" in Szelenyi's conceptualization, would really benefit more from the reforms than government bureaucrats and workplace leaders, the present study has demonstrated that government bureaucrats have been losing their favorable positions in the redistribution of income (particularly bonuses) in favor of workplace cadres, despite the fact that they are responsible for monitoring and controlling the economic reforms. It would be instructive to see the results of further study of the ways in which government bureaucrats have defended their interests and maintained their power and privileges. This line of research will be especially useful in identifying the political, bureaucratic, and socioeconomic bases of China's Communist regime in the continuing process of economic transformation.

Workplace Leadership and Workers. Do ordinary workers benefit more from the reforms than their work-unit leaders—party cadres, supervisors, shop-floor managers, and workplace directors? I have argued and shown with specific data that workplace leaders have become new redistributors and workers have been deprived of material incentives in the new environment of the urban workplace. The most interesting finding relevant to this matter is the greater inequality between cadres and ordinary workers in bonuses than in salaries. I have noted that the distribution of bonuses is controlled by workplace leadership, as that of salaries is subject to government bureaucrats. Thus, the shift of the redistributive power from a few government bureaucrats to a larger number of workplace leaders has in fact resulted in a greater inequality between the new redistributors and workers.

Deng Xiaoping's reformers did not intend to create greater inequalities between cadres and workers in the urban workplace. Their desire was to promote the economic effectiveness of work organizations by granting decision-making power to workplace leadership. But, because economic reform is a government campaign, and because the party-state relies on its cadres to execute the campaign and to protect its political regime, new decision makers' "corruption" has been widely tolerated by central and local authorities. On the other hand, Deng's reformers also underestimated the abuse of power by workplace and government decision makers, just as Mao's state administrators and planners failed to use their power in the interest of the Chinese people. Government-initiated economic reforms have not and may never change the relative position of the working class in the socialist society; in the short run, such changes will depend on the political actions of the working class.

APPENDIX A
SURVEY OF WORK AND OCCUPATIONS
OF TIANJIN URBAN RESIDENTS

PRINCIPAL INVESTIGATOR: YANJIE BIAN
July, 1988

Sampling and Data Collection Procedures

Tianjin's population resides in four areas: 41 percent reside in six high-density central-city districts, 10 percent in three developing coastal districts, 15 percent in four rural suburbs surrounding the central-city districts, and 34 percent in rural counties on the periphery of the Tianjin administrative area. The central-city districts are home for the municipal government's agencies, headquarters of industries, major institutions and enterprises, and their employees. The 1988 Tianjin survey was conducted in these districts.

Each central-city district is divided into subdistricts. Each subdistrict is further divided into neighborhood committees, which are the basic unit of residential organizations. In 1988, the six central-city districts had a total of eighty-seven subdistricts and 1273 neighborhood committees. On the average, a neighborhood committee had about 650 households.

The sample was drawn according to a multistage random sampling. The first stage randomly drew three subdistricts from each of the six districts, resulting in a total of eighteen subdistricts. The next stage randomly selected two neighborhood committees (residential blocs) from each of the eighteen subdistricts. The final stage of the sampling randomly drew twenty-eight households from each of the thirty-six selected neighborhood committees. These procedures resulted in a total sample of 1008 households.

The target respondents were adult residents who had any work experience. If more than one person in a selected household met this qualification, the following criteria were applied step by step for

choosing the target person for interviewing: (1) age above eighteen;
(2) currently employed; and (3) random selection (toss of a coin). If
no one in a selected household met this qualification (twelve cases
were found) or if people in the households refused to cooperate (five
persons did), the interviewer went to the third home (on the left first
and then, if needed, on the right) from the household previously
selected. As a result, 1008 respondents were interviewed. The average age of the respondents was forty-three years, and the sexual ratio
was 544 males to 464 females.

A group of thirty-six sociology majors at Nankai University
were hired as interviewers, with each person interviewing twenty-
eight households in a selected neighborhood committee. Data recorded in the questionnaires were transcribed by hand onto a record-
ing sheet, and were later entered into a computer in the United
States. A training session for the interviewers was conducted in
early June 1988, which was followed immediately by a pretest of ten
households. The formal data collection started on July 15th and
ended August 15th, 1988.

Data from 950 respondents who were currently employed in
the civilian labor force are used for the analyses presented in this
book. Excluded were retirees (forty-three respondents), military personnel (one), and full-time students (fourteen). This study sample is
representative of Tianjin's labor force in terms of the distribution of
respondents according to sex, education, sector, and occupation (see
Census Office of Tianjin 1984). The average age of the respondents is
40.7 years, which is higher than that for the total labor force in
Tianjin. This difference is expected because of the method used to
obtain household samples (Lin and Bian 1991).

Questionnaire

I. Basic Household Situation

1. Sex:
    1) male
    2) female
2. Date of birth: _____ year
3. Nationality:
    1) Han
    2) minority
4. Your ancestor is from
    1) rural area in a province
    2) town in a province

    3) city in a province
    4) rural area in Tianjin
    5) town in Tianjin
    6) city of Tianjin
5. Place of your birth:
    1) rural area in a province
    2) town in a province
    3) city in a province
    4) rural area in Tianjin
    5) town in Tianjin
    6) city of Tianjin
6. Marital status
    1) never married
    2) married
    3) divorced
    4) married again after divorce
    5) widowed
    6) married again after death of spouse
7. If you are now married or ever married, when were you first married: _____ year.
8. Have you and your spouse ever given birth to any children?
    1) yes
    2) no
    If so, how many boys and girls?
    1) boys _____
    2) girls _____
9. Are your parents alive?
    father: 1) alive _____ ; 2) dead _____
    mother: 1) alive _____ ; 2) dead _____
10. How many siblings do you have?
    brothers _____
    sisters _____
11. Whom do you live with ?
    1) your parents
    2) your parents-in-law
    3) your parents and parents-in-law
    4) your own family
    5) all by yourself
    6) others
12. If you live with your parents, how do you manage your income?
    1) spend separately

2) spend together
3) spend majority separately
4) spend majority together
13. What is your employment status?
   1) employed, in state or collective enterprise or institution
   2) working on your own private business
   3) retired, but still making some money in the form of "bu cha"
   4) retired, not being "bu cha"
   5) in school, but was employed before
   6) in school, never employed
   7) in military service
   8) unemployed
   9) homemaker
   10) others
14. When did you first start to work? (serving in the military or being sent to countryside to work is not included) year _____
15. Have you ever served in the military or been sent to the countryside to work?
   1) both
   2) neither
   3) worked in countryside
   4) served in military
16. Please fill table 1 in accordance with the description in the first column. (Those who were never employed skip to question 52.)
A. Education:
   1) illiterate or semiliterate
   2) 4-year elementary school
   3) 6-year elementary school
   4) middle school
   5) high school (including vocational school or technical school)
   6) 3-year college
   7) 4-year college
   8) graduate school
B. Occupation:
   0. peasant
   1) unskilled worker in commerce or service sector
   2) skilled worker in commerce or service sector
   3) unskilled worker in industrial enterprise
   4) skilled worker in industrial enterprise
   5) staff, clerical worker (below sub-branch or branch level)

TABLE 1

Occupation and Related Questions
(retirees fill in the status quo before retirement)

	*	A	B	C	D	E	F	G	H
Yourself, currently									
Yourself, by the end of 1983									
Yourself, by the end of 1978									
Yourself, when you started to work									
Your father, when you started to work									
Your mother, when you started to work									
Your spouse, currently									
Your spouse, when she/he started to work									
Your father-in-law, when your spouse started to work									
Your mother-in-law, when your spouse started to work									

*The numbers on the columns indicate the following.

6) middle-ranking cadre
7) high-ranking cadre
8) primary-school teacher
9) middle- or high-school teacher
10) college or university assistant instructor or instructor
11) college or university associate professor or professor
12) low-ranking technical professional (technicians or nurses)
13) middle-ranking technical professional (assistant researchers, engineers, or physicians)
14) high-ranking technical professional (senior engineers, associate researchers, or assistant chief physician)
15) student
16) military personnel

17) homemaker
18) other
C. Administrative position:
0) none
1) group head
2) section supervisor (at sub-branch rank)
3) department manager (at branch rank)
4) division chief
5) director of bureau
6) chairman of committee or above level
D. Political affiliation
1) none
2) democratic party
3) Communist Youth League
4) Chinese Communist party
E. Ownership of work unit:
1) private enterprise
2) new type of collectivity (you are responsible for loss or gain)
3) collectivity
4) state enterprise
5) state institution
6) government agency
7) others
F. Officially imposed rank of work unit
1) sub-branch
2) branch
3) division
4) bureau
5) deputy ministry or above
6) no idea
G. Size of the work unit
1) 10 employees or fewer
2) 11–50 employees
3) 51–100 employees
4) 101–500 employees
5) 501–1000 employees
6) 1001–2000 employees
7) 2001–3000 employees
8) 3001–5000 employees
9) 5001 or above
H. Average monthly income:

1) basic salary
2) bonus, average monthly bonus
3) others, including all the incomes relating to your work, such as fringe benefits and all kinds of allowances

II. Some Processes of Your Employment

17. Which of the following situations did you meet when you were first employed:
    1) completely assigned by government
    2) basically assigned by government, but there was some indirect manpower involved
    3) not assigned by government; assigned based on your own application and job search

WE WOULD LIKE TO ACQUIRE SOME INFORMATION ABOUT THE PERSON WHO PROVIDED YOU THE GREATEST HELP OR AFFECTED YOU MOST WITH YOUR FIRST EMPLOYMENT. PLEASE ANSWER THE FOLLOWING QUESTIONS.

18. Sex of the person
    1) male
    2) female
19. How was the person related to you:
    1) parent
    2) other family member
    3) spouse
    4) relative of father or mother
    5) relative of other family members
    6) relative of spouse
    7) friend of parents
    8) friend of other family members
    9) friend of spouse
    10) acquaintance of parents
    11) acquaintance of other family members
    12) acquaintance of spouse
    13) your friend
    14) your acquaintance
    15) relative of your friend
    16) relative of your acquaintance
    17) friend of your friend
    18) friend of your acquaintance
    19) acquaintance of your friend

    20)   acquaintance of your acquaintance
    21)   other
20. How well did you know each other?
    1)   very well
    2)   well
    3)   fairly well
    4)   not well
    5)   not at all
21. If you knew the person through a third party, how was the person related to the third party?
    1)   relative
    2)   friend
    3)   acquaintance
    4)   no idea
    5)   no third party
22. How well did they know each other?
    1)   very well
    2)   well
    3)   fairly well
    4)   not well
    5)   not at all
    6)   no idea
    7)   no third party
23. How was the third party related to you?
    1)   parent
    2)   other family member
    3)   spouse
    4)   relative
    5)   friend
    6)   acquaintance
    7)   other
    8)   no third party
24. How well did you and the third party know each other?
    1)   very well
    2)   well
    3)   fairly well
    4)   not well
    5)   not at all
    6)   no third party

(PLEASE REFER TO TABLE 1 WHEN YOU FILL IN THE FOLLOW-ING ITEMS.)

25. How much education did the person who most helped you get your first job complete?
26. What was the person's occupation?
27. What was the person's administrative position?
28. To which political affiliation did the person belong?
29. What was the type of ownership of the work unit in which the person was employed?
30. What was the rank of the work unit in which the person was employed?
31. What was the size of the work unit in which the person was employed?
32. Was the person working in the same work unit where you were about to work?
    1) yes
    2) no, but the person worked in a superior work unit
    3) no, but the person worked in a different work unit in the same administrative system
    4) no
33. Were any of your relatives working in the same work unit where you were about to work?
    1) yes
    2) no, but I had a relative who worked in a superior work unit
    3) no, but I had a relative who worked in a different work unit in the same administrative system
    4) no
34. Have you ever changed your job since you started to work? (This question refers to whether or not you have changed your occupation or work unit.)
    1) yes
    2) no

IF YOU HAVE CHANGED YOUR JOB, WE WOULD LIKE TO ACQUIRE SOME INFORMATION ABOUT THE PERSON WHO PROVIDED YOU THE GREATEST ASSISTANCE WITH YOUR RECENT JOB CHANGE.

35. The time when the person assisted you with your job change was _____ (year).
36. Sex of the person:
    1) male
    2) female
37. How was the person related to you:

 1) parent
 2) other family member
 3) spouse
 4) relative of father or mother
 5) relative of other family members
 6) relative of spouse
 7) friend of parents
 8) friend of other family members
 9) friend of spouse
10) acquaintance of parents
11) acquaintance of other family members
12) acquaintance of spouse
13) your friend
14) your acquaintance
15) relative of your friend
16) relative of your acquaintance
17) friend of your friend
18) friend of your acquaintance
19) acquaintance of your friend
20) acquaintance of your acquaintance
21) other

38. How well did you know each other?
 1) very well
 2) well
 3) fairly well
 4) not well
 5) not at all

39. If you knew the person through a third party, how was the person related to the third party?
 1) relative
 2) friend
 3) acquaintance
 4) no idea
 5) no third party

40. How well did the person and the third party know each other?
 1) very well
 2) well
 3) fairly well
 4) not well
 5) not at all
 6) no idea
 7) no third party

41. How was the third party related to you?
    1) parent
    2) other family member
    3) spouse
    4) relative
    5) friend
    6) acquaintance
    7) other
    8) no third party
42. How well did you and the third party know each other?
    1) very well
    2) well
    3) fairly well
    4) not well
    5) not at all
    6) no third party

(PLEASE REFER TO TABLE 1 WHEN YOU FILL IN THE FOLLOW-ING ITEMS.)

43. How much education did the person who most helped you change your job complete?
44. What was the person's occupation?
45. What was the person's job title?
46. To which political affiliation did the person belong?
47. What was the type of ownership of the work unit in which the person was employed?
48. What was the rank of the work unit in which the person was employed?
49. What was the size of the work unit in which the person was employed?
50. Was the person working in the same work unit where you were about to work?
    1) yes
    2) no, but the person worked in a superior work unit
    3) no, but the person worked in a different work unit in the same administrative system
    4) no
51. Were any of your relatives working in the same work unit where you were about to work?
    1) yes
    2) no, but I had a relative who worked in a superior work unit

3) no, but I had a relative who worked in a different work unit in the same administrative system
4) no

III. Household Financial Situation

52. (A) Please estimate the average monthly income of your family: _____ *yuan*

(B) Please choose one of the following saving situations which describes your family best (including municipal bonds or other securities):

0) no savings
1) under 100 *yuan*
2) under 500 *yuan*
3) under 1000 *yuan*
4) under 2000 *yuan*
5) under 5000 *yuan*
6) under 10,000 *yuan*
7) under 50,000 *yuan*
8) under 100,000 *yuan*
9) above 100,000 *yuan*

53. If you hold shares or own your private business or do some type of extra job, please estimate the amount of your fixed shares and variable assets:

0) none
1) under 100 *yuan*
2) under 500 *yuan*
3) under 1000 *yuan*
4) under 2000 *yuan*
5) under 5000 *yuan*
6) under 10,000 *yuan*
7) under 50,000 *yuan*
8) under 100,000 *yuan*
9) above 100,000 *yuan*

54. Please indicate whether you have the following durable household appliances:

	(1) Yes	(2) No
1) Color TV		
2) Black and white TV		
3) Refrigerator		
4) Electric fan		
5) Camera		
6) Stereo cassette radio		
7) Air conditioner		
8) Washing machine		
9) Motorcycle		
10) Bicycle		
11) Sewing machine		
12) Watch (above 120 *yuan*)		
13) Piano		
14) VCR		
15) Video camera		

IV. Interpersonal Relationships

55. Now, we would like to ask you an interesting question. Please think of three people: your father, your mother, and one of your siblings who is closest to you. Also, think of three of your most intimate friends with whom you keep close touch. Finally, think of three of your acquaintances with whom you don't maintain close contact, but you will help each other whenever needed. Please fill out Table 2, and see if you can record their sexes, ages, occupations, and related characteristics.

TABLE 2

Basic Family Ties and Social Contacts

Relationship*	(1)	(2)	(3)	(4)	(5)	(6)	(7)	(8)	(9)	(10)	(11)	(12)	(13)
Father													
Mother													
Sibling													
Friend 1													
Friend 2													
Friend 3													
Acquaintance 1													
Acquaintance 2													
Acquaintance 3													

*The numbers on the columns indicate the following.

1) Sex: 1) male; 2) female
2) Age:
3) Residence: 1) in the city; 2) out of the city
4) The number of times you have met during the past month
   0) never; 1) once or twice; 2) once a week; 3) two or three times a week; 4) almost every day; 5) at least once a day
5) The number of times you got together during the past month
   (referring to dining together, chatting, going to park, watching TV or a movie, playing games, etc.)
   0) never; 1) once or twice; 2) once a week; 3) two or three times a week; 4) almost every day; 5) at least once a day
6) Education
7) Occupation
8) Job title
9) Political affiliation
10) Ownership of work unit
11) Rank of work unit
12) Size of work unit
13) Average monthly income (referring to table 1)

V. Occupational Prestige

56. If you are asked to comment on the type of jobs for your children or friends, how do you rate the following conditions regarding the job selection? What do you consider first? What do you consider second? Please rank the following ten items in the order of preference. (The first preferred item is 1, then 2 . . . till 9; the least preferred one is 0)

Job authority
Working environment and condition
Income and bonus
Labor type and intensity
Housing
Distance from your home
Social prestige
Opportunity for promotion and salary raise
Fringe benefits
Contribution to society

57. Since there are different jobs, people have different views about these jobs. We would like to ask you to compare the following occupations within each of five sets. These comparisons are made according to your own judgment about which occupations are relatively better than others. (Rank them in order of preference: the best one is 1, then 2 . . . till 9; the worst is 0.)

Set 1: technician
        elementary-school teacher
        train conductor
        department manager
        college or university teacher
        journalist
        live-in maid and nanny
        foundry worker
        electrician
        painter

Set 2: entertainer
        draftsman
        machinist
        bureau director
        mail carrier

physician
elementary-school teacher
plumber
sales clerk
coal deliveryperson

Set 3: textile operator
scientist
cook
construction worker
official of municipal government
police officer
athlete
elementary-school teacher
mechanic
garbage collector

Set 4: accountant
official of central government
middle-school teacher
seaman
elementary-school teacher
ice cream vendor
cargo loader
barber
ticket agent
licensed driver

Set 5: carpenter
nurse
elementary-school teacher
hotel attendant
writer
shoe repairer
engineer
boiler worker
division chief
lathe operator

VI. Finally we would like to know your opinion on various aspects
and the degree of your satisfaction for the following
situations:

58. How satisfied are you with the following life domains?

	*	1	2	3	4	5
Relationship with your colleagues						
Relationship with your supervisor						
Labor type and intensity of your job						
Working environment and condition of your job						
Prestige of your job						
Income of your job						
Contributions of your job to society						
Benefits related to your job						
Technical complexity of your job						
Distance of your work unit from your home						
Authority of your job						
Opportunity for promotion and salary raise						
Overall view of the job						
Housing condition of your family						
Forestation around your neighborhood						
Security environment in your neighborhood						
Sanitary environment in your neighborhood						
Relationship with your neighbors						
Electricity and related service						
Water and related service						
Transportation						
Telephone						
Day care or kindergarten						
Primary and middle school						
Location/convenience of cinema						

Location/convenience of park					
Location/convenience of library					
Location/convenience of other cultural and recreational centers					

*The numbers on the columns indicate the following:
1. Very satisfied
2. Satisfied
3. Fairly satisfied
4. Somewhat unsatisfied
5. Very unsatisfied

59. What is your opinion on the recent situations that have occurred in your city or in the whole country?

	*	1	2	3	4	5
Development of housing construction						
Development of industrial production						
Development of road and transportation facilities						
Development of primary and middle-school education						
Kindergarten education						
Development of legal system						
Social security and morality						
Prices of goods and services						
Employment						
Coping with bureaucratic problems						
Coping with corruption of officials						
Face-to-face talk between municipal government and people						
Freedom to criticize municipal government						

	1	2	3	4	5
Election of representatives of people					
Efforts in rejuvenating leadership					
Policy or regulations concerning private owner-ship					
Policy or regulations concerning commercial-ization of housing					
Policy or regulations concerning one-child fam-ily planning					
Policy or regulations that give more respect to intellectuals					
Truthfulness of news reports					

*The numbers on the columns indicate the following:
1. Very satisfied
2. Satisfied
3. Fairly satisfied
4. Somewhat unsatisfied
5. Very unsatisfied

60. To what degree are you favorable or unfavorable toward the following statements?

	*	1	2	3	4	5
The more comfortable, the better life is.						
Life should be active and stimulating.						
There should be equal treatment among people.						
Be unselfish.						
Have self-respect.						
Try to acquire social recognition.						
Respect true friendship rather than make use of it.						
Have an open mind.						

Be truthful and honest.					
Be independent and self-reliant.					
Be rational, and not emotional.					
Be devoted and affectionate while doing your job.					
Be courteous and well-mannered.					
Be reliable and responsible.					
China has its own culture, and Chinese people should abide by the traditional norms.					
Films can be shown to the public only if they are totally in accordance with Chinese culture or custom; otherwise they should be cut off.					
If parents and children can't agree on their children's mate choices, children should be obedient to parents.					
Parents should confine children under the age of 16 from contacting persons of opposite sex.					
Children should be obedient and loyal to their parents.					
Every family should have boys so that family heredity can be carried on.					
It doesn't matter whether you have boys or girls.					

*The numbers on the columns indicate the following:
1. Very favorable
2. Favorable
3. Hard to say
4. Unfavorable
5. Very unfavorable

APPENDIX B
LIST OF PERSONAL INTERVIEWS

Interviews Conducted in Tianjin, China (1983–85). Pseudonyms given, age when interviewed, job in China.

1. Ms. Ding, 30, advisor of the Communist Young Pioneer League in an elementary school
2. Ms. Fang, 32, secretary of the Communist Youth League in a state-owned factory, who was later transferred to the factory's labor and wage office
3. Mr. Guo, 28, purchasing agent in a state-owned soy sauce plant, who took over his father's job through *dingti*
4. Mr. Han, 29, worker in a collective textile plant, who took over his mother's job through *dingti*
5. Ms. Fei, 31, typist working in the general office of a state-owned chemical material factory
6. Ms. Li, 28, two-year technical-school graduate who worked in a bureau-operated factory as a skilled worker
7. Ms. Lin, 41, director of a district-managed, collectively owned manufacturing factory
8. Mr. Liu, 30, lawyer whose work unit is the first law firm affiliated with the municipal government
9. Ms. Luan, 23, secretary of the Chinese Communist Youth League in a high school
10. Mr. Qi, 24, building construction worker affiliated with an employment service center
11. Ms. Qian, 36, party office staff member in a textile factory
12. Ms. Rui, 34, director of the political education office in a high school
13. Mr. Su, 55, director of the union organization in a state manufacturing factory
14. Mr. Tang, 57, party secretary in a railroad manufacturer
15. Mr. Wang, 48, head of the housing office of a large state-owned manufacturing factory
16. Mr. Wu, 45, history teacher in a high school
17. Mr. Yang, 55, director of municipal labor bureau

18. Ms. Yuan, 46, director of women's associations in a municipal company-managed, collectively owned textile plant
19. Mr. Zha, 21, worker in a railroad station, who took over his father's job through *dingti*
20. Ms. Zhai, 29, worker's union staff member in a state-owned textile needle factory
21. Ms. Zhang, 25, production assembly-line worker in a state-owned textile needle factory
22. Mr. Zhangh, 47, head of the general affairs office in a collectively owned manufacturing plant
23. Mr. Zhao, 31, cargo van loader, who quit his state farm job and was hired by his father's former work unit in a transportation company
24. Mr. Zhi, 41, senior deputy director of a municipal company-managed, collectively owned factory
25. Ms. Zhou, 27, train conductor, who was recruited through *neizhao* after graduation from high school

Interviews Conducted in the United States (1988–1992)

26. Ms. Feng, 52, university official
27. Mr. Ge, 38, municipal party committee's office staff member
28. Mr. Huang, 56, municipal official
29. Mr. Jiang, 47, municipal official
30. Mr. Li, 39, commercial school teacher
31. Ms. Ren, 26, math teacher in an elementary school
32. Mr. Sun, 33, bus driver
33. Mr. Wang, 37, university economics lecturer
34. Ms. Xue, 33, skilled worker before joining a university's library staff
35. Mr. Yan, 35, university finance lecturer
36. Mr. Yang, 46, head of worker's union in a collectively owned factory

APPENDIX C
MEASUREMENT OF KEY STATUS
VARIABLES USED IN
TABLES 2.2 TO 8.4

Name of Variable	Measurement or Description
Work-unit rank	0) nonranking 1) section (*gu*) 2) department (*ke*) 3) division (*chu*) 4) bureau (*ju*) 5) higher than bureau
Education	1) no formal schooling 2) elementary school 3) middle (junior-high) school 4) high school/technical-vocational school 5) college or above
Occupational categories used to calculate an occupational status scale using Lin-Xie (1988) index	1) unskilled worker in commerce or service sector 2) skilled worker in commerce or service sector 3) unskilled worker in industry 4) skilled worker in industry 5) staff, clerical worker (below section level) 6) middle-ranking cadre 7) high-ranking cadre 8) primary-school teacher 9) middle- or high-school teacher 10) college or university assistant instructor or instructor 11) college or university associate professor or professor 12) low-ranking technical professional (technicians or nurses) 13) middle-ranking technical professional (assistant engineers or physicians)

	14) high-ranking technical professional (senior engineers, chief physicians, etc.)
	15) student
	16) military personnel
	17) homemaker
	18) other
	19) private sector worker
Monthly salaries	Monthly salary in *yuan*
Bonuses per month	The sum of monthly bonuses plus last year's year-end bonuses divided by 12 months, in *yuan*

Note: These measurements apply to the respondent's first and current jobs and, wherever appropriate, the respondent's father and the respondent's social ties.

GLOSSARY

biaoxian (personal performance in work and nonwork activities) 表現

bu (ministry) 部

buguan wuzi (ministry-managed materials) 部管物資

cai gou yuan (purchasing agent) 采購員

cha (a *D* grade in school) 差

chu (division) 處

daiyie (waiting for jobs) 待業

daiyie qingnian (youths waiting for jobs) 待業青年

dan diao (one-way job transfer) 單調

dang, zheng, qi-shi-ye danwei fuzeren (party, administrative, and enterprise or institution leaders) 党,政,企事業單位負責人

danwei (work units) 單位

danwei jibie (work-unit rank) 單位級別

danwei lingdao (leaders of the work unit) 單位領導

danwei suoyouzhi (ownership of labor by the work unit) 單位所有制

de (morality and political thought) 德

diao dong gong zuo (job transfer, or change of workplace) 調動工作

dingti (taking over a parent's job) 頂替

duli hesuan danwei (independent accounting unit) 獨立核算單位

erlei wuzi (second-category materials) 二類物資

fujia gongzi (supplementary wages) 附加工資

fudong gongzi (floating salary) 浮動工資

gai bian gong zhong (change in the type of work or occupation) 改變工種

geren biaoxian (performance of the individual) 個人表現

geti laodong zhe (individual laborers or self-employed) 個體勞動者

getihu (family businesses) 個體戶

gongzuo danwei (work unit) 工作單位

gu (section) 股

guanxi (interpersonal connections) 關系

guojia fenpei (direct state assignment) 國家分配

guojia jiguan (government agency) 國家機關

hetong gong (contract workers) 合同工

hetongzhi gong (workers under a contract system) 合同制工

hong ("redness," or commitment to party ideologies) 紅

jianjie guojia fenpei (indirect state assignment) 間接國家分配

jiating chushen (the family's class origin) 家庭出身

jishu ganbu (technical cadre) 技術干部

ju (bureau) 局

ke (department) 科

lian xi ren (party members as sponsors for applicants) 聯系人

linshi gong (temporary workers) 臨時工

lixu (retirement plan for senior cadres) 離休

neizhao (internal recruitment) 內招

qiyie danwei (enterprise) 企業單位

quanmin suoyou zhi (all-the-people's ownership, or state ownership) 全民所有制

rencai jiaoliu zhongxin ("talent exchange centers," or employment service centers) 人才交流中心

sanlei wuzi (third-category materials) 三類物資

shiyie danwei (institution) 事業單位

shuang diao ("two-way job transfer," or exchange of one's place of employment with another person) 雙調

silei wuzi (fourth-category materials) 四類物資

siren gongsi (privately owned companies) 私人公司

ti (physical education and health) 體

tiaozi (a message) 條子

tie fan wan (iron rice bowl) 鐵飯碗

tongpei wuzi (centrally-allocated materials) 統配物資

tuixu (retirement at the official retirement age) 退休

tuizhi (early retirement) 退職

xiao zu zhang (small-group leaders) 小組長

yiban ganbu (ordinary cadre or clerical or office staff) 一般干部

yilei wuzi (first-category materials) 一類物資

you ren (having *guanxi,* or personal ties) 有人

yuan (unit of Chinese currency; $100 equal 550 *yuan* according to the 1991 official exchange rate) 元

zhanyou (comrade-in-arms) 戰友

zhengfu zhuguan bumen (government jurisdiction) 政府主管部門

zhengzhi mianmu (political background) 政治面目

zhi (academic credentials) 智

Zhongguo Gongchanzhuyi Qingniantuan (the Chinese Communist Youth League) 中國共產主義青年團

Zhongguo Gongchanzhuyi Shaonian Xianfengdui (the Chinese Communist Pioneer League) 中國共產主義少年先鋒隊

Zhongguo Gongzhandang (the Chinese Communist Party) 中國共産黨

zhuan (expertise) 專

zimou zhiyie (direct individual application) 自謀職業

NOTES

Chapter 1

1.   See also Kalleberg, Wallace, and Althauser (1981), Kaufman, Hodson, and Fligstein (1981), and Hodson and Kaufman (1982) for summaries and criticisms of these economists' studies.

2.   In China, membership in a unified union is a mandatory status assigned to every worker. Members pay 0.3 percent of their monthly salaries for the membership fee, and participate in both political and entertainment-oriented activities organized by the union officers of their workplaces. In the workplace, union leaders usually have posts in party committees to take responsibility for welfare programs and worker affairs. These characteristics are not unique to China; see Burawoy and Lukacs (1985) for Hungarian worker's unions.

3.   That is, to promote industries, agriculture, national defense, and science and technology to a high-tech standard.

4.   In two state-owned factories in Tianjin where I interviewed in 1981, items used as material prizes between 1977 and 1980 included radios and tape recorders, suits, T-shirts, bedspreads, pillowcases, summer sleeping mats, umbrellas, bath and hand towels, thermos bottles, teapots, glasses and teacups, cooking utensils, and metal lunch boxes. In both factories, these material prizes were distributed four times a year, with an additional year-end prize (one factory did not have year-end prizes for two years because of short finances). Prizes were divided into three grades each time. First prize would be an item worth 30 percent of an average worker's monthly salary, usually given out to 30 percent of the top-rated staff and workers. Another 30 percent, rated somewhat lower, received second prizes worth about 20 percent of the average monthly salary. Still another 35 percent received the lowest-grade prizes, worth 10 percent of the average monthly wage. The remaining 5 percent would be denied any prize because of failure to meet their quotas or for their political and personal mistakes during the effective period. The sizes of the additional year-end prizes would be much larger, worth on average an entire month's salary. In addition, free or factory subsidized foods such as rice, meat, and fresh vegetables were distributed equally to workers, both seasonally and at the end of the lunar year, as an extra incentive.

5.   I discovered that in a recent study by Peng (1992, p. 207) wage returns tied to the level of college education vary between rural and urban

sectors. But little difference was found in returns linked to cadre status, a variable that is critical to testing Nee's market transition theory.

6. These negative behaviors have been termed "weapons of the weak" in Scott's (1985) work.

7. To the best of my knowledge, the April–June prodemocracy movement of 1989 was the only large-scale, grass-roots movement in post-revolutionary Chinese history that was not led by the Communist party.

8. The percentages were recalculated by excluding the category of workers in farming, forest, hunting, and fishing sectors.

Chapter 2

1. Although *danwei* also can refer to a military unit, this study will focus only on nonmilitary organizations.

2. There are nine democratic parties in existence today: (1) the Revolutionary Committee of the Nationalist Party of China, (2) the Democratic Allies of China, (3) the Association of Democratic Reconstruction of China, (4) the Peasants-Workers Democratic Party of China, (5) the Zhi-Gong Party of China, (6) the Nine-Three Scholars' Society, (7) the National Federation of Industrialists and Merchants, (8) the Taiwanese Allies, and (9) the Federation of Overseas Chinese. This order has been used in the Communist Party's documents.

3. Workers' unions, women's federations, and Communist youth leagues function as branch organizations of the Communist party. At both the central and local levels, heads of these "mass" organizations are appointed by the party committees in which they are, usually, members.

4. *Dui zi-ben-shu-yi gong-shang-yie de she-hui-zhu-yi gai-zao.*

5. For wage regulations of collective enterprises, see Li (1990, chap. 6), and for descriptions of welfare benefits for workers in the collective sector, see Tang (1990, pp. 244–45).

6. In many cases, these "not ranked" or "nonranking" units are too small to have an official rank.

7. A comprehensive discussion of this fiscal structure and its impact on the ability of work organizations to retain "slack resources" has been offered by Walder (1992).

8. I obtained correlations between workplace size and these status variables for two industrial sectors: profit-making enterprises, on the one hand, and nonprofit institutions and government agencies, on the other.

The results are: (1) no correlation between education and enterprise size; (2) the correlation between occupational status and enterprise size was low and insignificant; (3) salaries and bonuses were nonlinearly associated with enterprise size, with the average salaries and bonuses being lower in the middle and higher on the two extremes; (4) the percentage of party members was poorly correlated with enterprise size; and (5) for agencies and institutions, none of the variables was significantly associated with workplace size, and occupational status and bonuses were negatively (but insignificantly) associated with workplace size.

Chapter 3

1.   "State labor agencies" here refer to the central government's Labor Ministry and local governments' labor bureaus.

2.   The gross difference in the number of urban staff and workers between 1960 and 1963 was 15.8 million jobs, revealing a 27-percent reduction (Statistical Bureau of China 1988, p. 123). There were 2.5 million new workers recruited over the period.

3.   Documents on employment policies include (1) "To Further Improve the Urban Employment Work" (*Jinyibu Zuohao Chengzhen Laodong Jiuye Gongzuo*), by the Central Committee of the CCP and State Council in 1980; (2) "Several Resolutions: Creating Alternatives, Promoting Economic Flexibility, and Solving Employment Problems in Cities and Towns" (*Guanyu Guangkai Menlu, Gaohuo Jingji, Jiejue Chengzhen Jiuye Wenti de Ruogan Guiding*), by the Central Committee of the CCP and State Council in 1981; (3) "Regulations of the Registration of Job-waiting People in Cities and Towns" (*Chengzhen Daiyie Renyuan Dengji Guanli Banfa*), by the Ministry of Labor and Personnel Affairs in 1984.

Documents on labor service companies include (1) "Suggestions Toward Several Issues About Labor Service Companies" (*Guanyu Laodong Fuwu Gongsi Ruogan Wenti de Yijian*), by the Ministry of Labor and Personnel Affairs in 1982; (2) "Temporary Regulations of the Use of Subsidies for Employment of Youth in Cities and Towns and the Management of Labor Service Companies" (*Guanyu Chengzhen Qinian Laodong Jiuye he Laodong Fuwu Gongsi Buzhufee Guanli Shiyong de Zhanxing Guiding*), jointly by the Ministry of Labor and Personnel Affairs and the Ministry of Finance in 1983; (3) "Suggestions Toward Several Issues in the Development and Construction of Labor Service Companies" (*Guanyu Laodong Fuwu Gongsi Fazhan he Jianshe zhong Wenti de Yijian*), by the Ministry of Labor and Personnel Affairs in 1989.

Documents on labor recruitment include (1) "Suggestions Toward the Recruitment of Workers Through All-aspect Examinations" (*Guanyu Zhaogong Shixing Quanmian Kaohe de Yijian*), by the National General Labor Bureau in 1979; (2) "Temporary Regulations of the Recruitment of

Best Qualified Workers Through Merit Examinations" (*Guanyu Zhaogong Kaoke Zeyou Luyong de Zhanxing Guiding*), by the Ministry of Labor and Personnel Affairs in 1983; (3) "Temporary Regulations of the Recruitment of Workers in State Enterprises" (*Guoying Qiyie Zhaoyong Gongren Zhanxing Guiding*), by State Council in 1986.

Documents on the labor contract system include (1) "Circular of Actively Implementing the Labor Contract System" (*Guanyu Jiji shixing Laodong Hetongzhi de Tongzhi*), by the Ministry of Labor and Personnel Affairs in 1983; (2) "Temporary Regulations of the Implementation of the Labor Contract System in State Enterprises" (*Guoying Qiyie Shixing Laodong Hetongzhi Zhanxing Guiding*), by State Council in 1986.

4. In the survey, the respondents were asked whether they found their first urban jobs (1) completely by government assignment, (2) basically government assignment, but some indirect processes involved, or (3) not government assignment, but individual application and job search. People who found jobs through "direct state assignments" between 1949 and 1952 were, in many cases, willingly using government job-introduction programs. Direct state assignments that were implemented after 1955 were more strict.

5. "Youths waiting for jobs" are those students who have failed in general examinations to enter college. Many of them were doing poorly in school.

Chapter 4

1. Lin and Bian (1991) did not find the effect of the father's work unit sector on the daughter's work unit and occupational attainments.

2. See also Davis (1990) for description and analysis of the *dingti* practices in the first half of the 1980s.

3. Therefore, membership in the dominant bureaucratic class is by a political and ideological standard.

4. Several schema have been offered to break down postrevolutionary Chinese history into periods. For example, Shirk (1984), Davis-Friedmann (1985), and Billeter (1985), in their conceptualizations about the criteria of social-class formations in China, considered three periods: (1) the founding of the PRC to the socialist reform (1949–56) favored the criterion of family origin, (2) the Anti-Rightist movement to the end of the Cultural Revolution (1957–76) emphasized the criterion of virtue or loyalty to the party, and (3) the post-Mao era (1977 to the present) favored the criterion of individual qualifications. Parish (1984) and Whyte and Parish (1984) show more concern with the Cultural Revolution and its effects on stratification and mobility. Thus, they differentiate between the pre-1966 and post-1966

periods for Mao's era. Lin and Xie (1988) and Lin and Bian (1990) utilized a four period scheme: 1949–57, 1958–65, 1966–76, and post-1977. The scheme I use in this book incorporates the viewpoints of American historians (Fairbank 1986) as well as the Chinese official position (Deng 1983).

5.   Lin and Bian (1991) used an ordinal measure containing four "sectors": state agencies and institutions, state enterprises, collective enterprises, and private businesses. The rank-order of the categories was justified in terms of respondents' education, occupation, party membership, income, and bonuses.

6.   The Lin-Xie index equation is: SEI score = −5.188 + 13.874 (eduction) + .262 (monthly salary) (Lin and Xie 1988, p. 830). It was obtained by regressing prestige ratings of fifty occupations rated by 1632 Beijing urban residents in 1983, on average education in occupation and average monthly salary in occupation. In the present analysis, socioeconomic index (SEI) scores were calculated for 19 occupations, based on average education in occupation and average monthly salary in occupation using respondents' current jobs. The SEI index then applies to occupational status for respondents' first occupation, fathers' occupation, and occupation of social ties.

7.   The father's education has a correlation of .139 with the respondent's first work-unit sector, .130 with first work-unit rank, and .200 with first occupation. But the father's education proved insignificant in the regression models for these three dependent variables.

8.   Neither pairwise deletion nor mean-substitution was the appropriate strategy (Anderson, Basilevsky, and Hum 1983). Because of the high percentage of missing values, pairwise deletion would unfortunately alter the sample distribution on independent variables not involving the missing cases, and therefore alter the correlations between these independent variables and the father's variables. Although mean-substitution does not alter variation of the father's variables nor alter the sample distributions on other independent variables that did not involve missing cases, it does change the correlations between the father's variables and the dependent variables, and the correlations between the father's variables and other independent variables. Consequently, model estimations will be significantly affected. It becomes necessary to include these missing cases in the analyses.

9.   The unreported father's sector exerts a significant coefficient of .48, smaller in magnitude than that of the father's state sector. It means that the nonreporting cases contain respondents whose fathers worked in state and nonstate sectors.

10.   Technological development in the city of Tianjin over the last forty years showed a similar trend. For example, manual workers in the state sector decreased from 89.2 percent in 1950 to 66.8 percent in 1983, whereas

technical and managerial staff increased from 8.7 percent to 15.8 percent (Tianjin Census Office 1986, p. 405).

11.   The calculations were obtained in two steps. The first is to obtain odds or antilog values for each level of education. The second is to obtain odds ratios for each level of education, based on the formula: odds ratio = odds / (1 + odds). The formula can be converted to: odds = odds ratio / (1 − odds ratio). The linearity for the education effect on sector attainment was tested with dummy variables in a separate preliminary analysis. In that analysis, with the omitted category of no school, the logit coefficients, which all were statistically significant, were: .31 for elementary, .65 for middle, .96 for high/vocational, and 2.46 for college or higher. These coefficients were obtained after predictors considered in the basic model were controlled for.

12.   The regression metric coefficient of .218 was insignificant for the 1973–83 cohort, compared with the significant .243 for the 1966–76 cohort.

13.   The father's sector was considered in the original model, but its correlation with the dependent variable (.13) was overshadowed by the correlation between the father's work-unit rank and the dependent variable (.35), and correspondingly its regression coefficient proved statistically insignificant.

Chapter 5

1.   The question used in the survey reads: "We would like to learn about someone who provided the greatest help or influence for you to get a job when you first entered the work force." Although the pronoun "someone" means *guanxi* in the Chinese context, I chose not to use *guanxi* because it was a sensitive word. Party policies opposed the use of *guanxi* or "back door" practices in job assignments, as in other government-imposed programs. It was considered inappropriate to use the word *guanxi* in a questionnaire study. In personal interviews, however, such a word is fine to use depending on the subject matter and the context in which the interviews are conducted. Throughout the data analysis that follows, the term "personal contacts" or "contact" is used.

2.   The percentages for the use of social ties in job search in U.S. studies are (1) 55.7 percent in Granovetter's Newton, MA sample (1974); (2) 34.8 percent in Ensel's New York State sample (1979); (3) 57.0 percent in Lin, Ensel, and Vaughn's Albany, NY study (1981); and (4) 57.4 percent in Bridges and Villemez's Chicago SMSA sample (1986).

3.   There are a variety of ways to measure strength of ties. One alternative that was considered in the Tianjin study is the degree of inti-

macy (Marsden and Campbell 1984). A preliminary analysis showed that in no place was it more effective than the role-relationship measure constructed herein. For this reason, I will report only the results regarding the role-relation strength of tie measure. After all, the role-relation measure is particularly meaningful in the Chinese context, since familial (kin) ties are substantively important in Chinese societies.

4.   Of the one hundred respondents who mentioned their parents as contacts, thirty-nine got jobs through indirect state assignment, in which the respondents took their parents' jobs (*dingti*) or were employed by their parents' work units. *Dingti* and *neizhao* are formal employment procedures; thus, it seemed problematic to treat these parents as contacts in network-analysis terms. To resolve this problem, indirect state assignment (and direct state assignment) as a method of job placement must be controlled for when the strength of tie and status characteristics of the contact are analyzed.

5.   As discussed in the first section of this chapter, the influence of contacts (*guanxi*) in the job-placement process is associated with the system of work units. Therefore, the contact's work-unit sector and rank indicate the degree of influence he or she has in the process. This particularly holds true when the contact intends to influence work-unit assignment. As for the first job variables, the contact's work-unit sector and rank are measured the same as those for the respondents. This is also true for the occupational status of the contact. The most important single indicator of the contact's status is cadre rank. Six major ranks are identified, from lower to higher: group head, section chief, department director, division chief, bureau chief, and higher. The higher the rank, the greater the authority and power.

6.   Studies conducted in the United States show that the use of personal contacts in a job search is fairly random, because neither the status attainment model variables nor any network characteristics predict use or non-use of personal ties (Lin, Ensel, and Vaughn 1981; Marsden and Hurlbert 1988; Lai, Leung, and Lin 1990). Lin and Bian (1989) found a similar pattern with their 1985 Tianjin sample, in which the same set of predictors as in cited U. S. studies were used. The present study shows different results. Based on a logistic model, use of personal contacts is predicted from variables that were considered in regression models (Chapter 4). In Marsden and Hurlbert's study, the use of personal contacts was considered as a method of job search, which contrasted with other methods such as direct application. Therefore, the method of job search in their analysis is the dependent variable. Lin and Bian did not consider the method of job placement.

7.   It is methodologically correct to predict these social resource variables from respondents' education and CCP membership, even for those respondents whose fathers are the contacts. Education and CCP membership determine the *likelihood* of whom one contacts for help.

8.   Different results were reported by Lin and Bian (1989) with their 1985 Tianjin study. In this study, education was not a significant predictor of the contact's sector, nor of the contact's occupation. The father's education and occupation had only marginal correlations with the two social-resource variables considered, which did not produce significant regression coefficients. Only the strength of tie proved to be negatively associated with the social-resource variables.

9.   At the national level, there were more than two hundred such systems before 1985. They were greatly reduced to about twenty major systems after the 1985 wage reform, which will be discussed in Chapter 7.

10.   This policy was first implemented in the early 1970s, following a Maoist ideology to select workers and peasants (who were thought to be politically pure or "red") rather than high-school students (who were trained by intellectuals thought of as academically oriented or "white") for college enrollments. The policy continued through the 1980s, but with a different intent. From 1977 to 1980, it was designed to select academically capable youth who had been denied the opportunity for a college education during the Cultural Revolution (1966–76). At the same time, selection of high-school graduates for college was resumed. From 1980 on, a large number of young workers received further training from television education centers (known as TV universities), workers' universities, regular universities' branch schools, and various vocational schools.

Chapter 6

1.   When I began writing this book between 1989 and 1991, unexpected changes took place in the Communist world, resulting in the decline of the Communist parties in the former Soviet Union and Eastern European countries. However, the Communist party still rules China. Although the 1988 Tianjin survey data do not reflect trends after 1989, they do provide us the opportunity to examine party membership attainment before and after China's market reform.

2.   In China, other political parties or associations also establish their organizations within the work-unit system. These parties or associations do not have branches in various levels of government administration, but they have local chapters in each locality. See note no. 2 to chapter 2 for these political parties.

3.   The dossiers are not open to employees, so in principle no one knows what is included in one's personnel dossier. Dossiers for ordinary staff and workers are kept in the work unit's party office, and those for work unit party secretary and director are kept in the party office of the next-higher level organization.

4.   Blau, Ruan, and Ardelt (1991) report 15.4 percent of party members in their sample of urban residents in Tianjin in 1986. But they include homemakers, students, and respondents with no jobs, and few of these respondents could be party members because joining the party usually takes place after people enter the workplace.

5.   Workplace size is not correlated with party membership for either subsample, and therefore is not considered in the model estimation.

6.   There are mixed data about public perceptions of party memberships during economic reforms. Walder (1989) reports that his Chinese informants, who were factory workers before coming to the U.S. in the late 1980s, believed that workers do not care about joining the party as much as they did before. Based on an interview I conducted with a college teacher in Beijing, however, more college students and intellectuals applied to the party in the 1980s than ever before.

7.   Several of the father's variables were considered in a preliminary analysis. These variables included work-unit ownership, work-unit rank, industrial sector, occupation, and party membership. But none of these is correlated at the zero-order level with the respondent's party membership both before or after 1978.

8.   Walder (1986), however, describes how important these group leaders are in the workshop. True, they manipulate the flow of information between "above" and "below," which is important in deciding production quotas, bonuses, and punishments for members of their groups. But most group leaders are young people, on the road to joining the party. Therefore, it seems inappropriate to use group leadership as a dependent variable. In the 1988 Tianjin survey, five percent of the respondents were group leaders, 16.3 percent of these group leaders were party members.

Chapter 7

1.   This is based on an official report of wage bills (Yuan 1990, p. 190). This wage structure was also revealed elsewhere (Li 1990).

2.   Price subsidies are generally imposed by the central government and at the national level. These included grain and coal subsidies for urban residents in 1965 (which were transformed into basic wages through several wage justifications afterward), subsidies for price increases in major groceries in 1979, meal price subsidies in 1985, and price subsidies for meat, vegetables, sugar, and eggs in 1988. There are also local price subsidies.

3.   For example, Tianjin workers who move to jobs in Tibet would earn compensations and subsidies roughly equivalent to their regular wages.

4.   This is a rephrasing of Marx's famous saying that religion is the "opium of the working class."

5.   National and regional prizes are recognized as special bonuses in the Chinese wage system. These prizes are generally awarded for scientific research, suggestions and innovations, scientific or technological improvements, high-quality products, and outstanding athletes. Except for outstanding athletes' prizes, prizes are funded by the central and local governments. They range from 200 *yuan* to 20,000 *yuan* ($36 to $363) each. These prizes are awarded to a very small number of people.

6.   Parish (1984) contends that there was a destratification trend during the Cultural Revolution decade (1966–76) in light of the egalitarian programs implemented. A similar hypothesis was proposed for Eastern Europe (Szelenyi 1978) and for rural-urban discrepancies in China (Whyte 1986) to predict the social consequences of a decentralized economy after reform. Walder (1990) finds supportive data for the latter hypothesis from a sample of one thousand wage earners in Tianjin in 1986.

7.   Originally reported nominal wages are used in the analysis to compare wage differentials for given years across industries. If the research focus here were in comparisons of changes in wage differentials over time, real wages would have been calculated to take into account the inflation effects on wages.

8.   This percentage is close to the 18.9 percent of party members obtained from a comparable study based a 1985 Tianjin sample (Lin and Bian 1991). Blau, Ruan, and Ardelt (1991) report 15.4 percent party members in their 1986 Tianjin sample. Homemakers, students, and respondents with no jobs were included in their analysis. In the 1988 Tianjin sample used in this study, only 1 percent of respondents excluded from the work force were party members, as compared to 75 percent of the party members who joined the party after entering the labor force.

9.   The respondents were also given a category of "nonranking" in the questionnaire denoting workplaces "not ranked." However, some respondents who were not sure how to rank their workplaces had mistakenly chosen this category. Due to this measurement error, all the respondents who reported their workplaces as "nonranking" were excluded from the analysis.

In his study, Walder (1990) uses a different rank variable to measure the level of government to which establishments are subject. He finds this to be significant in predicting basic wages and total income of workers, rather than bonuses. The noneffect on bonuses in his study may be due to the fact that enterprises under the same level of government control can actually have different bureaucratic ranks, because of differences in size, history, industry, managerial personnel's reputation, and unknown factors, which are all important for rank assignments. Managers of enterprises with higher bureaucratic ranks will have greater bargaining power than those of enterprises with lower bureaucratic ranks, even when the two enterprises are under the same ministry or bureau. Both Walder's and this study's measures of bureaucratic rank may be useful in future research to test which is the best predictor of earnings inequality.

10. Size is a simple measure but has complex meanings. In a capitalist market economy, firm or establishment size may indicate the degree to which they belong to a monopoly sector (Hodson 1984), a firm's internal labor markets become effective (Edwards 1975, 1979), and how labor unions are formed (Kalleberg, Wallace, and Althauser 1981). Size is also related to other dimensions of economic segmentation (Kalleberg, Wallace, and Althauser 1981). Brown and Medoff (1989) record six explanations for the positive relationship between workplace size and wages, focusing on the following variables: quality of workers, working conditions in organizations, prevention of unionization, financial ability of the firm, supply-demand relations, and labor control. Since large differences in wages still remain after all these variables are taken into account, the authors believe that further explanations of size effects on earnings are needed. In a centralized economy such as China's, workplace size may provide three forms of power: political power associated with the number of workers, economic power associated with the resources that an enterprise possesses, and inter-organizational power associated with the networks and social resources that organizations have.

11. An alternative to the three-step analysis presented here would be one starting with human resource predictors in the first equation and ending with workplace variables added to the model. Unfortunately, this alternative procedure would violate the actual process in which bonuses are distributed.

12. Size variable shows an independent, substantial effect on year-end bonuses ($b = .14$, beta $= .09$, $r = .12$, $p < .05$)—part of the reported dependent variable of bonuses per month—in a regression model using all work unit and individual predictors included in the third equation. Such an effect disappears in the regression of total bonuses per month, of which year-end bonus is only 25 percent. The consistent results on workplace size (no effects) across two dependent variables lead one to speculate whether size effects on rewards are conditional on other dimensions of segmentation. Given that large establishments are likely to be state-owned or to have higher bureaucratic ranks, interaction terms between workplace size and the other two variables were created. However, these interaction terms were not significantly correlated with (ln) bonuses and (ln) salaries.

13. Party membership has a correlation of .33 with salary and a correlation of .08 with bonuses.

Chapter 8

1.   These holidays are New Year's Day (one day), the Spring Festival (the new-year's day based on the lunar calendar, three days), Labor Day (May 1, one day), and National Day (October 1, two days).

2.   Subsidized meal halls are popular in many workplaces, especially large factories. Supplies are purchased at a wholesale price, and workplace subsidies are provided to cover labor costs incurred in their production and service of food. For these reasons, food served in meal halls is several times cheaper than that in markets. When there is a shortage of foods, workplace meal halls are protected by local governments with special supplies, in order to maintain the stability of the work force. On the workplace side, meal halls are committed to obtaining food through workplaces' ties to food suppliers, retail grocery stores, and farms, and resell these foods to employees. Scarce foods, beverages, and seasonal farm products are distributed to employees in workplaces free of charge or at a low price. In Tianjin in 1983, first-rate rice, solid meat, ribs, winter cabbage, and fresh fruits were items difficult to get in markets. These are made available in workplace meal halls occasionally, particularly before every year's Spring Festival, when these items are in high demand. For example, residents in Tianjin try to buy hundreds of pounds of cabbages to store at home for uses in the coming winter. Besides higher prices, cabbages sold in the market are not as good as those shipped directly to workplaces from farms. Another advantage of getting cabbages from workplaces is that people do not have to stand outdoor in long lines to buy them in grocery stores.

3.   Walder (1992) reported survey data on the availability of eleven workplace welfare facilities and benefits. These individual-level data support the fiscal-structure and resource dependence arguments.

4.   However, Ms. Fei (personal interview 5) and her husband lived in their new apartment for several weeks without water and power. They might not have chosen to do so if there was space in their parents' homes for them. They decided to eat at their parents' and use their own apartment for sleeping. Ms. Fei told me that the whole neighborhood in which she and her husband lived was like that for "quite a long time," and that there were other families living in the neighborhood at that time as well.

5.   Analyses presented in this section have benefited from a working paper by Logan and Bian (1992).

6.   Information on community resources is appended from a separate source. In 1990, researchers at the Tianjin Academy of Social Sciences solicited information on community resources available to the thirty-six neighborhoods as of 1988. A questionnaire was delivered personally to the officers of all thirty-six neighborhood committees. In addition, one or more officers from each of the neighborhood committees was interviewed to con-

firm the responses provided on the questionnaire. The data was integrated with the 1988 Tianjin survey, and is being used in a study of access to community resources in Tianjin (Logan and Bian 1992).

Chapter 9

1. This has been known as Deng Xiaoping's "theory of cats": "whether it is a black cat or white cat, the cat that catches rats is a good cat." A current rephrasing is, "put your right hand on the economy and put your left hand on the polity." In the Chinese political context, "black" or "right hand" imply the capitalist ways or economic capitalism, whereas "white" or "left hand" imply political correctness or party dictatorship.

BIBLIOGRAPHY

Althauser, Robert P., and Arne L. Kalleberg. 1981.
"Firms, Occupations, and the Structure of Labor Markets: A Conceptual Analysis." In *Sociological Perspectives on Labor Market*, edited by I. Berg, pp. 119–49. New York: Academic Press.

Anderson, Andy B., Alexander Basilevsky, and Derek P. J. Hum. 1983.
"Missing Data: A Review of the Literature." In *The Handbook of Survey Research*, edited by P. Rossi, J. D. Wright, and A. B. Anderson, pp. 415–94.

Averitt, Robert T. 1968.
The Dual Economy: The Dynamics of American Industry Structure. New York: Norton.

Bailey, Kenneth D. 1987.
Methods of Social Research (3rd edition). New York: Free Press.

Barnett, A. Doak. 1967.
Cadres, Bureaucracy, and Political Power in Communist China. New York: Columbia University Press.

Baron, James N. 1984.
"Organizational Perspectives on Stratification." *Annual Review of Sociology* 10:37–69.

Baron, James N., and William T. Bielby. 1980.
"Bringing the Firms Back In: Stratification Segmentation, and the Organization of Work." *American Sociological Review* 45:737–65.

———. 1984.
"The Organization of Work in a Segmented Economy." *American Sociological Review* 49:454–73.

Beck, E. M., Patrick M. Horan, and Charles M. Tolbert II. 1978.
"Stratification in a Dual Economy: A Sectoral Model of Earnings Determination." *American Sociological Review* 43:704–20.

Berk, Richard A. 1983.
"An Introduction to Sample Selection Bias in Sociological Data." *American Sociological Review* 48:386–98.

Bernstein, Thomas P. 1977.
Up to the Mountains and Down to the Villages: The Transfer of Youth from Urban to Rural China. New Haven: Yale University Press.

Bian, Yanjie. 1990.
"Work-Unit Structure and Status Attainment: A Study of Work-Unit Status in Urban China." Doctoral dissertation, State University of New York at Albany.

Bibb, Robert, and William H. Form. 1977.
"The Effects of Industrial, Occupational, and Sex Stratification on Wages in Blue-Collar Markets." *Social Forces* 55:974–96.

Billeter, Jean-Francios. 1985.
"The System of 'Class Status'." In *The Scope of State Power in China,* edited by S. R. Schram, pp. 127–69. London: University of London Press.

Blau, Peter M., and Otis Dudley Duncan. 1967.
The American Occupational Structure. New York: John Wiley.

Blau, Peter M., and Danqing Ruan. 1990.
"Inequality of Opportunity in Urban China and America." In *Research in Stratification and Mobility.* Vol. 8, edited by A. L. Kalleberg. Greenwich, CT: JAI Press.

Blau, Peter M., Danqing Ruan, and Monika Ardelt. 1991.
"Interpersonal Choice and Networks." *Social Forces* 69:1037–62.

Bluestone, Barry. 1970.
"The Tripartite Economy: Labor Markets and the Working Poor." *Poverty and Human Resources Abstracts* (Supplement) 5:15–35.

Bridges, William P., and Wayne J. Villemez. 1986.
"Informal Hiring and Income in the Labor Market." *American Sociological Review* 51:574–82.

Brown, Charles, and James Medoff. 1989.
"The Employer Size-Wage Effect." *Journal of Political Economy* 97:1027–59.

Brus, Wlodzimierz. 1989.
"Evolution of the Communist Economic System: Scope and Limits." In *Remaking the Economic Institutions of Socialism,* edited by V. Nee and D. Stark, pp. 255–77. Stanford, CA: Stanford University Press.

Burawoy, Michael, and Janos Lukacs. 1985.
"Mythologies of Work: A Comparison of Firms in State Socialism and Advanced Capitalism." *American Sociological Review* 50:723–37.

Campbell, Karen E., Peter V. Marsden and Jeanne S. Hurlbert. 1986.
"Social Resources and Socioeconomic Status." *Social Networks* 8:97–117.

Chaichian, Mohammad A. 1990.
"Urban Public Housing and Recent Reform Policies in China: The Case

of Tianjin." Paper presented at the annual meeting of the American Sociological Association, Washington, DC, May.

Chamberlain, Heath B. 1987.
"Party-Management Relations in Chinese Industries: Some Political Dimensions of Economic Reform." *China Quarterly* (December) No. 12:631–61.

Chandler, Alfred D. 1962.
Strategy and Structure. Cambridge, MA: MIT Press.

———. 1977.
The Visible Hand. Cambridge, MA: Harvard University Press.

Ciechocinska, Maria. 1987.
"Government Interventions to Balance Housing Supply and Urban Population Growth: The Case of Warsaw." *International Journal of Urban and Regional Research* 11 (March):9–26.

Coleman, James S. 1988.
"Social Capital in the Creation of Human Capital." *American Journal of Sociology* 94 (Supplement): S95-S120.

Connor, Walter D. 1979.
Socialism, Politics and Equality: Hierarchy and Change in Eastern Europe and the USSR. New York: Columbia University Press.

Dahrendorf, Ralf. 1959.
Class and Class Conflict in Industrial Societies. Stanford, CA: Stanford University Press.

Davis, Deborah. 1988.
"Unequal Chances, Unequal Outcomes: Pension Reform and Urban Inequality." *China Quarterly* 114:221–42.

———. 1990.
"Urban Job Mobility." Chapter 4 In *Chinese Society on the Eve of Tiananmen,* edited D. Davis and E. F. Vogel. Cambridge, CA: Harvard University Press.

———. 1992.
" 'Skidding': Downward Mobility among Children of the Maoist Middle Class." *Modern China* 18:410–37.

———. 1993.
"Urban Families and the Post-Mao Housing Reforms: Strategies of Supplication." Chapter 5 In *Chinese Families in the 1980s,* edited by D. Davis and S. Harrell.

Davis, Kingsley, and Wilbert E. Moore. 1945.
"Some Principles of Stratification." *American Sociological Review* 10: 242–49.

Davis-Friedmann, Deborah. 1985.
"Intergenerational Inequalities and the Chinese Revolution." *Modern China* 11 (April):177–201.

DeGraaf, Nan Dirk, and Hendrik Derk Flap. 1988.
"With a Little Help from My Friends: Social Resources as an Explanation of Occupational Status and Income in West Germany, the Netherlands, and the United States." *Social Forces* 67:452–72.

Djilas, Milovan. 1957.
The New Class. New York: Frederick A. Praeger, Publisher.

Doeringer, Peter, and Michael J. Piore. 1971.
Internal Labor Markets and Manpower Analysis. Lexington, MA: Heath.

Domanski, Henryk. 1988.
"Labor Market Segmentation and Income Determination in Poland." *Sociological Quarterly* 29:47–62.

———. 1990.
"Dynamics of Labor Market Segmentation in Poland, 1982–1987." *Social Forces* 69:423–38.

Duncan, Otis Dudley. 1961.
"A Socioeconomic Index For All Occupations." *Occupations and Social Status,* edited by A. J. Reiss, pp. 109–38. New York: The Free Press of Glencoe, Inc.

Duncan, Otic Dudley, David L. Featherman, and Beverly Duncan. 1972.
Socioeconomic Background and Achievement. New York: Seminar Press.

Edwards, Richard C. 1975.
"The Social Relations of Production in the Firm and Labor Market Structure." In *Labor Market Segmentation,* edited R. C. Edwards, M. Reich, and D. M. Gordon, pp. 3–26. Lexington, MA: Heath.

———. 1979.
Contested Terrain. New York: Basic Books.

Edwards, Richard C., Michael Reich, and David M. Gordon (eds.) 1975.
Labor Market Segmentation. Lexington, MA: Heath.

Ensel, Walter M. 1979.
"Sex, Social Ties, and Status Attainment." Doctoral dissertation, Department of Sociology, State University of New York at Albany.

Fairbank, John King. 1986.
The Great Chinese Revolution, 1800–1985. New York: Harper & Row.

Featherman, David L., and Robert M. Hauser. 1978.
Opportunity and Change. New York: Academic Press.

Galbraith, John K. 1973.
Economics and the Public Purpose. Boston: Houghton Mifflin.

Giddens, Anthony. 1979.
Central Problems in Social Theory: Action, Structure and Contradiction in Social Analysis. Berkeley, CA: University of California Press.

———. 1981.
A Contemporary Critique of Historical Materialism. Berkeley, CA: University of California Press.

Gold, Thomas. 1985.
"After Comradeship: Personal Relations in China Since the Cultural Revolution." *China Quarterly* 104:657–75.

———. 1990.
"Urban Private Business and Social Change." In *Chinese Society on the Eve of Tiananmen,* edited by D. Davis and E. F. Vogel, pp. 157–78. Cambridge, MA: Harvard University Press.

Gordon, David M., Richard C. Edwards, and Michael Reich (eds.). 1982.
Segmented Work, Divided Workers. New York: Cambridge University Press.

Granovetter, Mark. 1973.
"The Strength of Weak Ties." *American Journal of Sociology* 78: 1360–80.

———. 1974
Getting a Job: A Study of Contacts and Careers. Cambridge, MA: Harvard University Press.

———. 1982.
"The Strength of Weak Ties: A Network Theory Revisited." In *Social Structure and Network Analysis,* edited by P. V. Marsden and N. Lin, pp. 105–30. Beverly Hills, CA: Sage Publications, Inc..

Hall, Richard. 1982.
Organizations: Structure and Process. Englewood Cliffs, NJ: Prentice-Hall.

———. 1986.
Dimensions of Work. Beverly Hills, CA: Sage Publications, Inc.

Haraszti, Miklos. 1979.
A Worker in A Worker's State. New York: Universe.

Hauser, Robert M. 1980.
"On 'Stratification in a Dual Economy': A Comment on Beck, Horan, and Tolbert." *American Sociological Review* 45:702–12.

Hegedus, J. 1987.
"Reconsidering the Roles of the State and the Market in Socialist Hous-

ing Systems." *International Journal of Urban and Regional Research* 11 (March):79–97.

Hegedus, J., and I. Tosics. 1983.
"Housing Classes and Housing Policy: Some Changes in the Budapest Housing Market." *International Journal of Urban and Regional Research* 7: 467–94.

Hershkovitz, Linda. 1985.
"The Fruits of Ambivalence: China's Urban Individual Economy." *Pacific Affairs* 58:427–50.

Hodson, Randy. 1983.
Workers' Earnings and Corporate Economic Structure. New York: Academic Press.

———. 1984.
"Companies, Industries, and the Measurement of Economic Segmentation." *American Sociological Review* 49:335–48.

Hodson, Randy D., and Robert L. Kaufman. 1982.
"Economic Dualism: A Critical Review." *American Sociological Review* 47:727–39.

Honig, Emily, and Gail Hershatter. 1988.
Personal Voices: Chinese Women in the 1980's. Stanford, CA: Stanford University Press.

Howe, Christopher. 1968.
"The Supply and Administration of Housing in Mainland China: The Case of Shanghai." *China Quarterly* 10:73–97.

———. 1973.
Wage Patterns and Wage Policy in Modern China, 1919–1972. Cambridge: Cambridge University Press.

Hu, Teh-wei, Ming Li, and Shuahong Shi. 1988.
"Analysis of Wages and Bonus Payments Among Tianjin Urban Workers." *China Quarterly* 113:77–93.

Jenkins, Robert M. 1987. "Social Inequality in the State Socialist Division of Labor: Earnings
Determination in Contemporary Hungary." Doctoral dissertation, University of Wisconsin at Madison.

Johnson, Kay Ann. 1976.
"Women in the People's Republic of China." In *Asian Women in Transition,* edited by S. A. Chipp and J. J. Green, pp. 62–103. University Park, PA: Pennsylvania State University Press.

Kalleberg, Arne L. 1983.
"Work and Stratification: Structural Perspectives." *Work and Occupations* 10: 251–59.

———. 1988.
"Comparative Perspectives on Work Structures and Inequality." *Annual Review of Sociology* 14:203–25.

Kalleberg, Arne L., and James R. Lincoln. 1988.
"The Structure of Earnings Inequality in the United States and Japan." *American Journal of Sociology* 94 (Supplement):S121-S153.

Kalleberg, Arne L., and A. B. Sorensen. 1979.
"The Sociology of Labor Markets." *Annual Review of Sociology* 5:351–79.

Kalleberg, Arne L., Michael Wallace, and Robert Althauser. 1981.
"Economic Segmentation, Worker Power, and Income Inequality." *American Journal of Sociology* 87:651–83.

Kaufman, Robert L., Randy Hodson, and Neil D. Fligstein. 1981.
"Defrocking Dualism: A New Approach to Defining Industrial Sectors." *Social Science Research* 10:1–31.

Kerkhoff, Alan C. 1976.
"The Status Attainment Process: Socialization or Allocation." *Social Forces* 55:368–81.

Kornai, Janos. 1986.
Contradictions and Dilemmas: Studies on the Socialist Economy and Society. Cambridge, MA: MIT Press.

Kornai, Janos. 1989.
"The Hungarian Reform Process: Vision, Hopes, and Reality." In *Remaking the Economic Institutions of Socialism: China and Eastern Europe,* edited by V. Nee and S. Stark, pp. 32–94. Stanford, CA: Stanford University Press.

Korzec, Michael, and Martin King Whyte. 1981.
"Reading Notes: The Chinese Wage System." *China Quarterly* 86:248–73.

Kraus, Richard. 1981.
Class Conflict in Chinese Socialism. New York: Columbia University Press.

Lai, Gina, Shu-yin Leung, and Nan Lin. 1990.
"Network Resources and Contact Resources: Structural and Action Effects of Social Resources." Paper presented at the annual meetings of the American Sociological Association, Washington, DC, August.

Lane, David. 1982.
The End of Social Inequality? Class, Status and Power under State Socialism. London: George Allen & Unwin (Publishers) Ltd.

Lardy, Nicholas R. 1975.
"Centralization and Decentralization in China's Fiscal Management."
China Quarterly 61:25–60.

———. 1989.
"Dilemmas in the Pattern of Resource Allocation in China, 1978–
1985." In *Remaking the Economic Institutions of Socialism*, edited by
V. Nee and D. Stark, pp. 278–305. Stanford, CA: Stanford University
Press.

Laumann, Edward O. 1966.
Prestige and Association in an Urban Community. Indianapolis:
Bobbs-Merrill.

Lee, Yok-shiu F. 1988.
"The Urban Housing Problem in China." *China Quarterly* 115:387–
407.

Lenin, Vladimir I. 1965 [1916].
Imperialism: The Highest State of Capitalism. Beijing, China: Foreign
Language Publishing House.

Lenski, Gerhard. 1984.
Power and Privilege. New York: McGraw Hill.

Lin, Cyril Zhiren. 1989.
"Open-Ended Economic Reform in China." In *Remaking the Economic
Institutions of Socialism*, edited by V. Nee and D. Stark, pp. 95–136.
Stanford, CA: Stanford University Press.

Lin, Nan. 1976.
Foundations of Social Research. New York: McGraw-Hill Book Company.

———. 1982.
"Social Resources and Instrumental Action." In *Social Structure and
Network Analysis*, edited by P. Marsden and N. Lin, pp. 131–47. Bev-
erly Hills, CA: Sage Publications, Inc.

———. 1989.
"Chinese Family Structure and Chinese Society." *Bulletin of the Institute of Ethnology at Academia Sinica* 65 (Spring):59–129.

Lin, Nan, Walter M. Ensel, and John C. Vaughn. 1981.
"Social Resources and Strength of Ties: Structural Factors in Occupational Status Attainment." *American Sociological Review* 46:393–405.

Lin, Nan, John C. Vaughn, and Walter M. Ensel. 1981.
"Social Resources and Occupational Status Attainment." *Social Forces*
59:1163–81.

Lin, Nan, and Wen Xie. 1988.
"Occupational Prestige in Urban China." *American Journal of Sociology* 93:793–832.

Lin, Nan, and Yanjie Bian. 1989.
"Social Connections and Social Resources in the Status Attainment Process." Paper presented at the Sunbelt International Conference of Social Networks, San Diego, February.

———. 1990.
"Status Inheritance in Urban China." Paper presented at the annual meeting of the American Sociological Association, Washington, DC, August.

———. 1991.
"Getting Ahead in Urban China." *American Journal of Sociology* 97:657–88.

Logan, John R., and David Molotch. 1987.
Urban Fortunes: Political Economy of Place. Berkeley, CA: University of California Press.

Logan, John R., and Yanjie Bian. 1992.
"Access to Community Resources in a Chinese City." Working Paper.

Mao, Zedong. 1957.
"On the Correct Handling of Contradictions Among the People." In *Selected Works of Mao Tsetung* (Zedong), V.5. Peking (Beijing), China: Foreign Language Press.

Marsden, Peter V., and Karen E. Campbell. 1984.
"Measuring Tie Strength." *Social Forces* 63:482–501.

Marsden, Peter V., and Jeanne S. Hurlbert. 1988.
"Social Resources and Mobility Outcomes: A Replication and Extension." *Social Forces* 66: 1038–59.

Marx, Karl. 1978 [1859].
"A Contribution to the Critique of Political Economy." In *The Marx-Engels Reader* (2nd edition), edited by R. C. Tucker. New York: W. W. Norton & Company, Inc.

Meyer, John W., Nancy Brandon Tuma, and Krzysztof Zagorski. 1979.
"Education and Occupational Mobility: A Comparison of Polish and American Men." *American Journal of Sociology* 84:978–86.

Mills, C. Wright. 1956.
White Collar: The American Middle Classes. New York: Oxford University Press.

Misztal, Barbara A., and Bronislaw Misztal. 1986.
"Uncontrolled Processes in the Socialist City: A Polish Case Study." *Politics and Society* 15:145–56.

Moore, Wilbert. 1963.
"But Some Are More Equal than Others." *American Sociological Review* 46:951–64.

Musil, Jiri. 1987.
"Housing Policy and the Sociospatial Structure of Cities in a Socialist Country - The Example of Prague." *International Journal of Urban and Regional Research* 11 (March):27–36.

Nee, Victor. 1989.
"A Theory of Market Transition: From Redistribution to Markets in State Socialism." *American Sociological Review* 54:663–81.

———. 1991.
"Social Inequalities in Reforming State Socialism: Between Redistribution and Markets in China." *American Sociological Review* 56:267–82.

Nee, Victor, and David Stark (eds.). 1989.
Remaking the Economic Institutions of Socialism: China and Eastern Europe. Stanford, CA: Stanford University Press.

Nee, Victor, and Su Sijin. 1990.
"Institutional Change and Economic Growth in China: The View from the Villages." *Journal of Asian Studies* 49:3–25.

O'Connor, James. 1973.
The Fiscal Crisis of the State. New York: St. Martin's Press.

O'Rand, Angela M. 1986.
"The Hidden Payroll: Employee Benefits and the Structure of Workplace Inequality." *Sociological Forum* 1:657–83.

Parish, William L, Jr. 1981.
"Egalitarianism in Chinese Society." *Problems of Communism* 29:37–53.

———. 1984.
"Destratification in China." In *Class and Social Stratification in Post-Revolution China*, edited by J. Watson, pp. 84–120. New York: Cambridge University Press.

Parkin, Frank. 1979.
Marxism and Class Theory: A Bourgeois Critique. New York: Columbia University Press.

Parsons, Talcott. 1940
"An Analytical Approach to the Theory of Social Stratification." *American Journal of Sociology* 45:841–62.

Peng, Yusheng. 1992.
"Wage Determination in Rural and Urban China: A Comparison of

Public and Private Industrial Sectors." *American Sociological Review* 57:198–213.

Perkins, Dwight H. 1986.
"The Prospects for China's Economic Reforms." *Modernizing China: Post-Mao Reform and Development*, edited by A. D. Barnett and R. N. Clough, pp. 39–61. London: Westview Press.

Pickvance, C. G. 1988.
"Employers, Labour Markets, and Redistribution Under State Socialism: An Interpretation of Housing Policy in Hungary, 1960–1983." *Sociology*:193–214.

Prengers, Maarten, Prits Tazelaar, and Hendrik D. Flap. 1988.
"Social Resources, Situational Constraints, and Re-Employment." *The Netherlands' Journal of Sociology*, Vol. 24.

Schurmann, Franz. 1968.
Ideology and Organization in Communist China. Berkeley, CA: University of California Press.

Scott, James C. 1985.
Weapons of the Weak: Everyday Forms of Peasant Resistance. New Haven, CT: Yale University Press.

Sewell, William H., and Robert M. Hauser. 1975.
Education, Occupation, and Earnings: Achievement in the Early Career. New York: Academic Press.

Shirk, Susan. 1982.
Competitive Comrades. Berkeley, CA: University of California Press.

Shirk, Susan. 1984.
"The Evolution of Chinese Education: Stratification and Meritocracy in the 1980s." In *China: The 80s Era*, edited by N. Ginsburg and B. Lalor, pp. 245–72. Boulder, CO: Westview Press.

Shue, Vivienne. 1988.
The Reach of the State: Sketches of the Chinese Body Politics, Stanford, CA: Stanford University Press.

Stacey, Judith. 1983.
Patriarchy and Socialist Revolution in China. Berkeley, CA: University of California Press.

Stark, David. 1986.
"Rethinking Internal Labor Markets: New Insights from a Comparative Perspective." *American Sociological Review* 51:492–504.

Stolzenberg, Ross M. 1978.
"Bringing the Boss Back in: Employer Size, Employee Schooling, and

Socioeconomic Achievement." *American Sociological Review* 43:813–28.

Szelenyi, Ivan. 1978.
"Social Inequalities in State Socialist Redistributive Economies." *International Journal of Comparative Sociology* 19:63–87.

———. 1983.
Urban Inequalities Under State Socialism. New York: Oxford University Press.

———. 1989.
"Eastern Europe in an Epoch of Transition: Toward a Socialist Mixed Economy?" In *Remaking the Economic Institutions of Socialism*, edited by V. Nee and D. Stark, pp. 208–32. Stanford, CA: Stanford University Press.

Szelenyi, Szonja. 1986.
"Social Inequality and Party Membership: Patterns of Recruitment into the Hungarian Socialist Workers' Party." *American Sociological Review* 52:559–73.

Treiman, Donald J. 1970.
"Industrialization and Social Stratification." In *Social Stratification: Research and Theory for the 1970's*, edited by E. O. Laumann. Indianapolis: Bobbs-Merrill.

———. 1977.
Occupational Prestige in Comparative Perspective. New York: Academic Press.

Treiman, Donald J., and Kam-Bor Yip. 1989.
"Educational and Occupational Attainment in 21 Countries." In *Cross-National Research in Sociology*, edited by M. L. Kohn, pp. 373–94. Newbury Park, CA: Sage Publications, Inc.

Unger, Johnason. 1982.
Education Under Mao: Class and Competition in Canton Schools, 1960–1980. New York: Columbia University Press.

Villemez, Wayne J., and William P. Bridges. 1988.
"When Bigger Is Better: Differences in the Individual-Level Effect of Firm and Establishment Size." *American Sociological Review* 53:237–55.

Vogel, Ezra. 1965.
"From Friendship to Comradeship: The Change in Personal Relations in Communist China." *China Quarterly* 21:46–65.

———. 1990.
One Step Ahead: Guangdong under Reform. Cambridge, MA: Harvard University Press.

Wachter, Michael L. 1974.
"Primary and Secondary Labor Markets: A Critique of the Dual Approach." *Brookings Papers on Economic Activity* 3:637–80.

Walder, Andrew G. 1986.
Communist Neo-Traditionalism: Work and Authority in Chinese Industry. Berkeley: University of California Press.

———. 1987.
"Wage Reform and the Web of Factory Interests." *China Quarterly* 109:22–41.

———. 1989.
"Factory and Manager in an Era of Reform." *China Quarterly* 118:242–64.

———. 1990.
"Economic Reform and Income Distribution in Tianjin, 1976–1986." In *Chinese Society on the Eve of Tiananmen,* edited by D. Davis and E. F. Vogel, pp. 135–56. Cambridge, MA: Harvard University Press.

———. 1992.
"Property Rights and Stratification in Socialist Redistributive Economies." *American Sociological Review* 57:524–39.

Wallace, Michael, and Arne L. Kalleberg. 1981.
"Economic Organization of Firms and Labor Market Consequences: Toward a Specification of Dual Economy Theory." In *Sociological Perspectives on Labor Markets,* edited by I. Berg, pp. 77–118. New York: Academic Press.

Wegener, Bern. 1991.
"Job Mobility and Social ties: Social Resources, Prior Job, and Status Attainment." *American Sociological Review* 56:60–71.

White, Gordon. 1987.
"The Politics of Economic Reform in Chinese Industry: The Introduction of the Labour Contract System." *China Quarterly* 111:365–89.

Whyte, Martin King. 1975.
"Inequality and Stratification in China." *China Quarterly* 64:685–711.

———. 1984.
"Sexual Inequality under Socialism: The Chinese Case in Perspective." In *Class and Social Stratification in Post-Revolution China,* edited by J. L. Watson, pp. 198–238. New York: Cambridge University Press.

———. 1986.
"Social Trends in China: The Triumph of Inequality?" In *Modernizing China: Post-Mao Reform and Development,* edited by A. D. Barnett and R. N. Clough, pp. 103–23. London: Westview Press.

Whyte, Martin King, and William L. Parish, Jr. 1984.
Urban Life in Contemporary China. Chicago: University of Chicago Press.

Whyte, Martin King, Ezra F. Vogel, and William L. Parish, Jr. 1977.
"Social Structure of World Regions: Mainland China." *Annual Review of Sociology* 3:179–207.

Williamson, Oliver A. 1975.
Markets and Hierarchies: Analysis and Antitrust Implications. New York: Free Press.

Wolf, Margery. 1985.
Revolution Postponed: Women in Contemporary China. Stanford, CA: Stanford University Press.

Wong, Siu-lun. 1988.
Emigrant Entrepreneurs: Shanghai industrialists in Hong Kong. New York: Oxford University Press.

Wright, Erik Olin. 1978.
Class, Crisis, and the State. London, New Left Books.

Xie, Wen, and Nan Lin. 1986.
"The Process of Status Attainment in Urban China." Paper presented at the annual meeting of the American Sociological Association, New York, August.

Xiong, Ruimei, Qingshan Sun, and Zhisong Xu. 1986.
"Strength of Ties and Job Change Behaviors of Employees in Manufacturing Industries." *Sociological Journal of National University of Taiwan* Vol. 18 (November):1–24.

Yang, Mayfair Mei-hui. 1986.
"The Art of Social Relationships and Exchange in China." Doctoral dissertation, University of California at Berkeley.

Yanowitch, Murray. 1977.
Social and Economic Inequality in the Soviet Union. New York: M. E. Sharpe.

Yudkin, Marcia. 1986.
Making Good: Private Business in Socialist China. Beijing: Foreign Languages Press.

Zagorski, Krzysztof. 1984.
"Comparisons of Social Mobility in Different Socioeconomic Systems." In *International Comparative Research: Social Structures and Public Institutions in Eastern and Western Europe*, edited by M. Niessen, J. Peschar, and C. Kourilsky, pp. 13–41. Oxford: Pergamon.

Chinese-Language References

Chen, Wenchun, and Huateng Wei (eds.). 1991.
Laws and Practices of "Three Capitalist Enterprises" (Sanzi Qiyie De Falu Yu Shijian). Guangzhou: People's Press of Guangdong.

Chen, Yun. 1956.
"The State Economic Planning" (Guanyu Guomin Jingji Jihua). In *Chen Yun's Strategy for China's Development (Chen Yun Lun Zhongguo Fazhan Zhanlue)*. Beijing: Foreign Language Press.

Deng, Xiaoping. 1983.
Deng Xiaoping's Selections: 1975–1982 (Deng Xiaoping Wenxuan: 1975–1982). Beijing: People's Press.

Duan, Zhenkun (ed.). 1987.
Economic Yearbook of Tianjin: 1987 (Tianjin Jingji Nianjian: 1987). Tianjin: People's Press of Tianjin.

Yearbook of China's Education (Zhongguo Jiaoyu Nianjian). 1989. Beijing: Chinese Educational Press.
Yearbook of the Encyclopedia of China (Zhongguo Dabaike Nianjian. 1983. Shanghai: Chinese Encyclopedia Press.

Fang, Weizhong, and associates (eds). 1984.
Chronicles of the Great Economic Events in the People's Republic of China (1949–1980) (Zhonghua Renmin Gongheguo Jingji Dashiji (1949–1980)). Beijing: Chinese Social Sciences Press.

Gu, Shutang (ed.). 1984.
General Economic Situations of Tianjin (Tianjin Jingji Gaikuang). Tianjin: People's Press of Tianjin.

Han, Fanglun, Zhitao Ren, and Maosheng Tian (eds.). 1991.
Modern Practical Personnel Management (Xiandai Shiyong Renshi Guanlixue). Beijing, China: Chinese Personnel Affairs Press.

He, Guang, and associates (eds.). 1990.
The Labor Force Management in Contemporary China (Xiandai Zhongguo Laodongli Guanli). Beijing: Chinese Social Sciences Press.

Huai, Wanrui (ed.). 1991.
State Taxes (Guojia Shuishou). Beijing: Chinese Financial Economics Press.

Jin, Rungui (ed.). 1988.
Material Management in Township Enterprises (Xiangzhen Qiyie Wuzi Guanli). Shanghai: Shanghai Social Sciences Press.

Li, Gan, and associates (eds.). 1986.
Economic Yearbook of Tianjin: 1986 (Tianjin Jingji Nianjian: 1986). Tianjin: People's Press of Tianjin.

Li, Weiyi. 1991.
China's Wage System (*Zhongguo Gongzi Zhidu*). Beijing: Chinese Labor Press.

Li, Yang. 1990.
An Economic Analysis of Subsidies (*Caizheng Butie Jingji Fenxi*). Shanghai: Life, Reading, and New Knowledge Publishing House.

Liu, Zhongli, and Guang Xu (eds.). 1991.
Current Fiscal Situations in Chinese Industry (*Zhongguo Gongyie Caiwu Xianzhuang*). Beijing: Chinese Financial Economics Press.

Rui, Guangzhao (ed.). 1988.
Chinese Labor Policies and System (*Zhongguo De Laodong Zhengce He Zhidu*). Beijing: Economic Management Press.

Sun, Qinghua, Shuling Chen, and Cunxian Li. 1991.
Housing Reforms and Perceptions (*Zhufang Zhidu Gaige Yu Zhufang Xinli*). Beijing: Publishing House for Chinese Construction Industry.

Tang, Yunqi (ed.). 1990.
A General Inquiry into China's Labor Management (*Zhongguo Laodong Guanli Gailan*). Beijing: Chinese Cities Press.

Xue, Muqiao. 1986.
"A Review of the Reform of the Labor Wage System" (*Tantan Laodong Gongzi Zhi De Gaige*). *Chinese Labor Sciences* (*Zhongguo Laodong Kexue*) 1:6–11.

Yuan, Baohua (ed.). 1990.
Current Situations of China's Industry (*Zhongguo Gongyie Xianzhuang*). Beijing: People's Press.

Zhang, Jian, and associates (eds.). 1986.
The Atlas of Chinese Education: 1949–1984 (*Zhongguo Jiaoyu Baikequanshu*). Changsha: Educational Press of Hunan Province.

Zhang, Zuoyi, and associates (eds.). 1991.
The Labor Force Management and Employment (*Laodongli Guanli Yu Jiuyie*). Beijing: China's Labor Press.

Chinese Government Documents and Statistics

Central Committee of the Chinese Communist Party and the State Council. 1980.
"To Further Improve the Urban Employment Work" (*Jinyibu Zuohao Chengzhen Laodong Jiuyie Gongzuo*).

———. 1981.
"Several Resolutions: Creating Alternatives, Promoting Economic

Flexibility, and Solving Employment Problems in Cities and Towns" (*Guanyu Guangkai Menlu, Gaohuo Jingji, Jiejue Chengzhen Jiuyie Wenti de Ruogan Guiding*).

Financial and Economic Committee of the Central Government (FECCG). 1952.
"Instructions for Resolving Several Problems of the Incentive Wage System (Draft)" (*Guanyu Tuixing Jiangli Gongzi Zhi Yixie Wenti de Jianyi (Caoan)*).

Grain Bureau of Jinghai County. 1978.
"Jinghai County Grain Bureau Documents on Wages and Benefits" (*Jinghai Xian Liangshiju Gongzi Ji Gexiang Daiyu Wenjian*). (Internally circulated documents).

Ministry of Labor and Personnel Affairs. 1982.
"Suggestions Toward Several Issues About Labor Service Companies" (*Guanyu Laodong Fuwu Gongsi Ruogan Wenti de Yijian*).

———. 1983a.
"Temporary Regulations of the Recruitment of Best Qualified Workers Through Merit Examinations" (*Guanyu Zhaogong Kaoke Zeyou Luyong De Zhanxing Guiding*).

———. 1983b.
"Circular of Actively Implementing the Labor Contract System" (*Guanyu Jiji Shixing Laodong Hetongzhi De Tongzhi*).

———. 1984.
"Regulations of the Registration of Job-waiting People in Cities and Towns" (*Chengzhen Daiyie Renyuan Dengji Guanli Banfa*).

———. 1989.
"Suggestions Toward Several Issues in the Development and Construction of Labor Service Companies" (*Guanyu Laodong Fuwu Gongsi Fazhan he Jianshe Zhong Wenti De Yijian*).

Ministry of Labor and Personnel Affairs and the Ministry of Finance. 1983.
"Temporary Regulations of the Use of Subsidies for Employment of Youth in Cities and Towns and the Management of Labor Service Companies" (*Guanyu Chengzhen Qinian Laodong Jiuyie he Laodong Fuwu Gongsi Buzhufee Guanli Shiyong De Zhanxing Guiding*).

Municipal Financial and Trade Office of Tianjin. 1977.
"Temporary Regulations of Wage and Benefits for Tianjin Financial and Trade Industries" (*Tianjin Caimao Shangyie Xitong Gongzi Ji Zhigong Daiyu De Zhanxing Guiding*). (Internally circulated documents).

People's Congress's Law Committee (ed.). 1985.
Compilation of Laws of the People's Republic of China (1979–1984) (*Zhonghua Renmin Gongheguo Fagui Huibian*). Beijing: People's Press.

Population Census Office of Tianjin. 1984.
Compilation of Data from the Third Population Census of Tianjin (*Tianjin Disanci Renkou Pucha Ziliao Huibian*). Printed by Census Office of Tianjin.

————. 1986.
Demographic Statistics of Tianjin: 1949–1983 (*Tianjin Renkou Tongji Ziliao: 1949–1983*). Tianjin: Nankai University Press.

State Council. 1978.
"Circular of the Reward and Piece-Rate Wage System" (*Guanyu Jiangli He Jijian Gongzi De Tongzhi*).

————. 1985a.
"Circular of Wage Reform Problems in State Enterprises" (*Guanyu Guoying Qiyie Gongzi Gaige Yixie Wenti de Tongzhi*) (January 5).

————. 1985b.
"A Plan for the Reform of the Wage System for Personnel in Government Agencies and Institutions" (*Guojia Jiguan he Shiyie Danwei Gongzuo Renyuan Gongzi Zhidu Gaige Fangan*). (June).

————. 1986a.
"Temporary Regulations of the Implementation of the Labor Contract System in State Enterprises" (*Guoying Qiyie Shixing Laodong Hetongzhi Zhanxing Guiding*).

————. 1986b.
"Temporary Regulations of the Recruitment of Workers in State Enterprises" (*Guoying Qiyie Zhaoyong Gongren Zhanxing Guiding*).

————. 1988 (February 27).
"Temporary Regulations of Contract Responsibility System for State Industrial Enterprises" (*Guanyu Guoying Gongyie Qiyie Shixing Chengbao Zeren Zhi de Zhanxing Guiding*).

State Economic Reform Commission, State Planning Commission, Financial Ministry, People's Bank of China, and State Council's Production Office. 1992 (May 15).
"Measures for Experimental Units of Stock-Shared Enterprises" (*Gufenzhi Qiyie Shixing Danwei de Banfa*). *People's Daily* (Overseas ed.) (*Renmin Ribao Haiwai Ban*), June 19, 1992.

State General Labor Bureau. 1979.
"Suggestions Toward the Recruitment of Workers Through All-Aspect Examinations" (*Guanyu Zhaogong Shixing Quanmian Kaohe De Yijian*).

State Statistical Bureau of China. 1982.
Statistical Yearbook of China: 1981 (*Zhongguo Tongji Nianjian: 1981*). Beijing: Statistical Press of China.

———. 1983.
China's 1982 Population Census: 10 Percent Sampling Tabulation (Computer Tabulation) (Zhongguo 1982 Nian Renkou Pucha: Baifenzhishi Chouyang Jieguo (Jisuanji Jieguo). Beijing: Statistical Press of China.

———. 1984.
Statistical Yearbook of China: 1984 (Zhongguo Tongji Nianjian: 1984). Beijing: Statistical Press of China.

———. 1986.
Statistical Yearbook of China: 1986 (Zhongguo Tongji Nianjian: 1986). Beijing: Statistical Press of China.

———. 1988.
Statistical Yearbook of China: 1988 (Zhongguo Tongji Nianjian: 1988). Beijing: Statistical Press of China.

———. 1989.
Statistical Yearbook of China: 1989 (Zhongguo Tongji Nianjian: 1989). Beijing: Statistical Press of China.

———. 1990.
Statistical Yearbook of China: 1990 (Zhongguo Tongji Nianjian: 1990). Beijing: Statistical Press of China.

INDEX

and employment, 57, 63, 64,
   69, 101, 122
and job mobility, 109, 113, 115
and types of social ties, 101,
   103. *See also* Social networks and social ties
as social resources, 98, 99
meanings of, 95, 96

Han, 14, 67, 71, 96, 149
Haraszti, 12
Hauser, 74
He, 51–56, 66
Hershatter, 82, 87, 161
Hodson, 3, 4
Honig, 82, 87, 161
Housing
   and collective consumption,
      177, 189
   and mobility, 75
   as incentives, 13, 48, 198
   as labor rewards, 198
   funding of, 191–194
   in Beijing, 200
   markets, 195–197
   quality, 201
   types of, 49, 190, 191
Howe, 190
Hu, 4, 13, 161
Huai, 29
Hurlbert, 99, 104

Inequalities
   and economic reforms, 163
   and segmentation, 209
   economic, 15
   in access to community re-
      sources, 201
   in access to housing, 189, 198
   in collective consumption, 177
   in income, 170, 174, 175, 217
   of opportunities, 109
   socioeconomic, 210
Institutions, 14, 23
   and wages, 153

Jenkins, 5
Job assignments, 10, 11
   and *guanxi*, 97, 99, 100. *See
      also Guanxi* and job
      mobility
   and job mobility, 119
   and party membership attain-
      ment, 143
   as a national policy, 52
   causal mechanisms of, 77, 78
   personal experiences with, 62–
      64
   practices, 59
   process of, 35, 59, 62
Job change. *See* Job mobility
Job mobility, 109, 110. *See also* Job
   transfer
   and *guanxi*, 100, 109. *See also
      Guanxi* and job mobility
   in Tianjin, 115, 117
   practices of, 110
Job search, 69
   and *guanxi*, 95, 102. *See also
      Guanxi* and job mobility; Job
      assignments and *guanxi.*
Job transfer, 110. *See also* Job
   mobility
   and change of occupation, 112
   by individual application, 112
   factors in, 113, 114
   formal, 112
   meaning of, 111
   recent trends in, 114
Johnson, 82

Kalleberg, 2, 4, 175, 213
Kornai, 7, 14
Korzec, 148, 161
Kraus, 77

Labor
   agencies, 10
   allocation of, 35, 36
   as a national resource, 10, 51
   cohorts, 78, 79, 86

collective consumption in, 178
distribution of labor in, 52, 73
distribution of resources in,
  28, 33, 34
firms in, 5
in China, 7, 8
worker power in, 6
Political
  activists, 13
  adviser, 61, 63
  background, 60, 75–77
  campaigns, 18–20, 47
  dimension to occupational
    groups, 131–133
  evaluation of party-
    membership applicants,
    128–130, 135
  functions of work units, 46, 47
  ideology, 76
  incentives, 12, 127, 138
  mobility, 142
  parties in China, 23, 46
  party membership, 124
  performances, 61, 64
  power of cadres, 109
  power of work units, 118, 119
  power of work units and hous-
    ing, 197, 198
  promotions, 45
  rationalization, 8, 206
  resources, 50
  status, 80, 81, 136
  status effects on wages, 161,
    173, 174
  studies in the workplace, 47
  virtue, 57, 76–78
  virtue and job assignments, 78,
    86–88, 94

Reforms in state socialism, 19, 21,
  163
  and inequality, 213, 215, 217
  and labor markets, 114
  and wages, 27, 145, 147, 157
  effects of, 14–16, 24, 26, 77,

86, 87, 127, 135, 139, 142–
  144
Reich, 2
Ren, 14, 67, 71, 96, 149
Ruan, 74, 75, 80, 89, 108

Segmentation
  and inequality, 209
  by industry in China, 9
  economic, 2–4
  effects of, 73, 162, 172
  in planned economy, 14, 15
  labor market, 2, 43
  measurement of, 80
  research, 2–5
  structural, 1–2, 211–213
  workplace, 7
Sewell, 74
Shi, 4, 13, 161
Shirk, 76, 77, 135
Social networks, 62
  and guanxi, 95, 96. See also
    Guanxi
  and job mobility, 117. See also
    Guanxi and job mobility
  and job search, 75, 109, 122
  and social contacts, 99, 102–
    105, 108, 117, 122
  and social ties, 75, 96, 98–100,
    104, 108. See also Guanxi
  and types of social ties
Social resources, 95
  and job status, 108, 109
  measurement of, 99–101
  theory of, 98, 99
Stacy, 82
Stark, 5, 213
State Council of China, 148, 157
State socialism, 5, 7, 16, 210
State Statistical Bureau of China,
  14, 19–21, 30, 39, 56, 147, 188
Status attainment
  and economic sectors, 84–88
  causes of, 74, 78
  modeling, 78